FACING MY FEELINGS

A Series of Distinctively Christian Support-Group Curriculum Guides

Making Wise Choices
Facing My Feelings
Living in My Family
Growing Through Changes

Illustrations by Jared D. Lee Studio, Inc.
Cover design by Barry Ridge Graphic Design
Photography and art direction by Coleen Davis
Text designed and edited by SETTINGPACE
Project direction by Linda Ford

The Standard Publishing Company, Cincinnati, Ohio
A division of Standex International Corporation

Printed in the United States of America

04 03 02 01 00 99 98 97 5 4 3 2 1

ISBN 0-7847-0643-3

FACING MY FEELINGS

by Linda Kondracki Sibley

Cincinnati, Ohio

Guidelines for Using Reproducible Pages

You may make copies of the sessions, activity pages, and forms in this book for your Confident Kids ministry. Please observe the following guidelines:

- Authorized copies may be made by the original purchaser or by someone in the same Confident Kids organization.
- Copies must be used for a noncommercial purpose within your Confident Kids program or to promote your Confident Kids program.
- It is illegal for you to make copies for other ministry programs or for Confident Kids programs in other ministries or churches.
- If you or your organization is not the original purchaser of this material, it is illegal for you to copy these Confident Kids materials.

These guidelines allow you to provide copies of all materials needed by the staff of your Confident Kids program while protecting copyrights for both author and publisher.

The Standard Publishing Company continues its commitment to offering reproducible products at affordable prices.

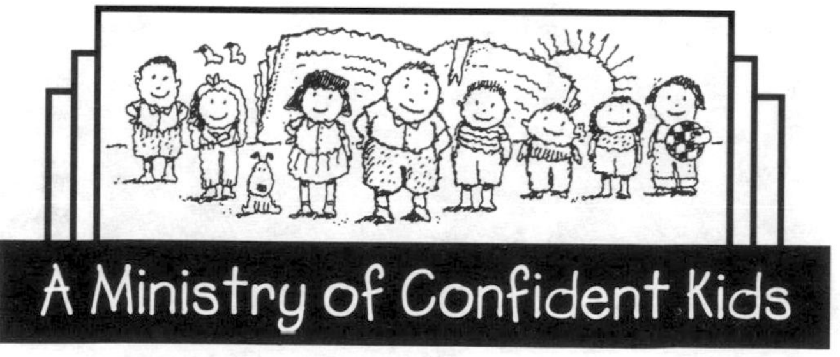

Facing My Feelings

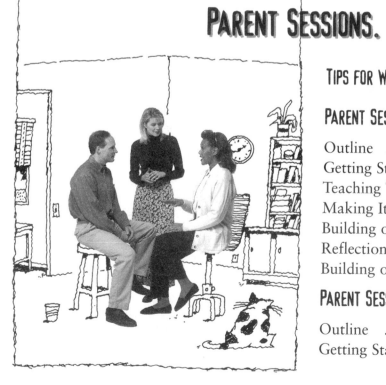

Facing My Feelings
Topic Overview

Unit Slogan

All My Feelings Are OK!

Key Verses
Joshua 1:9 and Philippians 4:6, 7

Be strong and courageous. Do not be terrified; do not be discouraged, for the Lord your God will be with you wherever you go. (*NIV*)

Do not be anxious about anything, but in everything present your requests to God. And the peace of God will guard your hearts and your minds in Christ Jesus. (*NIV*, condensed)

Bible Lessons

Stories from the life of David in 1 Samuel 16–26, and selected Psalms

Key Concepts

- There are no "good" or "bad" feelings; all are necessary to living a healthy life.
- It is dangerous to stuff (avoid) our feelings by using feelings defenses.
- There are healthy ways to express our feelings; following a few basic rules can keep us from expressing our feelings in inappropriate ways.
- Our feelings can tell us when it's time to ask for help.
- Jesus understands all our feelings and His presence within our hearts is the greatest resource we have to deal with them.

Preschool Sessions

1 I Have Lots of Feelings

2 All My Feelings Are OK!

3 Some Feelings Are Not Fun to Feel

4 I Can Talk About My Feelings

5 I Can Name My Feelings

6 Asking for Help

7 Jesus Helps Me With My Feelings

8 Family Night

Elementary/Preteen/Parent Sessions

1 Feelings Are an Important Part of Life

2 All My Feelings Are OK!

3 What Are My Feelings Defenses?

4 Express Those Feelings!

5 Some Feelings Are Difficult to Handle

6 Asking for Help

7 Jesus Helps Me With My Feelings

8 Family Night

Facing My Feelings

This unit addresses one of the most fundamental, and yet difficult parts of living a healthy life—the ability to feel the whole range of feelings God has placed within us. When properly understood, the capacity to experience feelings is an incredible gift from God. Feelings enrich our lives, help us connect with others and God, and warn us when we are in danger or need help. Yet most of us are not always sure if our emotional life is a blessing from God, or a curse! On one hand, we have the ability to feel love, pleasure, excitement, and pride. But on the other hand, we also feel great pain, anger, and loneliness. And here's the problem—we cannot have one without the other! We cannot pick and choose which emotions we want to feel. The only way we can avoid "bad" feelings is to shut down our ability to feel anything at all, or use unhealthy behaviors (feelings defenses) to keep them under control.

Children learn early in life that some feelings are not very much fun to feel. Unfortunately, *they also come to believe that if they feel bad, they are bad*, and therefore they must avoid or get rid of bad feelings at all costs! That one basic misconception is at the heart of much unhealthy behavior, learned in childhood and carried into adulthood. As you and your children work through the sessions in this unit, your primary goal will be to replace this misconception with the truth that there are no "bad" feelings, recognize the importance of opening up to all your feelings, and develop the skills necessary to handle them in helpful and appropriate ways.

Build a Feelings Vocabulary

An important part of this unit is teaching children (and yourself) how to *name what they are feeling, when they are feeling it*. Throughout the weeks of this unit, be aware of times you can help your children learn new feelings words and apply them to their life experiences. Using the Alphabetical List of Feelings Words (page 353) can help you expand your own feelings words vocabulary.

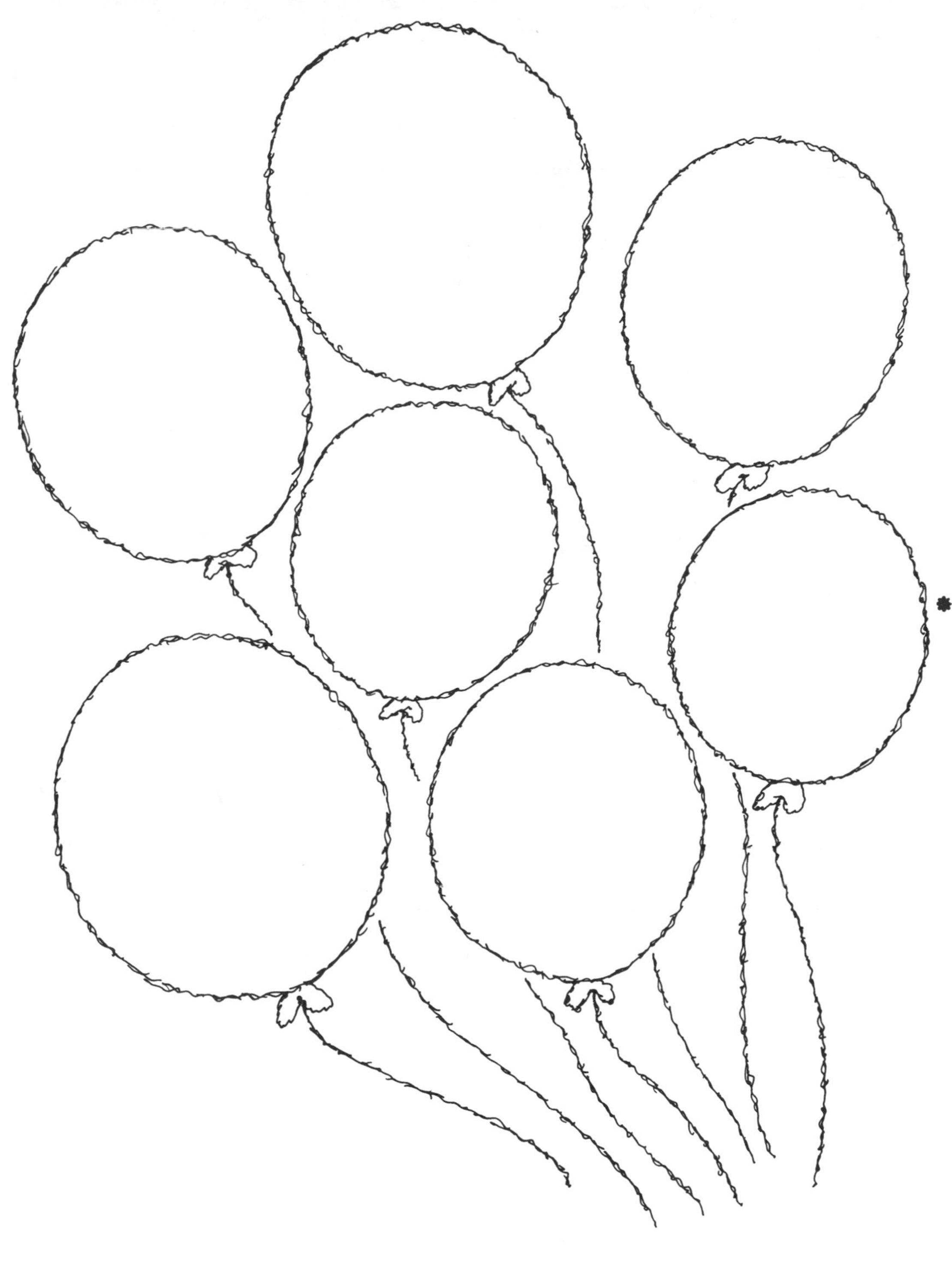

GETTING STARTED

- ABOUT CONFIDENT KIDS
- STARTING A CONFIDENT KIDS PROGRAM
- USING THE SESSION PLANS

As you read this section, you will want to review the forms and information in Appendices A and B.

About Confident Kids

Why a Support Group for Children?

Because times have changed. The emotional needs of children growing up in America today are greater than ever before. Growing up with divorce, stepparents and stepsiblings, drugs and alcohol, gangs, community violence, absent parents—and more—is taking its toll. Children often spend less than one hour per week in church, so children's workers simply do not have time to teach Bible stories, memory verses, missions, and music *and* be responsive to the deepest emotional needs of so many of today's kids! As a result, many of us live with the feeling that we aren't helping the kids who need us most.

What Is Confident Kids?

Have you ever thought, *"Wouldn't it be great if we had a place to give focused time and attention to struggling kids? A place where we could support and encourage them, pray with them, and teach them skills to cope with their life circumstances? And wouldn't it truly be a dream come true if we could help their parents, too?"* Well, Confident Kids is that place!

Confident Kids is a Bible-based support-group program that helps families with children ages 4–12 deal with the stresses of living in today's world. Since 1989, Confident Kids has been used by churches and other Christian organizations to offer hope, help, and healing to struggling families. The heart of the program is the Confident Kids curriculum:

- **Facing My Feelings**
  Using the theme "All my feelings are OK," children learn how to name their feelings, how to express them in healthy and appropriate ways, and how to use their feelings to know when it's time to ask for help.
- **Living in My Family**
  Using the theme "There are no perfect families," children are encouraged to see the family as their primary place of belonging and practice a variety of family-living skills.
- **Growing Through Changes**
  Using the theme "Nothing stays the same forever," children learn to deal with change by grieving the losses that occur when things change. They learn to identify and manage the six stages of grief: denial, anger, bargaining, depression, acceptance, and hope.
- **Making Wise Choices**
  Using the theme "I always, always have choices," children learn the difference between wise and unwise choices, practice six steps for making wise

choices, and decide how to find wise adults who can help them choose when needed.

What's in This Manual?

This manual contains all the materials you need to conduct one of the four Confident Kids units. This includes the basic information you need to start a Confident Kids support-group program in your area, and the necessary curriculum material.

- **Age-graded session plans**

  Each of the unit's eight sessions has a complete session plan for the following age groups: preschool (ages 4 years through kindergarten), elementary (grades 1 through 4), preteen (grades 5 and 6), and parents.

- **Session summaries for parents**

  These materials tell parents what their children are learning each week and provide suggestions for reinforcing the session themes at home each week.

- **Resources**

  Game and activity ideas as well as media resources are given.

Can I Use This Series in Settings Other Than a Support Group?

Yes! Although designed as a support-group curriculum for high-stress families, Confident Kids' life skills emphasis makes it a valuable teaching tool in a variety of settings. Here are some of the ways you can use the Confident Kids series:

- **A life skills educational curriculum for all kids**

  Use Confident Kids in Sunday morning classes, vacation Bible schools, weeknight youth programs, and camp or retreat settings.

- **A family life enrichment program for families with preschool and elementary age children**

  Because everyone studies the same life skills curriculum and parents learn how to reinforce the concepts at home, Confident Kids can dramatically impact entire families.

- **A community outreach/evangelism tool**

  Churches that begin a Confident Kids program can be helpful with neighborhood families who may never come to their church for any reason other than seeking help for their struggling children.

- **Single-parent ministry**

  Confident Kids helps children with divorce recovery, as a follow-up after divorce recovery, and in retreat settings for single parents and their kids.

- **A supplement to classroom curriculum**

  School teachers can add a life skills component to their curriculum by using segments of the Confident Kids curriculum in their classrooms.

Understanding How Confident Kids Works

Program Goals

The Confident Kids program seeks to:

- Teach children the skills necessary to understand, talk about, and cope with their life circumstances in healthy and positive ways
- Encourage children to talk about their experiences in a loving, safe environment

- Build self-esteem and a sense of trust through relationships with caring adults (program facilitators)
- Influence homes by teaching parents the same skills being taught to their children
- Guide children and parents into a relationship with God and teach them to value prayer and Scripture as resources

The Power Source: Scriptural Foundations

Confident Kids seeks to help kids who may withdraw from God find Him a personal friend and source of strength. The session plans include carefully selected Bible stories, memory verses, and small group prayer times to communicate four Scriptural truths.

- **God is a loving caregiver who is always present and gives us support in difficult times.**

  Joshua 1:9; Romans 8:38, 39; 1 Peter 5:7

- **Jesus knows what it means to suffer and feel pain and therefore can help us when we experience suffering and pain.**

  Hebrews 2:18, and the Easter events and themes (which help kids connect with Jesus' suffering and difficult choices)

- **When we pray honestly about what we are feeling, God helps us find comfort and peace.**

  Philippians 4:6, 7

- **God intends a hopeful, purposeful future for us, no matter how painful the present may seem.**

  Jeremiah 29:11

Limitations of Confident Kids

Like all programs, Confident Kids has limitations:

- **Support groups are not therapy groups**

  Support groups at any age level never replace professional help. In cases where children or parents are significantly damaged by their life circumstances, a referral to other appropriate sources of help must be made.

- Confident Kids **cannot "cure" all the problems of children!**

  Confident Kids is just one program. It is not a cure-all for helping kids grow up healthy in the midst of our confusing world. It is important for both leaders and parents to maintain reasonable expectations as to the results of participating in the support-group experience (i.e., participating in Confident Kids does not guarantee kids will not have struggles in their teen years)!

Three Program Elements
The Keys to Success

Life Skills Education
• Feelings
• Family
• Changes
• Choices
Concurrent Parent Group
• Life skills education
• Safe, supportive environment
• Impacts the family
A Support-Group Setting
• Small groups
• Safe, supportive environment to talk
• Trained facilitators

Successful support groups for children blend three program elements:

Life Skills Education

Since high-stress children are at risk for developing unhealthy and destructive coping skills, Confident Kids begins by teaching children healthy ways to deal with life's pain and stress.

A Support-Group Setting

The life skills curriculum is taught in a caring, supportive setting. This environment helps make it easier for the kids to develop trust and talk about their lives.

Concurrent Parent Group

By taking parents and the kids through the same material, the entire family is helped. Parents also receive support from meeting other parents who are dealing with the same or similar issues.

How to Start a Confident Kids Program

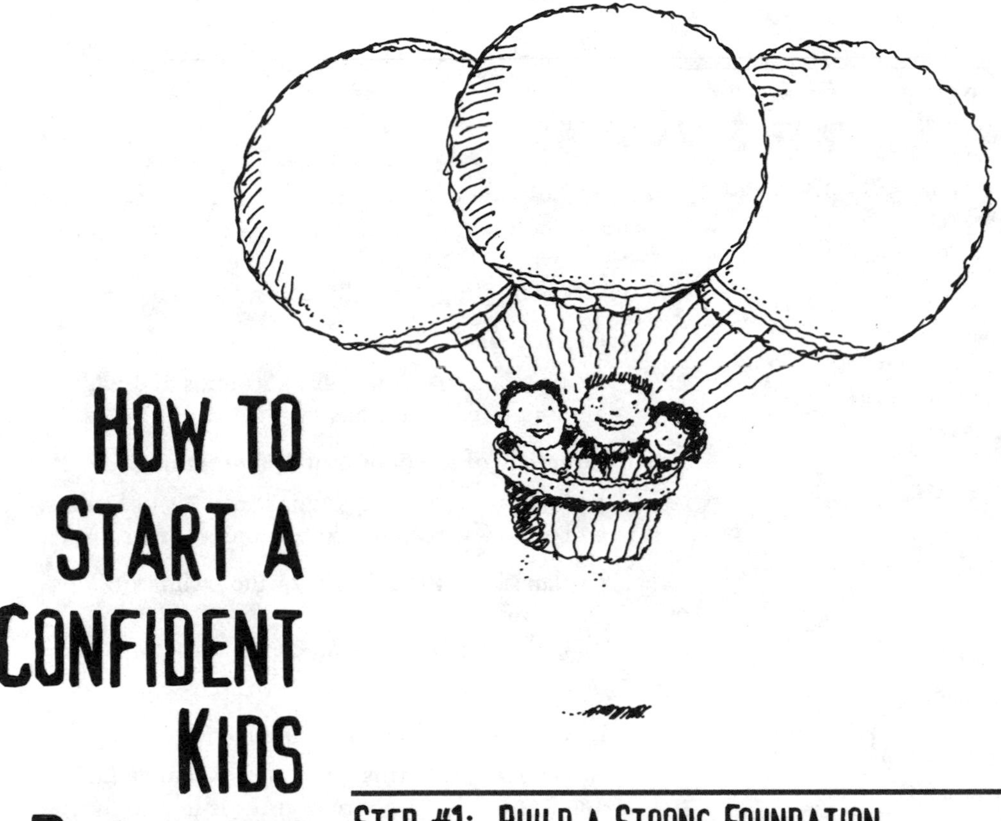

Step #1: Build a Strong Foundation

Determine the Target Audience

Whom do you want to come to your Confident Kids groups? High-stress families in your church? In your community? Both? Single-parent families? Know the people you want to help. The target audience you select will influence the way you organize the program.

Recruit Leaders

Perhaps the most difficult part of any ongoing children's ministry is recruiting and maintaining qualified leaders. Many churches are concerned that beginning a support group for children will further drain their already overtapped leadership pool. However, experience has taught us that Confident Kids often attracts new leaders. Follow these guidelines as you recruit.

Successful Confident Kids leaders exhibit the following characteristics:

- A deep love for children
- A high degree of responsibility and dependability
- Some experience in working with children in group or class settings
- A concern for hurting children
- A level of understanding and sensitivity to hurting children that is crucial to the Confident Kids program. This sensitivity is prevalent in leaders who experienced a painful childhood.

In addition, successful leaders must be committed to the following three principles:

- **Consistently "being there" emotionally and physically**

  Leaders must be totally committed to being at Confident Kids each week, both physically and emotionally. This is crucial because many of the children have been hurt by adults they trusted.

- **Being nonjudgmental**

  Leaders must realize that children may reveal family secrets or behave in certain ways that go against their personal value systems. Although leaders do not have to condone these issues, they must realize that unconditional love and acceptance are important to the healing process.

- **Confidentiality**

  All leaders must realize they will be called upon to use wisdom and discretion as the kids reveal details of their lives. In most cases, the leaders must be able to keep what children or parents say in the group setting confidential, with a few notable exceptions. See "Handling Sensitive Issues" (page 9) for more information on this vital subject.

The Leadership Team

The Program Administrator

This person oversees the entire program. Ideally, this is a paid staff member or someone with easy access to the administrative resources of the organization (i.e., office equipment, publicity vehicles, room allocation schedules, knowledge of potential volunteers, etc.). The responsibilities of the program administrator include:

- Introducing the program to the sponsoring organization
- Securing the time and place for the meetings
- Recruiting and training the facilitators
- Arranging child care for younger siblings
- Publicity
- Registration
- Securing all needed supplies
- Maintaining records
- Evaluation and follow-up

Parent Group Facilitator

It is helpful if the parent group facilitator has had some experience teaching or leading parenting groups, but not required. This person's responsibilities include:

- Knowing the Confident Kids curriculum thoroughly
- Conducting the group, using the Confident Kids parent group guide
- Attending all facilitator training sessions and meetings
- Being involved in parent conferences and/or referrals, when necessary

Small Group Facilitators

The small group facilitators work directly with the kids. Each facilitator is assigned three to five children (usually four), and then grouped with two or three other facilitators and their kids to form a room. Using the Confident Kids curriculum, these facilitators conduct the meetings each week.

Leadership Training

Facilitator training generally takes place in three stages:

Orientation

The first step in the training process is a "no-obligation" orientation. This gives both the potential leaders and the program administrator a chance to explore whether this ministry will be a good match for both. This meeting generally is conducted as follows:

- **Get-acquainted time**

  Participants share their backgrounds and why they are interested in a ministry like Confident Kids.

- **Overview of the Confident Kids program**

  Includes program goals, qualifications of leaders, and a look at the curriculum and meeting format.

- **Explanation of the details of the facilitator commitment**

  Expectations and the importance of follow through once commitment is made are discussed.

- **Distribution of facilitator applications**

  Appendix A ("Forms") contains a sample facilitator application. For legal reasons, it is important to have an application on file for every facilitator. Prospective participants can fill out applications at home, and return them before the basic training session, should they decide to continue.

Basic Training

Once the team is in place, training begins. Confident Kids leaders are trained in:

- **Small group facilitation**

  Skills are needed in listening and responding, keeping the group on track, and recognizing behaviors that indicate a need for professional help. Your church or organization's policy for handling sensitive issues should be discussed as well.

- **Classroom management**

  Maintaining discipline and control, providing smooth transitions between program segments, and having well-prepared lessons are important to the success of Confident Kids.

- **Teamwork**

  Facilitators work together to plan sessions, discipline consistently, solve problems, and pray.

On-the-Job Training

Training does not stop once the sessions begin. Leaders will continue to learn if they meet briefly immediately following each session. Use this time to:

- **Debrief the meeting**

  What happened? Was there anything you didn't know how to handle? Was anything said by a child that concerned you?

- **Plan for the next meeting**

  Take time to prepare for the next session.

- **Pray**

  Prayer should be a priority.

- **Write postcards**

  Kids love to get mail! Sending a postcard each week helps the kids and facilitators bond. Taking time to write them at this meeting ensures every child will receive a card.

Getting Help With Training

Program administrators can get help with the Confident Kids training process from several sources:

Training Seminars. Learn from the creators of the Confident Kids program and those who have used it. The Confident Kids national office offers two-day program administrator training seminars several times a year in various parts of the country as well as four-day leadership institutes. See Appendix B ("Resources") for contact information.

Training Series on Tape. The Confident Kids office also makes available six-hour training programs in audio- or videocassette formats. Program administrators can use these as a self-study program, or to train their facilitators.

Nearby Churches That Have Completed a Confident Kids *Unit.* If another church in your area has offered a Confident Kids program, ask their leaders for help with your training, or send a key leader or two to participate in their program to gain some firsthand experience.

Local Professionals. Therapists, social workers, children's pastors, and teachers can train leaders.

Set Policy for Handling Sensitive Issues

Most of the time, Confident Kids groups are straightforward and predictable. However, from time to time children or parents may reveal sensitive matters. Decisions about how these matters will be handled must be made *before you begin* a support-group program so you will not be caught off guard, should the occasion arise in your program. Many churches now have *written* policies for handling sensitive issues. If your church does not have written policies, encourage your church leaders to establish some before beginning any Confident Kids unit. See Appendix B ("Resources") for resources that can help you with this task.

Handling Confidentiality

Our Confidentiality Agreement With the Kids. In the children's groups, confidentiality is the first rule placed on the "group rules" posters. The facilitators will explain to the children that Confident Kids is meant to be a safe place where they can talk about whatever they want to talk about, and in order to feel safe, everyone needs to know that what they say in group will stay in group. This will be explained further to mean that when they leave the group, they cannot tell anyone else about personal, private things another child has shared in the group. They can talk about whatever else they want. The kids will also be told that the confidentiality agreement extends to the facilitators. The facilitators will not tell anyone what the kids share with them without their permission, and *this includes their parents*. We cannot be helpful to the kids if they believe we will repeat everything they say in the group to their parents.

Our Agreement With the Parents About Getting Information to Them About Their Kids. Although we respect and will hold to the confidentiality agreement with their kids, parents need to know that we will find a way to get information that concerns us to them. This is usually not difficult to do; remember, the key phrase is "without their permission." Most often, when we ask the kids if we can talk to their parents about a particular issue, they are very happy to have us do so; some kids are even relieved. Even when they do not give us permission, we can usually find a way to get information to parents without violating confidentiality, such as making observations of behavior we see. Parents can be assured that it is not our intent to hide things from them. Rather we want to make it as easy as possible for the kids to find help.

Children's Understanding of Confidentiality. The distinction between what is acceptable to talk about outside the group, and what is to be kept confidential is very blurred at the elementary age level. Therefore, parents need to be prepared that their children may come home and say that they were told that they could not tell Mom or Dad anything that happened in the group. In fact, this is the very issue that started Confident Kids parent groups! We want every parent to know that we value confidentiality so much we will not compromise it.

Exceptions to Confidentiality. There are two exceptions to the confidentiality rule:

- **Confidentiality among the Confident Kids leaders**

  If we are to be as helpful as possible to all participants, Confident Kids facilitators must be free to share information about what happens in the groups each week. Facilitators can then be given guidance as to the best way to deal with the issues their group members discussed. This sharing also allows the program administrator to note any information that seems out of the ordinary.
- **Reports of abusive behaviors**

  Any reports of abusive behavior against the kids must—by law in most states—be reported to authorities.

Making Referrals

When families have problems that go beyond the scope of the support-group program, refer them to other sources for help. If your church does not have an approved list of counselors or agencies, build one of your own. Look for the following.

- Counselors and counseling agencies that include one or more counselors on their staff who specialize in working with children and/or family therapy *and* include a sliding scale fee structure
- Lawyers and legal aid services to assist parents with legal issues
- Community resources for specialized issues such as chemical dependency treatment, ADHD diagnosis and treatment, shelters for women and children, etc.
- Local meetings of Alcoholics Anonymous, Al-Anon, and other twelve-step groups
- Other professionals who specialize in issues common to families in your community

Reporting Abuse

In most states, church workers are required by law to report any reports of suspected abuse. Be sure you know in advance the signs to look for and the proper procedures for making reports.

Preventing Legal Problems

It is not likely that your church will encounter any legal difficulties from your Confident Kids program. However, you can safeguard against this possibility by giving attention to the following three issues:

- **Have parents sign a release form**

  The purpose of this form is to make it clear to parents that they are attending a support group only, and not a therapy group. Most courts will recognize that support groups are peer-led groups, and do not incur the same legal liabilities as professionally-led therapy groups.

  A sample enrollment/release form is included in Appendix A ("Forms").

- **Know when and how to report abusive behaviors**

  Never act alone in reporting abuse. Make this decision in consultation with your Confident Kids program administrator, and any other program supervisors (e.g., pastors, counselors). The main point to emphasize here is the need to know the proper procedure to follow in your church or organization *before* the issue actually comes up. *Don't wait until you are in a crisis situation to ask these questions!*

- **Screen your Confident Kids facilitators carefully**

  This is a very important responsibility of the program administrator. It is mentioned here for emphasis. For more information, see Appendix B ("Resources").

STEP #2: RECRUIT FAMILIES AND SET UP THE GROUPS

PUBLICIZE YOUR PROGRAM

Publicize your program in as many of the following as seem appropriate:

- Place announcements in church bulletins and newsletters, school newsletters, etc.
- Distribute informational brochures to selected audiences (i.e., families with elementary-age children, single parents, families living within a five-mile radius of the sponsoring organization)
- Invite teachers and counselors to make referrals to the program
- Place articles and advertisements in your local newspaper(s)

All publicity materials should include the purpose of the program and a clear statement of registration procedures.

REGISTER FAMILIES

Advance registration is necessary to control the size of the groups, gather information about each family, and ensure that parents understand the goals of the group and the commitment that is necessary.

Advance registration is handled through a phone interview. See Appendix A ("Forms") for a sample parent phone interview guide sheet.

Following the phone interview, send a release form to the parent and ask him or her to sign it and return it to you. For legal reasons, it is wise to keep these signed release forms on file for approximately two years.

Appendix A ("Forms") contains a sample parent release form.

SET UP THE CHILDREN'S GROUPS

In a support-group program, how children are grouped and the size of the groups is crucial. In Confident Kids, a "small group" comprises one facilitator and no more than five children. The "large group" is no more than three or four small groups in one room (e.g., nine to fifteen children with three facilitators, or twelve to sixteen children with four facilitators). You can have many rooms running at one time, but never place more than sixteen children in a room.

Children are assigned to a small group and remain in that group for eight weeks. When assigning children to small groups, follow these guidelines:

- Do not place siblings or other family members in the same small group

- Age-grade the groups as closely as possible
- Use same-sex groups, as long as doing so does not violate the first two guidelines

Don't Forget the Parent Group

As stated earlier, an important part of the Confident Kids program is to involve parents in a parent group, unless they are involved in another support group or parenting class meeting at the same time. In general, parents are quite willing to attend the parent group, especially when it is presented to them as an important part of the program. Normally, only one parent group is offered, with all parents meeting together. It is helpful to provide child care for younger children, since many who come to the parent group are single parents.

Welcome Everyone to the First Session

The first meeting is crucial! Since most children attending will have been enrolled by a parent, the kids may be apprehensive and possibly even resistant. The primary goal of the first meeting is to put children at ease and help them begin bonding to the group. We recommend you use the "Welcome to Confident Kids" session (page 19). In this session, all age groups meet together and are introduced to the Confident Kids program.

Step #3: Wrap Up the Unit

Family Night

The last meeting of each session, Family Night, brings everyone together for a closing program and party. Many relationships are built during the seven weeks, and saying good-bye is important. Be sure any parents who may not have participated in the parent group are invited to this session.

Schedule Additional Units

It is likely that at the end of each eight-week unit, your groups will want to continue meeting. If this is the case, you can offer one of the other Confident Kids topics. Start by inviting current parents to enroll their children for another unit. Then add new families to fill any spaces left by those who may choose not to return. Churches that have used Confident Kids for a long period of time simply cycle through all four of the books, adding families at the beginning of each unit as space allows.

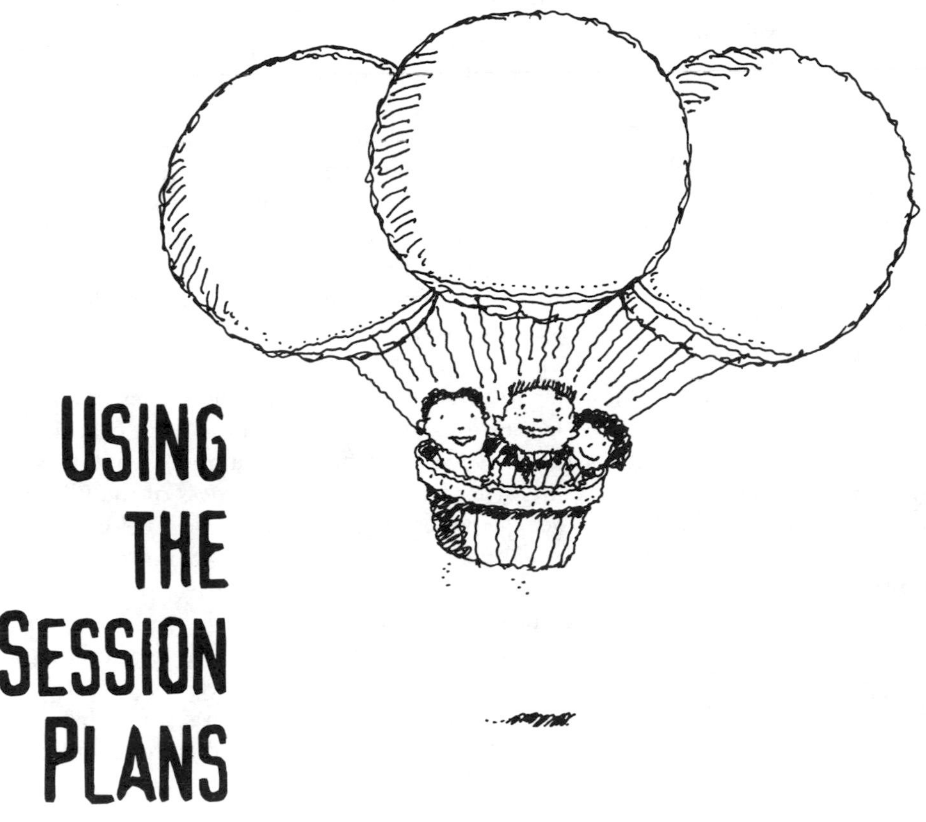

Using the Session Plans

Kids Sessions

Materials Needed for the Group Meetings

Each session plan contains a list of materials needed for that session. This is only a listing of the materials *unique* to that session, such as activity sheets, posters, craft materials, etc. In addition, each room should be stocked with the following basic supplies:

- Pencils, fine-tip markers, and broad-tip markers
- Scissors and staplers
- Glue or glue sticks
- Masking and clear adhesive tape
- Assortment of construction paper and poster board
- *Optional:* A costume/props box for role plays and skits
- *Optional:* An audio- or video-cassette recorder/player
- *Optional:* Games
- Snack tin(s)

Session Plan Components

Each session lasts 90 minutes and includes the following segments.

Getting Started (Large Group)—25 Minutes

Gathering Activity. The gathering activity is usually a game or a craft designed to involve the kids as soon as they arrive, to begin the meeting in a positive and fun way. Facilitators should be available to greet the kids warmly and immediately direct them to this activity.

Group Rules. Some children have never been given clear expectations of appropriate behavior. It is important to establish what is expected of them in Confident Kids almost immediately. This is done through the use of group rules. Most facilitators find it best to have the children help establish these rules. The following four rules should always be included:

1. What is said in group, stays in group (confidentiality)
2. No name-calling or putdowns (respect one another)
3. The "right to pass" (although participation is desired, every child must feel free not to participate if the activity or discussion feels threatening or hurtful)
4. Let the leaders lead (children need to know that the adults are in control, and that they are to be respected)

Once the list of rules has been established, discuss with the group what will happen when the rules are not followed. Most groups have successfully used a simple time-out system. Consistent disruptions result in a consultation with a parent. If a satisfactory change is not made, the child is removed from the group permanently.

Introduction to the Session Theme. The lesson theme is introduced each week through a skit or activity to which the kids can easily relate. In most cases, the story will end with a question or issue designed to stimulate discussion of the session theme. Immediately following the skit, the kids are dismissed to their small groups where this discussion takes place.

Small Groups—35 Minutes

The small group experience is the heart of the Confident Kids program. It is here that the dynamic of teaching life skills in a support-group setting emerges in a powerful way. The small group time comprises these elements:

- **Discussion of the opening skit/activity**

  Each session plan contains questions to debrief the opening skit or activity the kids have just watched.

- **Teaching**

  The life skill being taught is presented.

- **Reinforcement activity**

  A role play, activity sheet, or other involvement activity is used to reinforce the teaching, and help kids to apply it to their own lives.

- **Prayer**

  Prayer is a vital part of Confident Kids. It is during this time that many kids share their most personal concerns, and facilitators can encourage children who are disappointed that God has not answered their prayers in the past (e.g., "I prayed and prayed my parents wouldn't get a divorce, and they did anyway, so what's the point?"). Facilitators can optimize this time by using a prayer journal or some other means to keep a record of kids' requests and answers.

Bible Time (Large Group)—25 Minutes

Regathering. The transition from the small groups to the Bible time should be handled well. Since not all of the small groups will end at exactly the same moment, use music or a short game to draw the kids back into the larger group. Assign one facilitator to lead this time. Use songs or games your kids know and like, or see Appendix B ("Resources") for ideas. *Note:* A tape of songs that correspond to the Confident Kids curriculum for preschoolers through grade four is available from the Confident Kids office. (See Appendix B for ordering information.)

Bible Story/Skit. The Bible stories in all Confident Kids sessions are presented in the form of a skit or puppet show. Careful thought and preparation of these skits will increase the effectiveness of the Bible teaching. (See "Tips for Successful Meetings" below.)

Key Verse. Each unit has two or three key verses, which can be taught using a variety of memory verse games. (See Appendix B.)

Closing Prayer Huddle. This method of closing each meeting brings a sense of ritual to the group, which helps to develop a sense of belonging. Instructions for the prayer huddle are included in each session plan.

Snacks—5 Minutes

Snacks are an important part of Confident Kids meetings. The kids love bringing the treats as well as eating them! Bringing treats in a special Confident Kids snack tin provides a reminder and keeps the snack simple. Of course, in areas where families cannot afford to send treats, they can be provided each week.

Tips for Successful Meetings

Years of experience have revealed some pitfalls you can avoid as you run a program like Confident Kids. You can benefit from others' mistakes by carefully observing the following guidelines:

- **Maintain the ratio of one adult per four children**

  Small groups are a key element to the success of your program. Don't let anything compromise this standard! If you have three leaders, twelve children is ideal. Take no more than fifteen. It is better to hold families on waiting lists for the start of another unit than to take too many kids into your program.

- **Enforce the group rules consistently**

  New facilitators who are eager to work with high-stress, hurting kids are often reluctant to deal with kids' inappropriate behavior. Since high-stress kids often act out their feelings in disruptive ways, all facilitators must work together to see that the group rules are enforced from the very first meeting. The adults must maintain control of the room, or the kids will never let down their defenses and trust the group experience.

- **Give attention to transitions**

  Be sure all facilitators are well prepared. Most of the difficulties encountered in Confident Kids groups happen during transition times when the facilitators are trying to gather materials or practice skits instead of leading the kids smoothly from one activity to another.

- **Insist on after-group staff meetings**

  Getting all Confident Kids leaders together after each meeting to debrief, share information, plan for the next meeting, and pray together is important. Even though everyone may be tired and want to go home, do not skip this vital communication link! See "Step #1: Build a Strong Foundation" (page 7) for more information about the after-meetings.

- **Send postcards every week**

  Anything we can do to let the kids know we are thinking about them is valuable. The simple exercise of having facilitators write postcards to the kids in their small group every week says volumes to the kids. These can be written out in the after-meeting before facilitators go home, and mailed a few days later by the program administrator. That way, every child is sure to receive a card.

Parent Sessions

The parent group sessions follow their own format. Each session follows the same basic outline.

Getting Started—20 Minutes

In this time, you will need to accomplish the following:

Check-In

This is merely a time of conversation to relax group members and give everyone a chance to visit.

Group Rules

As with all support groups, the parent group has several rules, which are designed to keep the group emotionally safe for all participants. The three rules for parent groups are:

- **Confidentiality**

  Confidentiality is foundational to the Confident Kids program. It is also new to many parents, and therefore needs some careful explanation in the group at the beginning of each unit. See page 9 for more information.

- **No advice giving**

  This rule keeps parents from telling other parents what they "should" do to solve their problems, which is not helpful to anyone. Tell parents that they are not to use phrases such as: "What you should do is—" or "Why don't you just—" or "If I were you, I'd—". It *is* helpful when parents share with each other from their own experiences. Encourage parents to use phrases such as: "When we faced that in our family, we found _____ to be helpful." Or, "We have the same problem in our family, and we found _____ to be not helpful." Or, "Here are some resources we found that helped us with _____."

- **The right to pass**

  To feel emotionally safe, parents need to know they will never be put on the spot to share something they feel uncomfortable sharing. Let parents know that when you go around the circle and ask for responses to questions, they may simply say, "I pass," and you will move on to the next person.

Review Session Summary for Parents

Each week you will review with the parents a handout containing an outline of the lesson material the kids will be covering in their groups, with a suggested activity to do at home. These handouts begin on page 343. You need not spend much time on this summary; the purpose is merely to give parents a concise picture of what their kids are doing in their groups each week.

Teaching Time—20 Minutes

This segment is an expansion of the children's material for parents. This material has been written to accomplish two goals:

1. To help the parents better understand what we are teaching their children and how to apply it at home
2. To guide the parents in their own personal growth

The material in the teaching section contains lecture material, plus a few skits, activities, and discussion questions.

Making It Personal—35 Minutes

The Confident Kids parent group is a support group, not a parenting class. Therefore, we try to give the parents opportunity to personalize the material being presented each week. This is accomplished through a personal reflection sheet, which parents fill out during the session and discuss during an open sharing time. These sheets help parents make connections with how they were raised as children (family-of-origin issues) and how they are functioning as parents today. We believe that these insights help break cycles of destructive behavior patterns that parents may unknowingly be following.

Some parent group leaders like to collect the reflection sheets at the end of each session, providing a personal link between them and the parents. This also gives the parents the experience of having an interested person "listen" to their personal issues. Other parent group leaders feel it is best to keep these sheets completely private, and encourage parents to use them during the week at home, to think through the issues at a deeper level.

Building on God's Word—15 Minutes

Each session ends with a time for Scripture emphasis and prayer. A second take-home sheet, "Building on God's Word," is included with each session for this purpose. It is not necessary to teach directly from this sheet, unless you want to. It is more important to encourage parents to use this sheet at home as an aid to spending some quiet time with God during the week. Devote most of this time to focusing on prayer requests and emphasizing the power of prayer.

Preparing to Lead a Session

Your effectiveness will be greatly increased by following these steps:

- **Read the children's curriculum before preparing your session.**

  Remember that the parent group is an expansion of the same material the kids are learning. The goal is for the *whole family* to feel they have experienced the same program. You will be better prepared to coordinate the total experience for the parents if you are well acquainted with what the kids are doing in their groups.

- **Take time to make the material your own.**

  There is nothing magical about the session plan; it is simply a tool. Therefore take time to personalize it. You will be effective as a parent group leader only to the extent you feel personally connected to the material you are presenting. Add personal examples and illustrations, expand on the material from your area of expertise and past experience, and add activities or approaches you feel are appropriate to your group of parents. Obviously, the session plan does not know you or your parents; it is *you* as the parent group leader who must add life to your session!

- **Choose which parts of the session seem to be most effective for your style and your setting.**

  You will probably not be able to do everything the session plan calls for each week. You will need to make some choices about what you will do. For example, if you are a good teacher, you may want to spend more time teaching. Or, if you feel the parents are benefiting more from the personal reflection time, keep your teaching time short and spend more time doing that. In the beginning, remain flexible and don't become frustrated if you don't get through everything. It takes time to discover the best format for you and your group!

- **Pray.**

  The families in your group will grow and change as God's Spirit moves in their hearts and lives. Therefore, you can facilitate the most powerful change of all by holding them up to God during the weeks of this unit!

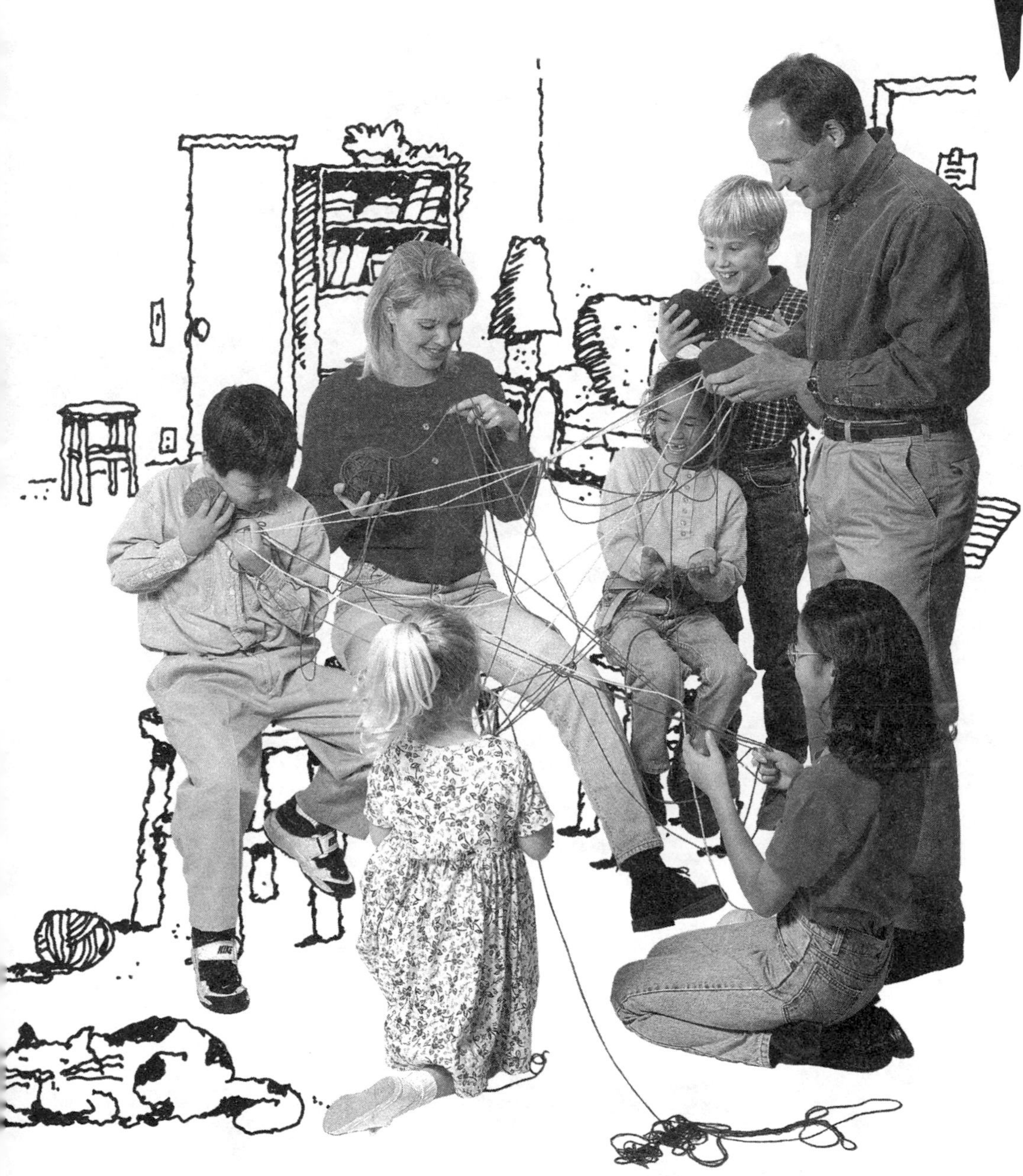

WELCOME TO CONFIDENT KIDS!

If this is your first Confident Kids unit and all the participants are new to the program, consider adding this optional introductory session to your schedule.

Introducing all the family members together to Confident Kids helps them relax and feel more comfortable. This session is only necessary when *all* the families are new. Once at least some of your participants have experienced a Confident Kids unit, this session is no longer necessary.

Goals

- Reduce participants' anxiety by establishing a warm, caring, and fun environment
- Introduce the Confident Kids program and purpose of the group
- Develop the group rules
- Use Joshua 1:9 to assure children of God's presence and care for them

Needed

- Family Shield activity sheet (one per family)
- Ball of yarn
- Blank poster boards (one for each room)
- "Welcome to Confident Kids" letter (one per family)
- Theme verse (Joshua 1:9) posters
- Snacks

Welcome to Confident Kids

Outline

Opening (40 Minutes)

Family Shields

Group Game and Introductions

Introduction of the Confident Kids Program

Dismissal to Individual Rooms

Getting Acquainted (25 Minutes)

The Reporter Game and Parent Group

Group Rules

Small Groups

Bible Time (15 Minutes)

Confident Kids Theme Verse

Prayer Huddle

Snack (10 Minutes)

WELCOME TO CONFIDENT KIDS

"God Be
With You"
Joshua 1:9

OPENING (40 MINUTES)

FAMILY SHIELDS

As children and parents arrive, have Family Shield activity sheets (page 26) and markers available. Say:

> **As a family, work together to complete your shields by filling in the quarters of the shields as follows:**
>
> 1. **Draw a picture of your family.**
> 2. **Draw or write about a favorite family activity.**
> 3. **Draw or write about something you would like to change about your family.**
> 4. **Draw or write the best thing about your family!**

When completed, ask them to bring their shields and move to the group area for the next part of the program.

GROUP GAME AND INTRODUCTIONS

Play the "Spider Web" game, or use any game that the parents and kids can play together. If you have preschoolers present, ask parents to help them play along.

Spider Web

You will need a ball of yarn for this activity. Have everyone stand in a circle. One person begins by holding onto the strand of yarn in one hand. Then he says his name before throwing the ball to a person somewhere else in the circle (without letting go of the strand). Whoever catches the ball is next, and repeats the process, also holding onto the yarn. As group members continue to throw the ball back and forth, the middle of the circle will transform into a "spider web." After everyone has had a turn, tell the group that they must now do something with their web (e.g., lay it on the floor, get into the middle of it, undo it). It's fun to see what they choose to do!

After the game, ask everyone to sit in a circle. Use the Family Shields as a way for families to introduce themselves.

Introduction to Confident Kids

The program administrator (or another leader) should make the following presentation to help the group understand what Confident Kids is all about:

> **Welcome to Confident Kids. This is a group especially for kids. It is your group and we want you to feel comfortable here!**
> *(Ask the following questions)*
>
> **Why do you think we named the group Confident Kids?**
>
> **What does it mean to be confident?**
>
> **What do you think we will be doing in this group?**
>
> **There are many special things about being a kid and growing up. When life is going well, you are exploring new things and spending time with people who will help you become all you can be. It is a time for you to be loved and cared for and to learn what things make you special and unique.**
>
> **But sometimes life is not what we want it to be, and even kids feel hurt and disappointed. Sometimes things change when we don't want them to, sometimes people hurt us without knowing it, and sometimes we don't feel like anyone could love us or we are good at doing anything. Those kinds of things happen to everyone from time to time. You are in this group because we care about you and want to help you learn how to handle those kinds of things—now—while you're still a kid.**
>
> **In Confident Kids, we will play games, do activities, have snacks, watch and act in skits, learn from the Bible, and pray together. While we are having fun doing those things, we'll also have lots of time to talk about things that we really want to talk about. That's all I want to say right now, except that we are on an adventure, and we're really glad you are with us!**

Dismissal to Individual Rooms

At this time, send everyone to their respective rooms, with their facilitators. Participants will spend the rest of the session there, coming back together for snacks at the end of the session.

Parent Group

Parents will spend their time introducing themselves, going over their group rules (below), and discussing the "Welcome to Confident Kids" letter (page 347). Build in enough time to answer any questions parents may have.

Getting Acquainted (25 Minutes)

The Reporter Game

Preschool

If you have a preschool room (kids age 4 years through kindergarten), use a variation of the reporter game. Use a microphone and act as a reporter. Interview each child by asking one or two questions such as:

> **How many brothers and sisters do you have?**

Do you have any pets?

What is your favorite _________ ?

Do you go to preschool? kindergarten?

Note: You can add interest by using a real tape recorder and playing the tape back for the kids to hear.

Grades 1–6

Divide the groups into pairs, being sure that brothers and sisters and kids that know each other are separated. Tell the kids that they are newspaper reporters and their assignment is to find out as much as possible about the other person in their pair. Encourage them to find out unusual things like famous relatives, unusual hobbies, awards won in the past, etc. Give them five minutes to talk to each other. Then reconvene the circle and ask each child to share one interesting fact they learned about their partners.

Group Rules

Establishing the group rules is an important part of this meeting. As you discuss the rules, write them down on a blank piece of poster board. (*Note:* In the preschool groups, prepare a rules poster in advance, using pictures and simple words to depict the rules.) A facilitator begins by saying:

This is our group, and we are going to be together for the next few weeks. All groups—like families, school classes, and even groups of friends—have rules.

What do rules do for us? *(Help us get along better, have fun, and stay safe)*

What would life be like if we didn't have any rules? *(Refer to what it would be like to play games, drive on roads, etc. if there were no rules)*

So, today we will spend some time making a list of rules that will make our group a good place to be. I'll start us off with one rule that is important to me—confidentiality. *(Write on board)* **What do you think that word means?** *(Allow for responses)* **It means that when the others in your group share something that is really personal—maybe something about their family or how they are feeling inside—you agree not to tell those personal stories to anyone else outside of this room. Confidentiality goes for the leaders, too. When you share with us, we will not tell your stories to anyone else *without your permission.***

Exception! There is one exception to confidentiality. If we find out you are being hurt by someone, particularly an adult, we will not keep that confidential. We will tell someone, and get you some help. We will never let you stay in a place where you are unsafe.

At this point, invite the kids to help you add rules to the poster. Keep this moving and keep it serious! Don't let the kids make fun of the rules. Let them know you take them very seriously, and expect them to as well. Periodically, the facilitators add rules. Be sure these are included:

—No put-downs or name-calling

—Leaders lead (kids follow directions and participate)

—The right to pass (no one has to do or say anything that make them uncomfortable)

When you have six or seven good rules, move on to talking about what will happen when the rules are not followed. This will have been determined in advance and communicated to facilitators during the training process (page 8). Communicate this to the kids now. Then display your group rules poster in a prominent place and be absolutely sure that every facilitator works together to maintain the rules consistently!

Small Groups

Divide the kids into their small groups to get acquainted with their facilitator for a few minutes. During this short time, the facilitator should introduce himself by telling a few personal things the kids would enjoy knowing, and ending with a short prayer for each child in the group.

Bible Time (15 Minutes)

Regathering

Gather everyone back together into the larger group for the remainder of the session.

Confident Kids Theme Verse

Before the meeting, print the Confident Kids theme verse (Joshua 1:9) on two posters: one for preschoolers and one for first through sixth graders. The preschool verse should use pictures instead of words. Use the versions listed below. Say:

> **Each week in Confident Kids, we are going to talk about how God helps us become confident kids. We will learn that no one has to face difficult things in their lives alone. We can find lots of people to help us. We're also going to learn that the best source of help we have is God! We have a theme verse that tells us about this. Let's say it together:**
>
> *Preschool:* **"So don't be afraid. The Lord your God will be with you everywhere you go." (*ICB*)**
>
> *Grades 1–6:* **"Have I not commanded you? Be strong and courageous. Do not be terrified; do not be discouraged, for the Lord your God will be with you wherever you go." (*NIV*)**

Conclude with a short personal example of how God's presence has helped you be strong and courageous when facing difficult things in your life.

Prayer Huddle

Teach the kids the traditional Confident Kids closing. Gather everyone into a tight circle and instruct them to "stack" their hands on top of each other in the middle of the circle. As they stand in this position, a facilitator says a short closing prayer. At the end, everyone yells out, "Amen!" as they raise their hands out of the stack and over their heads.

Snacks (10 Minutes)

Make this first meeting special by providing a nice refreshment table for families to enjoy. You might get a decorated cake, with the words "Welcome to Confident Kids!" or have make-your-own sundaes. This will make the kids feel welcome and comfortable with the program.

Draw a picture of your family

Draw or write about a favorite family activity

Draw something you would like to change about your family

Draw the best thing about your family

Preschool Sessions

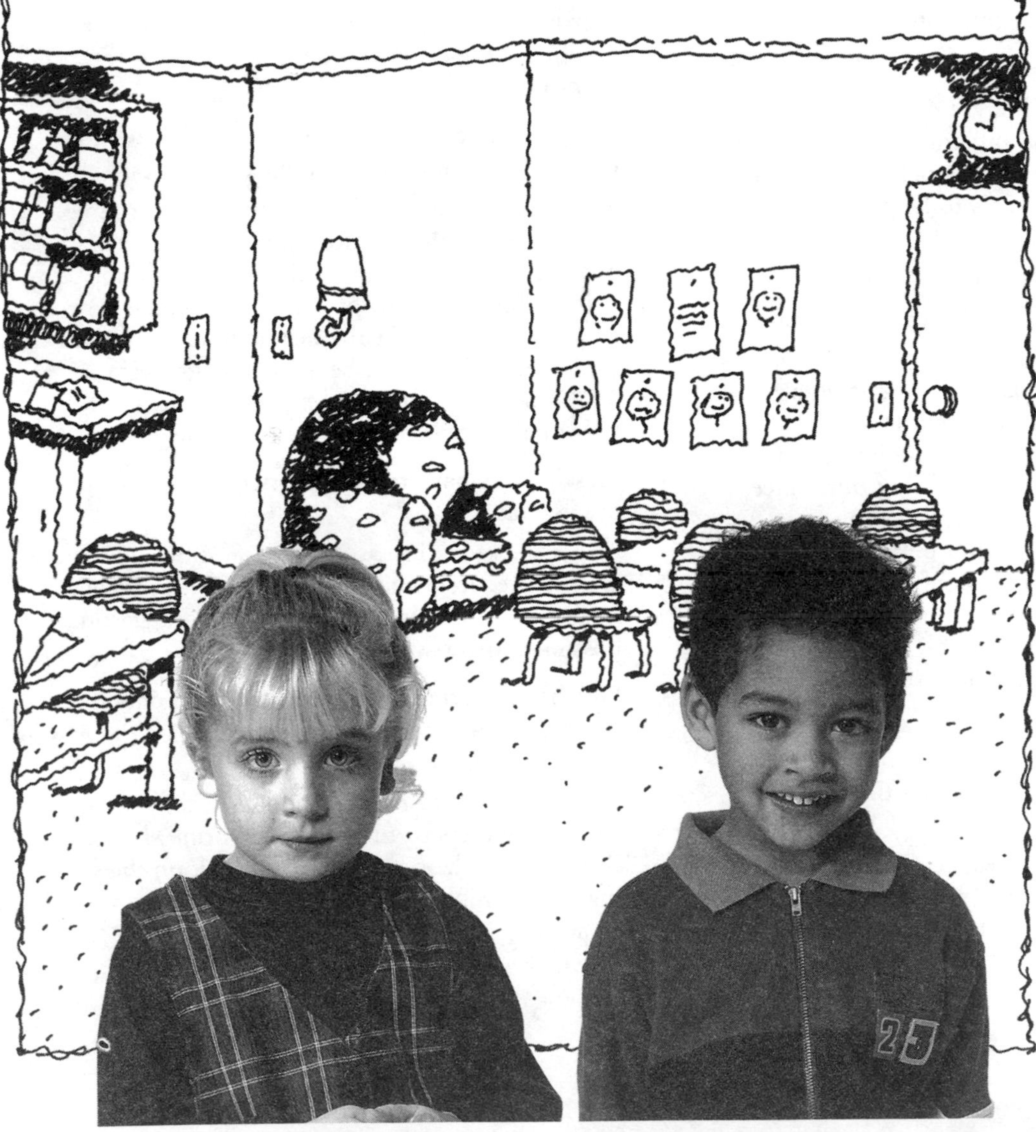

Tips for Working With Preschoolers in a Support-Group Setting

What to Expect From Preschoolers in Confident Kids Groups

Preschoolers are at a much different developmental level than elementary age kids, and function in and respond to the support-group experience uniquely. Here are a few key points about preschoolers to help you plan for your group:

- **Preschoolers hurt deeply but have few developmental skills to deal with emotional pain.**

  A preschooler cannot reason, "I feel guilty and abandoned because my parents are getting a divorce. I need to grieve this great loss in my life." Rather, she is confused by the intense pain she feels and responds by acting out. Since she cannot verbalize what is really going on, adults may miss the connection between a child's feelings and her behavior. In Confident Kids, we understand this connection and help preschoolers deal with their emotional pain by helping them name their feelings, release them through play and story activities, and by teaching them to ask for help when they need it.

- **Preschoolers express themselves best through play and pretending.**

  Preschoolers have limited verbal skills. Therefore, they are helped more through play centers, puppet role plays, and art activities than through dialogue and discussion. The most strategic time you have with your preschoolers may be in the opening play centers!

- **Preschoolers are concrete thinkers and have difficulty with the abstract concepts in the Confident Kids material.**

  Feelings, grief, and evaluating the results of choices are abstract concepts. Although the session plans make these concepts as concrete as possible, you may have to simplify them even further. Don't be alarmed if the children do not understand everything perfectly.

- **Preschoolers cannot think in terms of cause-and-effect relationships and complex processes.**

  This means your preschoolers may have trouble understanding the relationships between feelings and the events that caused them, and will not be able to think in terms of "layered" feelings. For example, "Are you really feeling hurt or are you feeling angry?" would be a confusing question. Therefore, focus on naming feelings and assuring kids that all their feelings are OK to feel.

- **Preschoolers have trouble participating in group discussions.**

  To get the kids to focus on the questions, go around the circle and ask each child a question. Be prepared to help them respond by suggesting possible answers.

- **Preschoolers remember and respond to only one direction at a time.**

  Make your directions clear and simple and stay focused on one task at a time. For example, don't tell preschoolers to finish their coloring sheets, clean up, get their snack, and then sit on the story rug for the Bible story—and expect them to get it all accomplished!

Activity Centers Maximize the Confident Kids Experience

Since preschoolers express themselves best through play and pretending, one of the most strategic times of the Confident Kids meeting is the opening activity centers. In each session plan you will find suggestions for opening centers that are related to the theme. However, any of the following centers allow children the opportunity to express their feelings through play:

- **Home Living Center**
  Have items available to "play house."
- **Doll House Center**
  Display a doll house complete with furniture and a family of dolls the kids can manipulate.
- **Stuffed Animal Center**
  This center can be effective when supervised and kids use the animals for cuddling and storytelling. Do not allow rough play with the stuffed animals.
- **Book Center**
  Display books that talk about feelings, family relationships, and problem solving. Preschoolers are particularly interested in animal and fantasy stories.
- **Puppet Box**
  Have a variety of puppets that can be used to act out scenarios or problem-solving situations.
- **Dress-Up Corner**
  A big box of old clothes, shoes, jewelry, hats, costumes, and a floor-length mirror will help kids express themselves through pretending and role playing.
- **Art Corner**
  Offer different art mediums throughout the unit.

Facilitators can make the activity centers places of healing by guiding the conversation and listening for key expressions from the kids. For example, if you are working in a puppet center, you could engage the kids in conversation by having a puppet pretend to have a problem typical of preschoolers. Kids can talk to the puppet about the problem, or take another puppet and have that "friend" talk to your puppet about his problem. In the art center, a facilitator can guide kids with simple suggestions such as: "What do you think happy looks like? Can you draw it? How about sad?" Listening to the children's responses and observing their behavior during these times will reveal a great deal about the kids and their experiences.

Skits and Bible Stories Are Key Learning Times

Another key time for preschoolers is story time. The preschool Confident Kids curriculum, like the elementary curriculum, offers both an opening skit and an ending Bible story. *Unlike the older kids, however, preschoolers respond best if you do not use facilitators as actors.* This confuses children at this age. Use one of the following ideas instead.

- **Recruit a drama team to do the skits and Bible stories.**
  Whatever format you use to tell the story, having someone else do it frees you from a large piece of the preparation. You can use live actors as long as the kids do not know them as their facilitators.
- **Use puppets to tell the story.**
  Puppets take some practice and equipment, but it is well worth the effort, as the kids respond unusually well to them. You might consider recruiting a puppet team whose only responsibility is to prepare and present the skits each week.
- **Prerecord the skits on videotape.**
  Videotaped skits allow you the freedom to be creative with the skits and give the kids the familiar experience of watching a "movie" on video. Again,

recruiting a team to produce the tapes would be ideal. High schoolers may really enjoy this "high-tech storytelling."

- **Involve the kids in the action.**

  Kids love to pretend, and can be recruited to act as a crowd, an army, or animals. Look for ways to get them to participate in the stories.

- **Use purchased visual aids or videos to tell the Bible stories.**

  Pictures, flannelgraph figures, objects, and animated videos are excellent ways to help the kids focus on the story. If you have an artist available to you, develop your own visual aids.

Have Basic Materials on Hand for All Sessions

Each session plan in the curriculum lists supplies unique to that session. However, before you begin any unit, be sure to set up your room with the following basic supplies. Adding the optional materials will further enhance the group's experience.

- **Basic Supplies**

  Confident Kids postcards and stamps
  Crayons, markers, pencils
  Colored drawing paper
  Tape, glue sticks, stapler
  Blunt scissors
  Paper towels and other supplies for clean up
  Paper cups and napkins for snack time
  Extra snacks (in case someone forgets to return the snack tin)

- **Optional Supplies**

  Roll of butcher paper
  Glitter, lace doilies, scraps of fabric and ribbon
  Paints and painting supplies
  Old magazines with lots of pictures
  Cassette tapes of songs for preschoolers
  A variety of stickers
  Preschool games and craft books to supplement the curriculum, if needed

Goals

- Introduce kids to the wide range of feelings God has given all of us
- Begin to teach a feelings vocabulary
- Assure kids that God understands and cares about everything we feel

Needed

- Supervised places around the room where kids can play
- Feelings faces flash cards
- Group rules poster
- Happy/sad face masks
- *Optional:* Feelings faces poster
- Props for skit
- Many pictures showing people expressing different feelings
- Prayer notebook or prayer boxes
- Children's praise music tape and/or other music items
- Costumes, props, or pictures for "Introducing David" Bible story (depending on how you choose to tell it)
- Joshua 1:9 poster
- Snacks or drinks
- Items for quiet games
- Story book
- Other: ______________

I Have Lots of Feelings!

Preschool Session 1 Plan

Fill in the name of the person responsible for each activity and post this sheet in the room.

Time: ______________ *Arrival and Play Centers (20 Minutes)*

Greeter ______________

Center #1: Free Play ______________

Center #2: Feelings Faces Flash Cards ______________

Time: ______________ *Circle Time (15 Minutes)*

Introduction of New Kids ______________

Group Rules and "How Are You Today?" ______________

"You Hurt My Feelings!" ______________

Time: ______________ *Small Groups (25 Minutes)*

Talk About It ______________

Feelings Faces Mural ______________

Prayer Time ______________

Time: ______________ *Bible Time and Closing Prayer Huddle (15 Minutes)*

Regathering ______________

"Introducing David" ______________

Memory Verse ______________

Closing Prayer Huddle ______________

Time: ______________ *Snack and Quiet Games/Stories (15 Minutes)*

Snack ______________

Quiet Games/Stories ______________

I Have Lots of Feelings!

Preschool Session 1

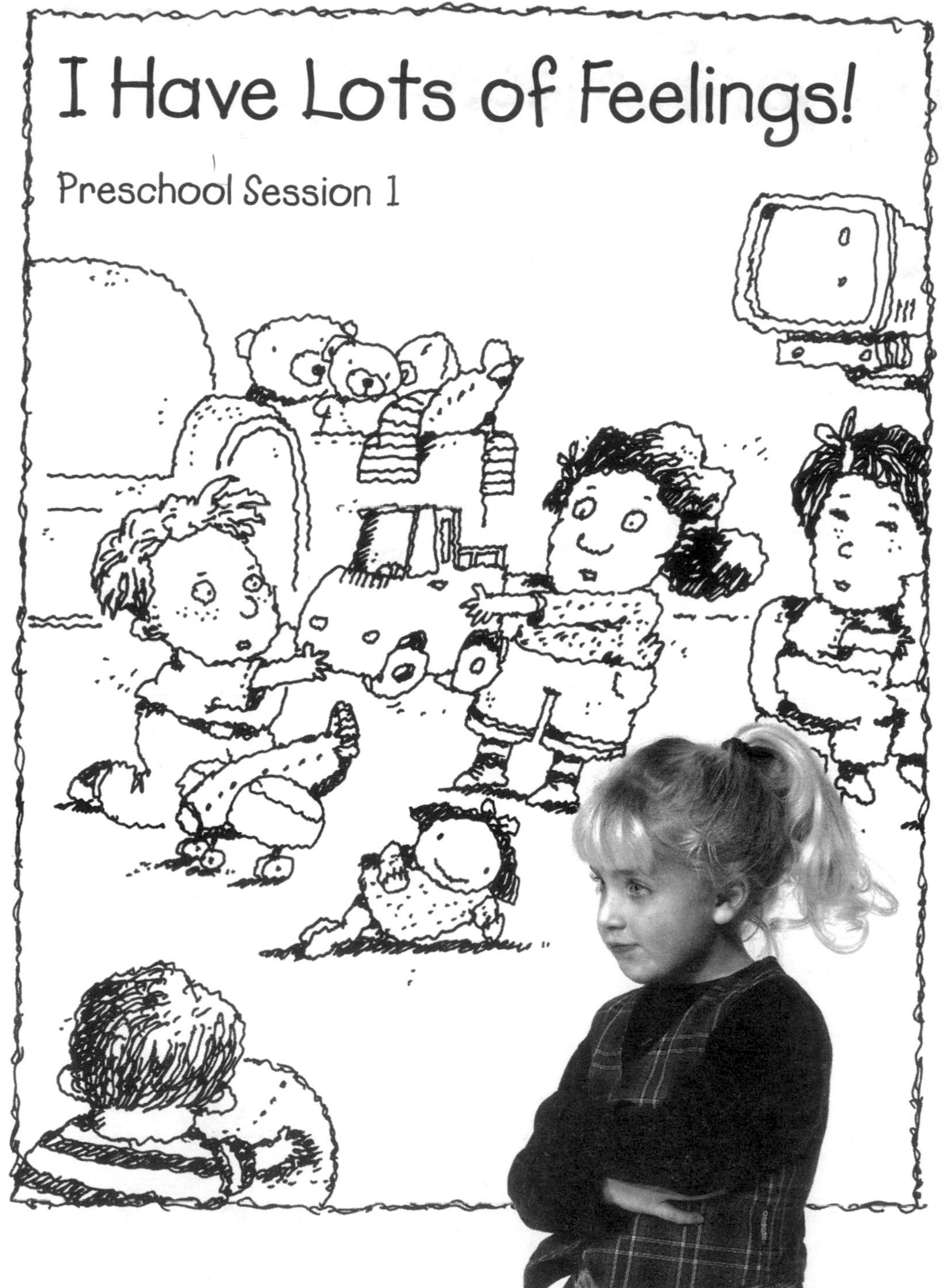

Opening Play Centers (20 Minutes)

Center #1: Free Play

Each week you can offer two centers where children can play safely (e.g., a home living area or doll house, blocks, modeling clay, puzzles, books, a sand table). One or two facilitators should supervise, encouraging kids to move freely between these areas and Center #2. Make sure all the kids are participating.

Center #2: Feelings Faces Flash Cards

Make two sets of feelings faces flash cards. Copy page 58 onto card stock and cut the cards apart. You will only need one set today (you will use two sets in future weeks). When kids arrive, begin by laying the cards out on the table. Ask kids to find various faces:

Where is the happy face?

Continue until all faces have been identified. Then add variety by letting kids pick up certain cards:

Jason, you can pick up the angry face.

When they are familiar with the faces, have them tell you what feelings the faces express as you point to them. Involve kids for as long as they are interested; remember, they can go back and forth between centers as often as they like.

Circle Time (15 Minutes)

Introduction of New Kids

If you have done a Confident Kids unit before, you will likely have both returning kids and new kids in the group. Welcome the new ones by calling each one to the front of the room. Ask the child to say his name and his favorite flavor of ice cream (or ask any other "ice breaker"). When the child is finished, lead the group in yelling, "Welcome, *(child's name)*!" and give each child a round of applause.

Group Rules

In advance, prepare a poster with the group rules on it, depicted in pictures and simple words. Display the poster and explain how the group rules work. Be sure all of the children understand the rules and the time-out system. (See page 15 for more information.) Use these rules with preschoolers:

1. We won't tell each other's secrets (be sure to explain this carefully)
2. Only one person talks at a time and everyone else listens
3. We will not hurt each other (e.g., no hitting, kicking, name-calling)
4. Listen to the teachers and follow directions carefully
5. You don't have to take a turn if you don't want to (i.e., it's OK to pass)

"How Are You Today?"

Ask the kids to think about how they are feeling today. Can they think of a feeling word to describe it? If you like, make happy/sad face masks out of two paper plates and dowel sticks. Draw a happy face on one plate and a sad face on the other. Fasten the plates to the dowels so you can hold up either a happy face or a sad face in front of your own. Invite kids to use the masks to tell you how they are feeling today. Pass them around the circle and let everyone have a turn. *Optional:* If you have a feelings faces poster, invite kids to come forward and point to the face that describes how they are feeling today.

"You Hurt My Feelings!"

Introduce the story:

> **We will be talking about our feelings in this unit of Confident Kids. We all have lots of different feelings. Some of them make us feel warm and happy, and others make us feel sad and hurt. Here's a story about a boy who had some hurt feelings.**

Use puppets, dolls, or a drama team to act out the skit. (See "Tips for Working With Preschoolers" on page 28 for ideas on story presentation.) The story script is on page 36.

Small Groups (25 Minutes)

Talk About It

Use these questions to discuss the story (*Optional:* Use a set of the feelings faces flash cards and have kids identify the appropriate feelings faces):

> **Carol said Clyde hurt her feelings when he called her stupid. Have you ever felt hurt because someone called you a name?** *(Let kids respond)* **What happened?** *(Let kids respond)*
>
> **What feeling do you think Clyde felt when he saw Carol crying?** *(Sad, sorry that he had done it)*
>
> **What feeling did Carol feel when Clyde said he was sorry and they started to play again?** *(Happy)*

When God made us, He gave us lots and lots of different feelings. Some of our feelings are fun—like when we feel happy or excited or loved. Others are not very fun at all—like when we feel sad or mad or lonely. But every single feeling we have is important—even ones that are not fun. It's OK to feel every feeling!

Feelings Faces Mural

Before the session divide a piece of poster board or butcher paper into four sections. Make a feelings face in the center of each one: happy, angry, hurt, and loved. Place this mural in the center of the table along with many pictures that show people expressing these feelings. Collect these from magazines, coloring books, children's story books, etc. Instruct the kids to find pictures that match the feeling face in the box on the mural and paste the pictures into that box. When complete, post the mural in the room. Encourage kids to show it to their parents at the end of the session.

Prayer Time

Each week you will spend the last few minutes of your small group time in prayer. The purpose of this time is to teach the kids how God's presence and power help them face the circumstances in their lives. To make this tangible, keep a prayer notebook or set up two boxes, one labeled *Requests* and the other *Answers*. Ask for prayer requests and write them in the notebook or write them on slips of paper and place them in the *Requests* box. Review past requests each week and talk about how God has responded to each one. When an answer has been given, put a happy face sticker in the notebook or on the slip of paper. Move the answered requests to the *Answer* box.

Bible Time and Closing Prayer Huddle (15 Minutes)

Regathering

Assign one facilitator each week to lead the kids in music as they come from their small groups to the Bible story area. During this unit on feelings, and with David as the principal Bible character, you may consider using a children's praise tape to teach the kids some Psalms set to music. You may prefer to use a favorite game or activity instead (see Appendix B, "Resources," for ideas). The facilitator will have to finish her small group time a few minutes early to be ready to gather the kids as they come from their groups.

"Introducing David"

As with the opening skit, you will have to decide how to present the Bible stories each week. See "Tips for Working With Preschoolers" (pages 28–30) for ideas. The Bible story script is on page 37. *Note:* Do not introduce David by name, as guessing his identity is part of the story.

Memory Verse

This week's memory verse is Joshua 1:9. Introduce the verse by making a poster the kids can "read." Put as many pictures together as possible, using words only as connectors. Use feelings faces for the feelings words, arms showing muscles for *strong*, a picture of Jesus for *God*, etc. Say the verse to the kids, using the poster. Then have them say it with you several times as you "read" it together.

> **So don't be afraid. The Lord your God will be with you everywhere you go.**
> **Joshua 1:9 (*ICB*)**

Closing Prayer Huddle

Each week the meetings will close in the same way. Gather all the kids into a tight circle and instruct them to stack their hands on top of each other in the middle of the circle. As they stand in this position, have them recite the following prayer together:

> **Dear God, thank You for loving me and giving me all my feelings! Amen!**

As they yell out "Amen," have them raise their hands out of the stack and over their heads.

Snack and Quiet Games/Stories (15 Minutes)

End each session with a snack. After the snack, have some quiet activities ready to fill any time left before parents arrive to collect their children. A story book, short video, or coloring page would work well.

Characters

- Clyde and Carol

Needed

- A doll
- A toy airplane
- A toy truck

"You Hurt My Feelings!"

Clyde and Carol are sitting on the floor playing. Clyde has the airplane and Carol has the doll. The truck is in front of them. Carol watches Clyde "zoom" the airplane for a few minutes, then puts the doll down and starts to play with the truck. Clyde notices, stops zooming the airplane, and watches her for a moment. Then he roughly takes the truck away.

Clyde Hey! You can't play with that!

Carol *(Looks surprised)* Why not?

Clyde Here, play with your dumb doll. Trucks are for boys, not girls.

Carol *(Tries to take it back)* I want the truck! Give it back!

Clyde *(Pushes her away)* No! It's mine now, and I want it. *(Holds it tight and moves away from her)* You're so stupid I don't even want to play with you! Why don't you just take your doll and go home?

Carol *(Looks shocked and hurt. Starts to cry and talks softly)* I'm not stupid.

Clyde *(Glances over his shoulder, slowly moves back)* Hey, why are you crying?

Carol Why do you think? You hurt my feelings! I'm not stupid and neither is Nellie! *(Hugs doll)* It hurts when you call me stupid.

Clyde It does? I didn't think about that. *(Pauses)* I'm sorry. You're not really stupid. You're my friend. Let's go play something else!

Carol *(Brightens)* OK!

From

- 1 Samuel (excerpted)

Characters

- David

Needed

- Biblical costume for David
- Props to help kids know who he is (e.g., a harp, a slingshot, a pouch with five pebbles)

Introducing David

David enters, carrying a few props to help the kids know who he is.

David Hi, everyone! Uh—you all look so sad! Am I in the right place? Is this the Down In the Mouth Club? No, that's not right. Are you the I Can't Do Anything Right Kids? No, no, that's not it either. I remember—you're Confident Kids, right? Well, then, let's say it like we mean it! *(Get kids to yell out, "We're Confident Kids!")*

I like your name! Do you know what it means? Being "confident" means we know there are things we can do really, really well. Like, how many of you can sing? *(Let kids respond)* Dance? *(Let kids respond)* Draw? *(Let kids respond)* Turn a somersault? *(Let kids respond)* Run fast? *(Let kids respond)* I know all of you can do at least one of those things really well! What else can you do? *(Ask specific kids for responses; "[Child's name], what can you do really well?" When they answer, add: "That makes you a confident [runner, artist, etc.]!")*

Being "confident" also means we know someone loves us very much. Like our moms and dads, or grandmas and grandpas, or friends, and of course, God! Who do you think loves you? *(Ask specific kids for answers)*

Say, I forgot something! Do you know who I am? *(Let kids guess)* Stories about me are told in the Bible, and I'll bet some of you have heard them. Like the time I fought the big giant named Goliath, using only my slingshot and pebbles. *(Show items. Lets kids try them, if there is time)* My name is David, and I'm here to tell you how I learned to tell all my feelings to God. I am famous for writing poems and songs to sing to God. *(Show harp)* That's how I tell God all my feelings.

We're going to have fun in the weeks ahead, but I'm all out of time today. I just want to say one more thing. Always remember, God gave you all your feelings, so you can always tell Him everything you feel, especially when you feel hurt or sad. It's easy! I'll show you how next week. Bye for now!

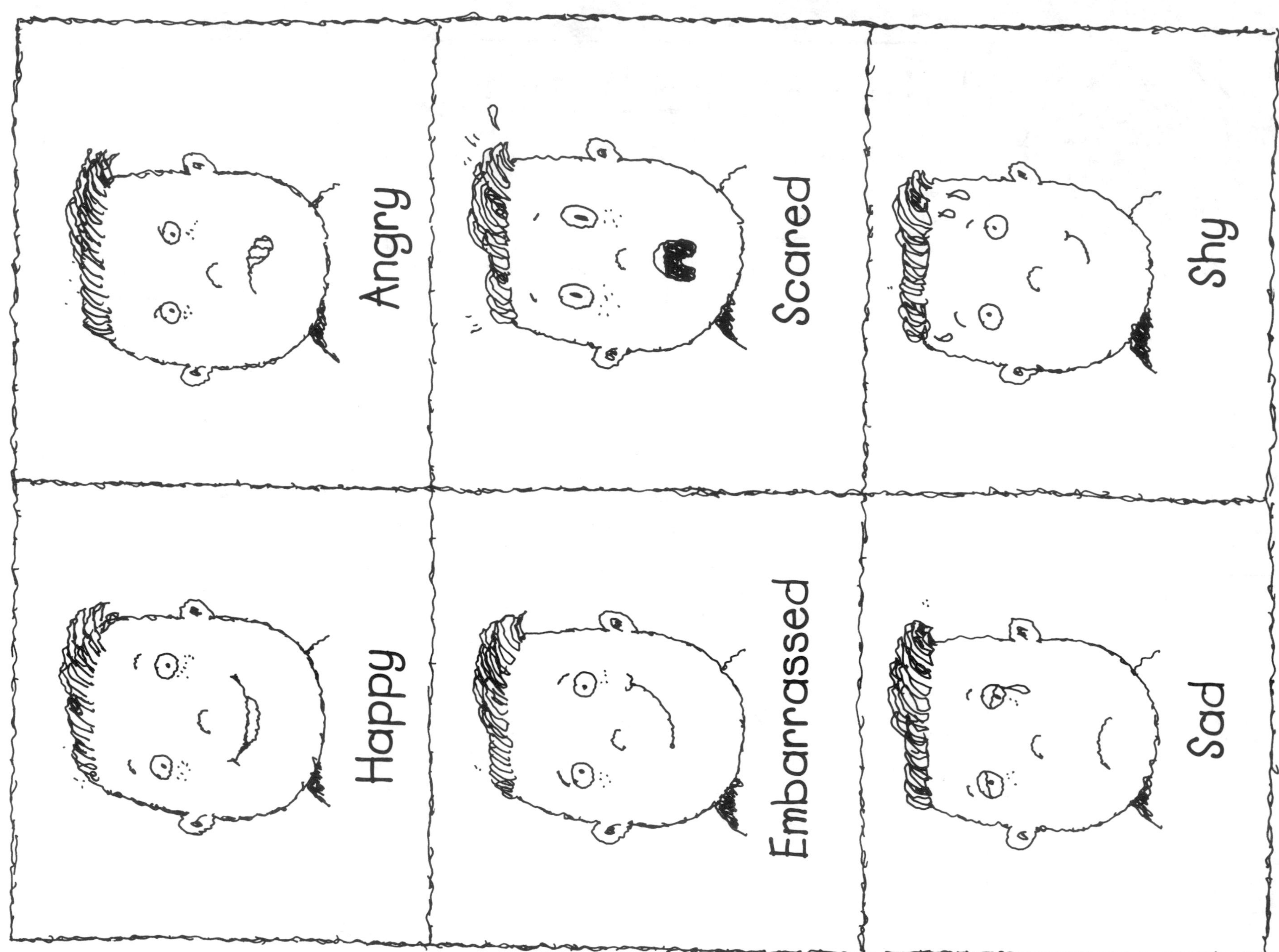

Angry
Scared
Shy
Happy
Embarrassed
Sad

Goals

- Continue to learn the feelings words introduced last week
- Do a movement exercise to show how our whole bodies are affected by our feelings
- Affirm that there are no bad feelings; even feelings that are uncomfortable are important

Needed

- Supervised places around the room where kids can play
- Coloring sheets
- Group rules poster
- Happy/sad face masks
- *Optional:* Feelings faces poster
- Feelings faces flash cards
- Puppets or props for skit
- Copies of "Feelings and My Body"
- Prayer notebook or prayer boxes
- Children's praise music tape and/or other music items
- Items for "David Will Be King" Bible story
- Joshua 1:9 poster
- Snacks or drinks
- Items for quiet games
- Story book
- Other: ______________

All My Feelings Are OK!

Preschool Session 2 Plan

Fill in the name of the person responsible for each activity and post this sheet in the room.

Time: ______________	***Arrival and Play Centers (20 Minutes)***
Greeter	______________________
Center #1: Free Play	______________________
Center #2: Coloring Sheets	______________________
Time: ______________	***Circle Time (15 Minutes)***
Group Rules and "How Are You Today?"	______________________
"The Merry-Go-Round"	______________________
Time: ______________	***Small Groups (25 Minutes)***
Talk About It	______________________
"Simon Says"	______________________
Prayer Time	______________________
Time: ______________	***Bible Time and Closing Prayer Huddle (15 Minutes)***
Regathering	______________________
"David Will Be King"	______________________
Memory Verse	______________________
Closing Prayer Huddle	______________________
Time: ______________	***Snack and Quiet Games/Stories (15 Minutes)***
Snack	______________________
Quiet Games/Stories	______________________

All My Feelings Are OK!

Preschool Session 2

EXIT

Opening Play Centers (20 Minutes)

Center #1: Free Play

Again offer two centers where children can play safely (e.g., a home living area or doll house, blocks, modeling clay, puzzles, books, a sand table). One or two facilitators should supervise, encouraging kids to move freely between these areas and Center #2. Make sure all the kids are participating.

Center #2: Coloring Sheets

Have available two or three coloring sheets that show situations in which preschoolers could have conflicting feelings, such as going to the zoo, or visiting the doctor or dentist. As kids arrive, let them choose one of the pictures to color. As they work, talk with them about what is happening in each situation, and ask them what feelings they would have in that situation:

> **What would you feel if you were going to the zoo?** *(Most would say happy. Encourage them to think of others. For instance, they may feel afraid of the animals, or worried the animals could get out of the cages. Be sure to resolve feelings that might be stirred up)*
>
> **It's OK to feel scared of the animals. Do you know the zookeepers are there to make sure none of the animals can get out?**

Do the same for the other scenarios.

Circle Time (15 Minutes)

Group Rules

Display your group rules poster from last session and remind kids how the group rules and the time-out system work.

"How Are You Today?"

Invite the kids to use the happy/sad face masks (or feelings faces poster) to tell you how they are feeling today. Let everyone have a turn.

"The Merry-Go-Round"

Introduce the story (script is on page 43) by using the feelings faces flash cards from last week's lesson. Show the cards to the kids and get them to say the name of the feeling with you. Make a game of it by asking kids to actually make the face that accompanies the feeling. Then say:

> **Have you ever been on a merry-go-round? Here's a story about two kids who learned more about their feelings when they took a ride on a merry-go-round!**

Small Groups (25 Minutes)

Talk About It

Use these questions to discuss the story (use your feelings flash cards or a feelings faces poster to help kids name the feelings):

> **Have you ever been on a merry-go-round?** *(Let kids respond)* **What other rides have you been on?** *(Let kids respond)*

> **What feelings did you have when you were on the rides?** *(Help the kids by suggesting the feelings words mentioned in the skit: "Did you feel scared at first? Did you feel sad when it was over?")*

> **Let's count all the different feelings Sally and Jeff felt when they went on the merry-go-round.** *(Review each one and what caused it. Help the kids count them)*

> **When God made us, He gave us lots of different feelings. Some of them are fun to feel—like when we are happy or excited to be doing something like going on a ride. Some are not very fun at all—like feeling angry because someone pushed us or embarrassed because we tripped and fell in front of someone. *But just because a feeling is not fun does not mean it is bad.* There is no such thing as a bad feeling. All our feelings are important and OK to feel. Let's say that together: All my feelings are OK!**

"Simon Says"

Distribute copies of "Feelings and My Body: Faces and Eyes and Eyes and Hands" (pages 45 and 46) and have kids begin to color them. As they work, talk about how we feel feelings in our whole body. For example:

> **Look at the mouths in the pictures. What do you think the kid who is smiling is feeling?** *(Happy, excited)* **How about the kid who is surprised? What about our hands? What might I be feeling if I am clapping my hands?** *(Happy, excited)* **But if I'm clenching my fists?** *(Angry, getting ready to hit someone)* **Can you think of something my eyes might tell me about my feelings?** *(Tears show I'm sad)*

Now play "Simon Says," using the feelings words on the flash cards. Before you begin, practice each one by getting the kids to use their whole bodies to show how the feeling looks. Then play "Simon Says" for a few minutes to reinforce how feelings affect our whole bodies.

Prayer Time

Use your prayer journal or boxes to review each prayer request from last week. Ask kids to report on each one. Then ask for new requests and offer a short prayer for each one.

Bible Time and Closing Prayer Huddle (15 Minutes)

Regathering

As you did last week, assign one facilitator to lead the kids in songs or an activity as they come back together again.

"David Will Be King"

Present the story as you did last week.
The Bible story script is on page 44.

Memory Verse

Use the Joshua 1:9 poster from last week to review the verse.

So don't be afraid. The Lord your God will be with you everywhere you go.
Joshua 1:9 (*ICB*)

Closing Prayer Huddle

Close the meeting with the prayer huddle, as you did last week. Use this prayer:

Dear God, thank You for loving me and giving me all my feelings! Amen!

Snack and Quiet Games/Stories (15 Minutes)

Have ready a story book, short video, or coloring page to use after the snack and before parents arrive.

Characters

- Sally and Jeff

The Merry-Go-Round

Sally and Jeff enter, laughing and carrying on.

Jeff Wasn't that great? That's got to be the best merry-go-round in the whole world!

Sally Yeah! And you didn't want to go!

Jeff So? I was a little scared, that's all. It looked so big when we first walked up to it. You were scared, too! I saw that look on your face!

Sally A little, but mostly I was excited. Hey, what did that really big kid do to you when we first got on?

Jeff He pushed me away from the horse I wanted! I was so mad I wanted to hit him!

Sally He probably would have sat on you if you had! Did you see me trip and fall when I first tried to get on my horse? I was so embarrassed! My face got all red.

Jeff Aw, lots of kids tripped. Those horses are really big.

Sally Gosh, Jeff. I feel all jumpy inside. I didn't know I could feel so many feelings all at the same time!

Jeff Me neither! But right now I feel sad because the ride is over. Come on! Let's ask Mom if we can go again!

Sally OK!

They run offstage.

From

- 1 Samuel 16:1–13

Characters

- David and Samuel

Needed

- Biblical costumes for David and Samuel

Suggested

- In advance, choose a verse from Psalms that expresses how you (as David) felt this week or write a sentence or two to make up your own Psalm to the Lord

David Will Be King

Samuel is standing off to one side as David enters and greets the kids.

David Well, I'm back and I'm glad each one of you are, too! Who am I again? *(Let kids respond)* Right! And I'm here to tell you how I learned to express my feelings to God by writing poems and singing to Him. Here's an example. One feeling I had this week was *[feeling]*. This is how I said it to God: *[Read or sing a verse from a Psalm or the one you made up]*

Now let me tell you something that happened to me a long time ago, when I was just a young boy. It all started when a man named Samuel—he's standing over there *(Points to Samuel)*—came to our house and told my dad that God had chosen one of his sons to become the next king! My dad was so excited! He called all of my older brothers (I was the baby of the family) in one at a time to talk to Samuel, but each time Samuel just shook his head and said:

Samuel *(Shakes his head and says his line)* Nope! This isn't the one! Who's next?

David Finally, there were no sons left, except me. My dad said, "That's all there is—except for David. But he's too little to be a king!"

Samuel Bring him to me!

David Well, I was so excited! And a little scared, too. What if God really chose me to be the next king? As soon as I entered the room—

Samuel *(Rushes over to David, bows down in front of him)* You are the one God has chosen! Don't be afraid. God will help you. Get ready and come with me. *(Exits)*

David I felt so many things! How would you feel if God chose you to be a king? *(Asks specific kids to suggest a feeling word)* I was excited and scared and sad to leave my family. But I knew God would take care of me, no matter what I was feeling and no matter what happened next. *(Sighs)* Well, there is so much more to tell you, but I have to stop now. Good-bye! See you all next week!

Faces and Eyes

Eyes and Hands

Goals

- Talk about feelings that are uncomfortable
- Identify two ways we try to pretend we don't have these feelings
- Affirm that talking about our feelings is a good way to handle them

Needed

- Supervised places around the room where kids can play
- Two identical sets of feelings faces flash cards
- Group rules poster
- Happy/sad face masks
- *Optional*: Feelings faces poster
- Story puppets or props for skit
- Copies of "Feelings Wheel," paper plates, and small brads
- Prayer notebook or prayer boxes
- Children's praise music tape and/or other music items
- Items for "Jonathan Warns David" Bible story
- Joshua 1:9 poster
- Snacks or drinks
- Items for quiet games
- Story book
- Other: ______________

Some Feelings Are Not Fun to Feel

Preschool Session 3 Plan

Fill in the name of the person responsible for each activity and post this sheet in the room.

Time: ______________ *Arrival and Play Centers (20 Minutes)*

Greeter ______________

Center #1: Free Play ______________

Center #2: Matching Game ______________

Time: ______________ *Circle Time (15 Minutes)*

Group Rules and "How Are You Today?" ______________

"The Bully" ______________

Time: ______________ *Small Groups (25 Minutes)*

Talk About It ______________

Feelings Wheels ______________

Prayer Time ______________

Time: ______________ *Bible Time and Closing Prayer Huddle (15 Minutes)*

Regathering ______________

"Jonathan Warns David" ______________

Memory Verse ______________

Closing Prayer Huddle ______________

Time: ______________ *Snack and Quiet Games/Stories (15 Minutes)*

Snack ______________

Quiet Games/Stories ______________

Some Feelings Are Not Fun to Feel

Preschool Session 3

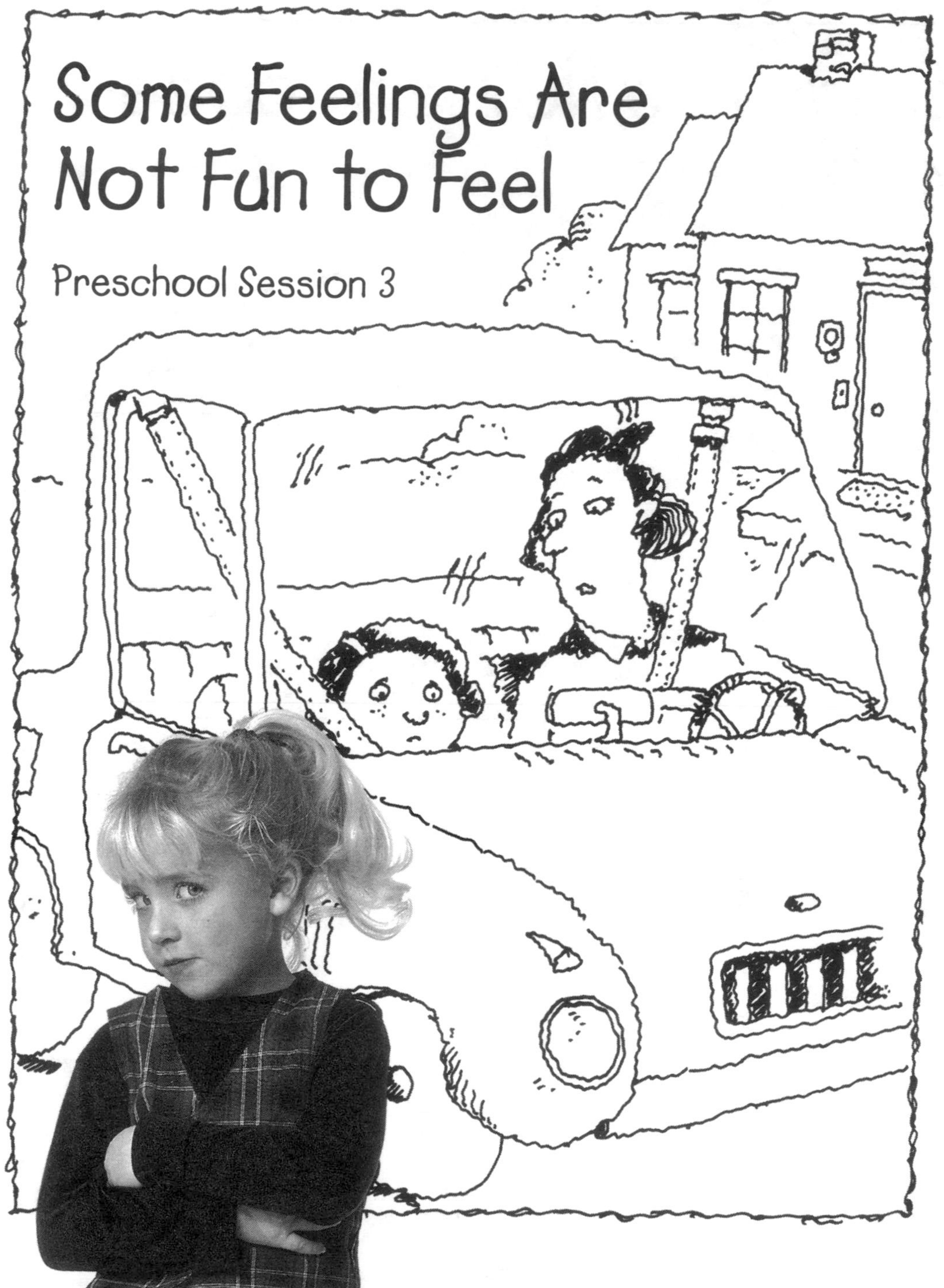

Opening Play Centers (20 Minutes)

Center #1: Free Play

As in weeks past, offer two or more areas where children can play freely.

Center #2: Matching Game

Place two identical sets of the feelings faces flash cards on a table. Have kids take turns picking up matching faces. Talk about what feeling the faces represent, and, if possible, have kids think of times they might feel that feeling.

Circle Time (15 Minutes)

Group Rules

Display your group rules poster from last session and remind kids how the group rules and the time-out system work.

"How Are You Today?"

Invite kids to use the happy/sad face masks (or the feelings faces poster) to tell you how they are feeling today. Pass them around the circle and let everyone have a turn.

"The Bully"

Introduce the story (script is on page 51) by having kids stand up and use their bodies to express a few feelings. One way to do this is to have kids take turns drawing a feelings faces flash card from the stack to determine which feeling the group will express. Then say:

We all have many, many feelings. Each one is important. But some of our feelings are not very much fun to feel. When we feel them, we might try to pretend we aren't feeling them at all. Let's watch a story about a girl who was having some feelings she did not like.

Small Groups (25 Minutes)

Talk About It

Use these questions to discuss the story (use your feelings flash cards or a feelings faces poster to help kids name the feelings):

What feeling did Melissa feel in the story? *(Afraid)*

Why was she afraid? *(Leonard was bullying her at preschool)*

Feeling afraid is not easy. Melissa did some things because she was afraid. Do you know what they were? *(Yelled at her brother, said she didn't want to go to preschool, and pretended to be sick so she wouldn't have to go)*

Do you think she felt better after she told her mom that she was afraid of Leonard? *(Let kids respond)*

When we have feelings we don't like to feel—like feeling afraid—the best thing we can do is to talk about our feeling and why we are feeling that way. If we don't, we will just keep on feeling sad or angry or afraid, and maybe start yelling at a brother or a friend, or hitting someone, or feeling sick. It's much easier to talk about our feelings!

Feelings Wheels

Prepare the activity in advance by copying the "Feelings Wheel" from page 54 onto card stock, and then cutting out the circles and spinners. Distribute these now, and help kids paste the circles in the middle of a paper plate and color them. Use a small brad to fasten the spinner to the center of the plate. Write each child's name on the spinner. Teach the kids how to use the spinner to help them talk about what they are feeling. They can put the spinner by the feelings face that describes their feeling and show it to mom or dad, or someone else. Or, they can post it on their door, so anyone who comes in will know how they are feeling! Encourage kids to keep their wheels in a place where they can use them every day.

Prayer Time

Conduct your prayer time as in weeks past.

Bible Time and Closing Prayer Huddle (15 Minutes)

Regathering

As you did last week, assign one facilitator to lead the kids in songs or an activity as they come back together again.

"Jonathan Warns David"

Present the story as you did last week. The Bible story script is on page 53.

Memory Verse

Use your Joshua 1:9 poster to help kids "read" the verse again. Begin to introduce one or two simple motions to put with the verse, such as making big muscles when you say the word *strong*, and pointing to Heaven when you say *God*.

> **So don't be afraid. The Lord your God will be with you everywhere you go. Joshua 1:9 (*ICB*)**

Closing Prayer Huddle

Close the meeting with the prayer huddle. Use this prayer:

> **Dear God, thank You for loving me and giving me all my feelings! Amen!**

Snack and Quiet Games/Stories (15 Minutes)

Have ready a story book, short video, or coloring page to use after the snack and before parents arrive.

Characters

- Melissa, her Mom, and the voice of her brother

Needed

- Two chairs set side by side (to represent the inside of a car)

The Bully

Mom is standing center stage.

Mom *(Calls off to the side)* Melissa! Let's go, honey! We're going to be late for preschool!

Melissa *(From offstage)* Stop it, you creep! I hate you!

Brother *(From offstage)* Why are you yelling at me? I didn't do anything! I was just looking at your stupid doll, that's all!

Mom Melissa! Greg! Stop it! The school bus will be here in a few minutes, Greg. Melissa, come on right now or we'll be late!

Melissa *(Enters, very upset)* Greg's mean and I hate him. And I'm not going to preschool. I think I'm sick.

Mom *(Guides her to the "car")* I think you are having a bad morning! *(Starts "driving")* What on earth was that all about?

Melissa He touched my doll! I told him never to touch my doll! He'll get her dirty! *(Lowers her head)*

Mom Is something wrong, Melissa? You don't seem like yourself today. *(Pauses)* Melissa?

Melissa No.

Mom Well, we all have days like that. Well, what do you think you'll do in preschool today?

Melissa I don't want to go! Let's go home, Mommy, please! I think I'm sick or something!

Mom OK, let's have it. What are you thinking about right now?

Melissa	I—I'm thinking about Leonard.
Mom	What about Leonard?
Melissa	He's gonna take my lunch away from me and push me down on the playground again, just like he always does! Please, Mommy! I don't want to go!
Mom	Is that what's bothering you? Are you feeling scared of Leonard?
Melissa	Yes! He hurts me sometimes and I don't like it when he's there.
Mom	Well, so that's why you yelled at your brother and think you are sick. You're feeling scared. I'm glad you told me! Anytime you feel afraid, you come and tell me and I'll help. Here we are. Come on. We'll talk to Mrs. Smith right now and she will take care of it for you. *(They exit from the "car")*

From

- 1 Samuel 18:1–16

Characters

- David and Jonathan

Needed

- An autoharp
- A spear

Jonathan Warns David

David enters carrying a spear and greets the kids.

David I'm so glad to be here again this week! I heard you talking about things you do when you are feeling feelings you don't want to feel. So, I want to tell you about something I did when I was afraid of King Saul.

Sometimes King Saul would have terrible dreams in the middle of the night and wake up upset. When things got really bad, I'd go in and play my harp for him. *(Show harp, and play a chord or two)*

Things went along pretty well—for awhile. But then Saul's bad dreams got worse and Saul got mad at me, too. One night he took a spear *(Show spear)* and threw it at me! It was only with God's help that I jumped out of the way in time. Boy, was I scared! Then Saul started hating me and throwing his spear at me a lot of times!

Now I was feeling afraid of Saul, and very sad because he hated me. But you know what? I pretended I wasn't feeling those things. Until one day—

Jonathan *(Enters, looking worried)* David, you have to listen to me! My father hates you and wants to kill you, and everyone in the palace knows it—except you! You have to do something to stay safe!

David *(Puts his arm around Jonathan and says to the kids)* This is my best friend, Jonathan. He is King Saul's son. *(To Jonathan)* Oh, come on, it isn't that bad.

Jonathan Yes, it is! Wake up, my friend, or you'll be dead very soon! *(He exits, shaking his head)*

David That night I felt really awful. So you know what I did? I ran away! That's not a very good thing to do when you are feeling scared, but that's what I did. Now I felt really awful! Only one thing made me feel better. I played my harp and sang to the Lord. I told Him how sad and lonely and scared I felt, and I knew He would take care of me. And He did! Next week I'll tell you more. Until then, keep telling God about all your feelings! *(Exits)*

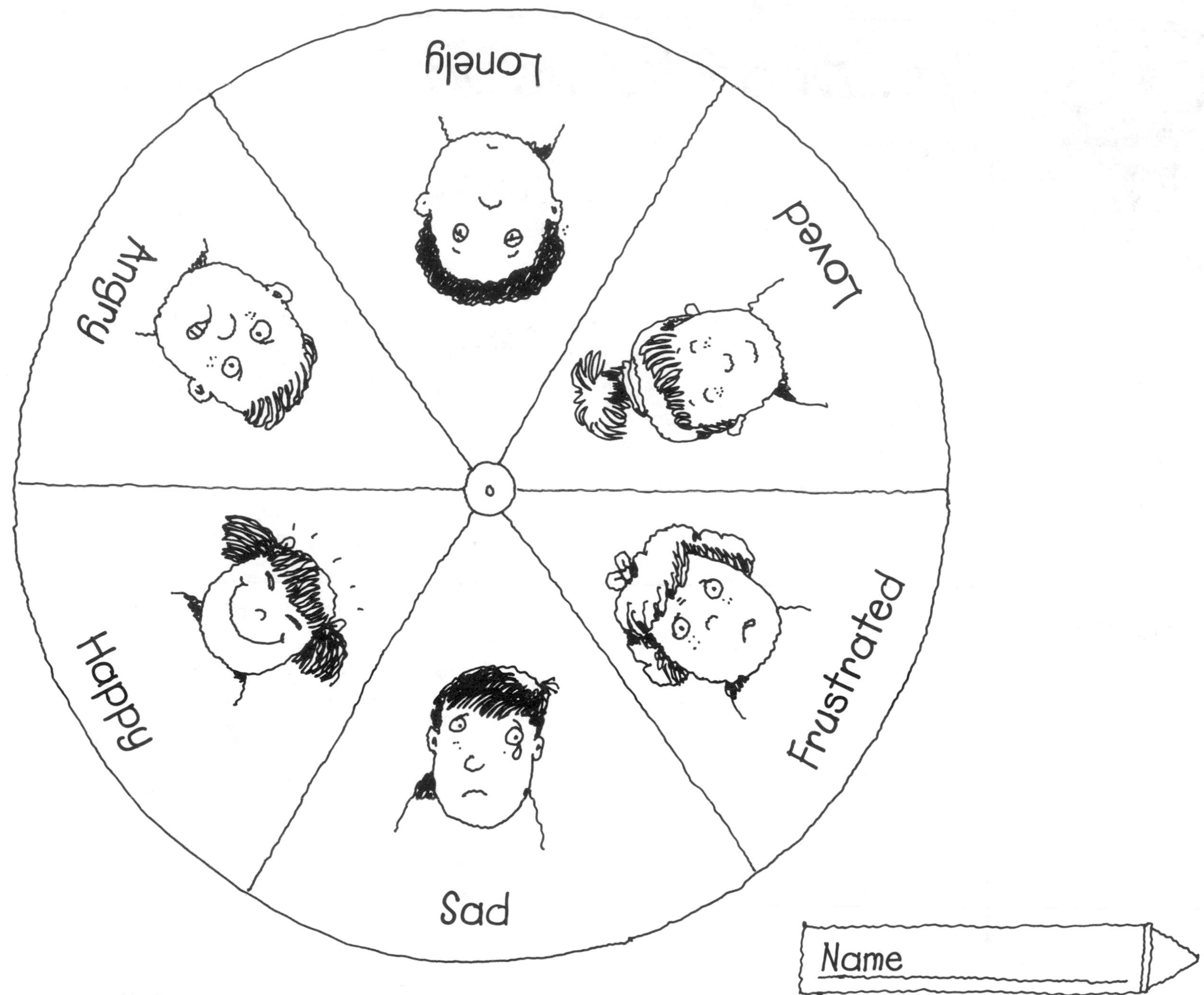

Name

Goals

- Affirm that it is important to express our feelings in positive ways
- Identify wrong (unhealthy) ways of expressing our feelings
- Identify and practice right (healthy) ways of expressing our feelings

Needed

- Supervised play areas
- Feelings faces flash cards
- Group rules poster
- Happy/sad face masks
- *Optional:* Feelings faces poster
- Props for skit
- A large bag or box containing a telephone, paper and crayons, running shoes, a picture of someone getting a hug, a box of tissues, and a pillow (one box or bag per facilitator)
- Feelings journals
- Prayer notebook or prayer boxes
- Children's praise music tape and/or other music items
- Items for "David Talks to God" Bible story
- Joshua 1:9 poster
- Snacks or drinks
- Items for quiet games
- Story book
- Other: ____________

I Can Talk About My Feelings

Preschool Session 4 Plan

Fill in the name of the person responsible for each activity and post this sheet in the room.

Time: ____________ — ***Arrival and Play Centers (20 Minutes)***

Greeter ____________

Center #1: Free Play ____________

Center #2: "Follow the Leader" ____________

Time: ____________ — ***Circle Time (15 Minutes)***

Group Rules and "How Are You Today?" ____________

"The Feelings Box" ____________

Time: ____________ — ***Small Groups (25 Minutes)***

Talk About It ____________

Feelings Journals ____________

Prayer Time ____________

Time: ____________ — ***Bible Time and Closing Prayer Huddle (15 Minutes)***

Regathering ____________

"David Talks to God" ____________

Memory Verse ____________

Closing Prayer Huddle ____________

Time: ____________ — ***Snack and Quiet Games/Stories (15 Minutes)***

Snack ____________

Quiet Games/Stories ____________

I Can Talk About My Feelings

Preschool Session 4

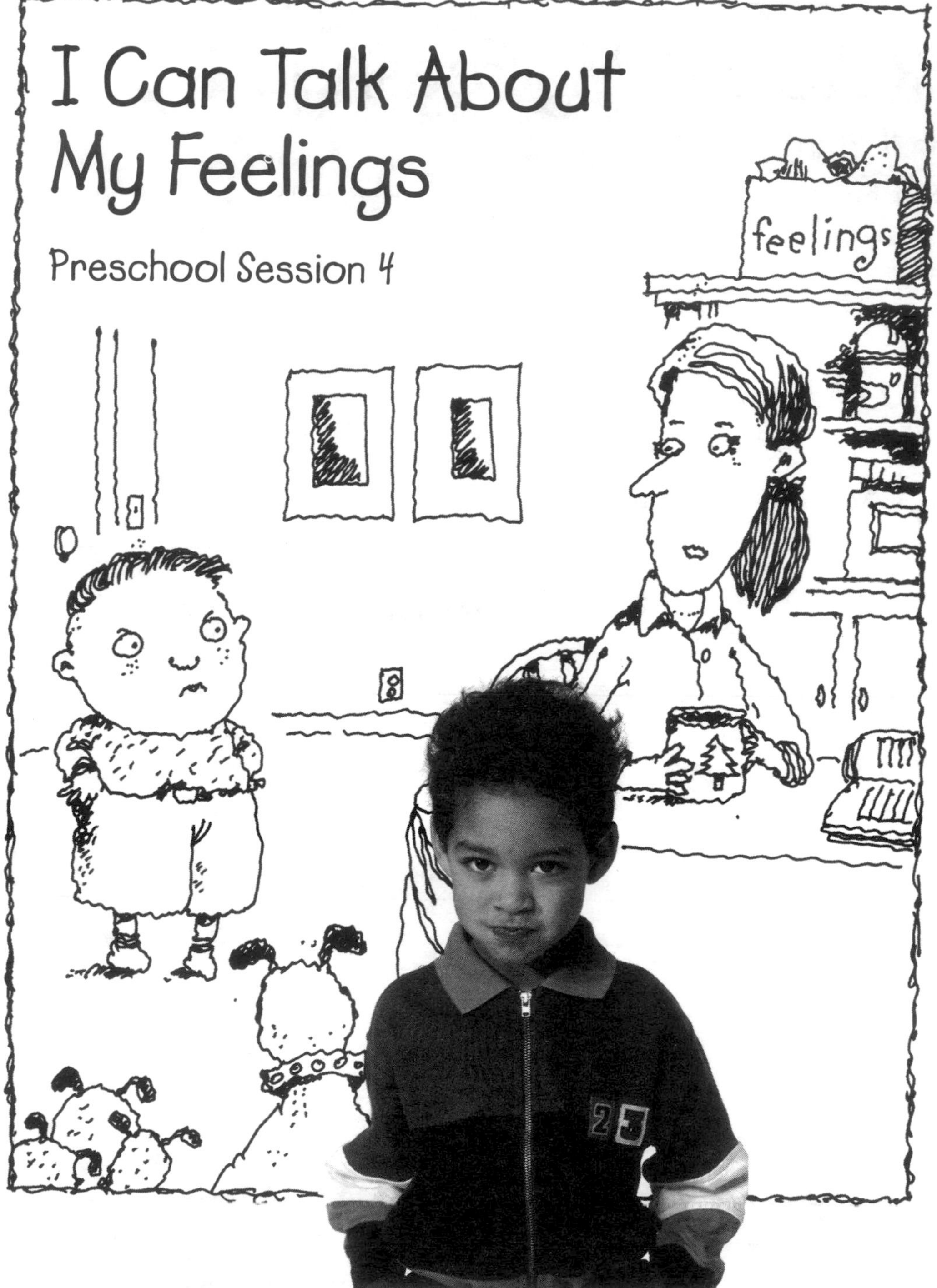

Opening Play Centers (20 Minutes)

Center #1: Free Play

As in weeks past, offer several safe places around the room for kids to play.

Center #2: "Follow the Leader"

When a number of kids have arrived, gather them together for a game of "Follow the Leader." To play this version, let kids take turns drawing one of the feelings faces flash cards and then leading the whole group in expressing that feeling. Have the kids use their whole bodies, and if possible, get them to move around the room while expressing the feeling. For example, if they are doing *happy*, they might skip around the room in a single-file line. If they are doing *shy*, they could lower their heads, clasp their hands in front of them, and "slink" around the room. Come up with other actions for the other feelings words.

Circle Time (15 Minutes)

Group Rules

Display your group rules poster from last session and remind kids how the group rules and the time-out system work.

"How Are You Today?"

Invite the kids to use the happy/sad face masks (or feelings faces poster) to tell you how they are feeling today. Pass them around the circle and let everyone have a turn.

"The Feelings Box"

Introduce the story (script is on page 59) by reminding the kids that we all have many kinds of feelings.

> **When something good happens, we feel happy. When someone is kind to us and takes care of us we feel love. When something scary happens we feel afraid. But even though we all feel the same things, we don't all do the same things. For instance, when I feel happy, I** *(Facilitator finishes this by telling what she does when she feels happy. Ask kids to share different ways they express happiness. Repeat, using love, sad, afraid)*
>
> **Now let's watch a story about a boy who learned lots of great things to do when he was feeling angry.**

Small Groups (25 Minutes)

Talk About It

Use the following questions to discuss the story (use your feelings flash cards or feelings faces poster to help kids name the feelings):

> **Why was Billy so angry?** *(Joshua called him a dumbhead)*
>
> **Billy wanted to punch Joshua for calling him a name. Have you ever felt so angry you wanted to punch someone?** *(Let kids respond)*
>
> **What did Billy do instead of punching Joshua?** *(Used crayons and paper from his feelings box to color his feelings)*

Bring to the group today your own feelings box (or bag). It should contain a pillow, a telephone, paper and crayons, a pair of running shoes, a box of tissues, and a picture of someone getting a hug. Place it in the middle of your group without opening it. Say:

> **Billy had a special box to help him know what to do when he was feeling angry. I have a feelings box, too. It helps me know what to do when I'm feeling lots of different feelings. But before I show you what's in my box, who remembers the rule Billy's mom taught him about what not to do with your feelings?**

Review the rule:

> **Never hurt someone else or yourself or break anything.**
>
> **Now let's look in my box and see what things we can do.**

Pull each item out of the box and hand it to a child in your group. Get the kids to talk about what they could do with each item. Keep this moving quickly. Then read each sentence below, and ask the children to tell how they would feel in that situation, and how the items in their hands could be used in that situation:

> **Someone hits you on the playground at preschool**
>
> **Your mom and dad are fighting**
>
> **You just got a brand new puppy**

Feelings Journals

Give kids purchased notebooks containing blank (no lines) paper, or booklets made by stapling blank paper inside the feelings journal covers (page 61). Tell kids these are their journals and they can "write" anything they want to in them. Give them time to color a page as this week's entry into their feelings journal. They can "write" about feeling happy, sad, or mad. As they work, ask each child what feeling they are writing about and why they chose that feeling. When the kids are finished, collect the journals. They will be used in the remaining sessions of this unit.

Prayer Time

Conduct your prayer time as in weeks past. This week, ask God to help each child know the best thing to do when they are feeling sad, angry, lonely, or afraid.

Bible Time and Closing Prayer Huddle (15 Minutes)

Regathering

As in weeks past, assign one facilitator to lead the kids in songs or an activity as they come back together again.

"David Talks to God"

Present the Bible story (script is on page 60).

Memory Verse

Use your Joshua 1:9 poster to review the verse again this week. Review the motions the kids learned last week. If they are doing well, add more.

Closing Prayer Huddle

Close your meeting as in weeks past. Use this prayer:

> **Dear God, thank You for loving me and giving me all my feelings! Amen!**

Snack and Quiet Games/Stories (15 Minutes)

Have ready a story book, short video, or coloring page to use after the snack and before parents arrive. The kids may enjoy coloring a picture or watching a video about the life of David.

Characters

- Billy and his mom

Needed

- A box containing paper and crayons, a pair of running shoes, a box of tissues, and a telephone

The Feelings Box

Mom is standing center stage, pretending to iron a shirt or make dinner. Billy is offstage.

Billy *(Runs in, very upset)* Mom! Do you know what happened? Joshua is so dumb! I don't ever want to play with him again! He cheated and then called me "stupid dumbhead." I'm not a stupid dumbhead. He is!

Mom Whoa, slow down, Billy. You're very angry, aren't you?

Billy Yes! Wouldn't you be if Joshua called you "stupid dumbhead?" I'm gonna go find him right now and punch his lights out!

Mom Wait a minute, cowboy. Let's think about what to do when you feel angry. What's the rule?

Billy *(Sighs loudly and recites the rule in a sing-song manner. He's obviously been through this before)* "It's never OK to hurt someone or myself or break things." But Mom, he deserves it!

Mom Why don't you go get out your feelings box and choose something there to help you? Go on.

Billy OK. *(Mom exits. Billy picks up his feelings box and sits down in front of the kids. He opens the box and pulls each thing out one at a time, names it, and says what he could do with it. For example, "Here are my running shoes—I could go run around the block until I feel better." "Here are my crayons and paper—I could draw how I'm feeling.")* I think I'll draw how I'm feeling about Billy. He's not very nice and this is how I feel about him! *(Uses dark colors and scribbles with big strokes as if he's angry. His artwork fills the whole page. When done, it's obvious his energy is spent)* Wow! Guess I was pretty angry! I wonder if Joshua wants to play some more? *(Exits)*

Characters

- David

Needed

- Biblical costume for David
- Confident Kids Psalm 1 written on poster board
- Confident Kids feelings journal

David Talks to God

David enters and greets kids. He is carrying a feelings journal and a poster with Confident Kids Psalm 1 (see script) written out.

David Wow! This is really good stuff! Now you're starting to express your feelings like I do! Whenever I'm feeling sad or mad or glad, I get out my pen and paper and write a poem to the Lord! And if that's not enough, I put it to music and sing it to the Lord! And if that's still not enough, I dance before the Lord! I've written a lot of songs and poems to God. They're in the Bible, in a book called Psalms. Can you say Psalms? *(Let kids try)* Good! That's another name for songs to God—Psalms!

Well, today I thought maybe you would all help me write another Psalm to the Lord. *(Display poster and read it to the kids, asking them to suggest words to fill in the blanks. Repeat it often, and have the kids say it with you so they get to know it)*

Confident Kids **Psalm 1**

O Lord, You are my friend *(Insert a picture of Jesus with children to represent the word "friend")* **and my helper.** *(Insert a picture of Jesus helping someone to represent the word "helper")*

You understand all my feelings. When I feel _______________, *(Write in the word of their choice and draw a feelings face to represent it)* **You help me ________________.** *(Insert word and simple picture that fits [e.g., "When I feel angry you help me feel calm." "When I feel sad you help me feel better."])*

And when I feel ________________, You help me ___________.

O Lord, You are my friend and my helper.

Good job! Keep sharing your feelings with God, OK? Good-bye! *(Exits)*

My Feelings Journal

Name________________________

Goals

- Teach kids to how to name their feelings
- Practice naming feelings

Needed

- Supervised places around the room where kids can play
- Copies of stick puppet figures
- Group rules poster
- Happy/sad face masks
- *Optional:* Feelings faces poster
- Story puppets or props for skit
- Stick puppets colored during the opening time and large craft sticks
- Feelings journals
- Prayer notebook or prayer boxes
- Children's praise music tape and/or other music items
- Items for "David Must Decide" Bible story
- Snacks or drinks
- Items for quiet games
- Story book
- Other: ______________

I Can Name My Feelings

Preschool Session 5 Plan

Fill in the name of the person responsible for each activity and post this sheet in the room.

Time: ______________ — *Arrival and Play Centers (20 Minutes)*

Greeter	______________
Center #1: Free Play	______________
Center #2: Stick Puppets	______________

Time: ______________ — *Circle Time (15 Minutes)*

Group Rules and "How Are You Today?"	______________
"The Bad Day"	______________

Time: ______________ — *Small Groups (25 Minutes)*

Talk About It	______________
Stick Puppet Role Plays	______________
Feelings Journals and Prayer Time	______________

Time: ______________ — *Bible Time and Closing Prayer Huddle (15 Minutes)*

Regathering	______________
"David Must Decide"	______________
Memory Verse	______________
Closing Prayer Huddle	______________

Time: ______________ — *Snack and Quiet Games/Stories (15 Minutes)*

Snack	______________
Quiet Games/Stories	______________

I Can Name My Feelings

Preschool Session 5

Opening Play Centers (20 Minutes)

Center #1: Free Play

As in weeks past, provide supervised safe areas around the room for kids to play.

Center #2: Stick Puppets

Have available copies of the stick puppet figures (pages 71 and 72) for kids to color. As they finish, cut them out and set them aside for use in the small groups later.

Circle Time (15 Minutes)

Group Rules

Display your group rules poster from last session and remind the kids how the group rules and the time-out system work.

"How Are You Today?"

Invite kids to use the happy/sad face masks (or feelings faces poster) to tell you how they are feeling today. Pass them around the circle and let everyone have a turn.

"The Bad Day"

Introduce the story (script is on page 67) by reminding kids that we are learning about feelings.

> **Everyone has lots of feelings. Some of them are fun and others are not fun at all.** *(Involve kids in making faces to depict feelings that are not fun: angry, sad, scared)* **But remember, even though some feelings are not fun, it's OK to feel them.**

Let's say this together: All My Feelings Are OK! *(Have kids repeat it several times)* **Now let's watch a story about a girl who had many feelings that were not fun—all in one day!**

Small Groups (25 Minutes)

Talk About It

Use the following questions to discuss the story:

Marcy was having a bad day. What are some of the things that happened to her? *(You may have to prompt kids to remember. As they name each thing, help them recall the feeling that accompanied it. For example, when she stubbed her toe and her brother called her a clumsy twerp, she felt hurt)*

Can you think of a time something happened to you and you had a feeling that was not fun to feel? *(Prompt kids with ideas that a preschooler might have. Examples include: someone calls them a name or hits them, they fight with a brother or sister, they break something and get in trouble, Mom or Dad breaks a promise to them)*

Everyone has feelings that are not fun to feel. When we feel those feelings, like feeling scared or mad or sad or lonely, we like to pretend we are not feeling them. But it is much better to think about what happened and then tell someone how we feel about it. *(Name and talk about feelings that are not fun to feel)*

Stick Puppet Role Plays

Help the kids glue the puppets they colored earlier onto large craft sticks to make stick puppets. Then tell Story 1 below. Have the kids work the puppets while you tell the story. Try to involve all the kids in some way. If time allows, repeat using Story 2.

Story 1

Mom and Dad are with Susie and Billy. Daddy tells the kids that he is moving away. Everyone feels very sad. Susie goes to her room and __________________. *(Ask kids what she does to handle her feelings)* Billy goes to his room and __________________. *(Ask kids what Billy does to handle his feelings)*

Later, Susie and Billy tell Mom how they are feeling. Susie says, "I feel so sad."

Billy says, "I feel scared. Who will take care of us now?"

Mom says, "Everything will be OK. Your dad and I still love you and will take care of you."

Story 2

Mom and Susie and Billy are at the pound looking at all the dogs. Mom says, "These dogs are all here because they don't have a home."

Susie says, "Can we give one a home?"

Billy says, "Can we take one with us today?"

Mom says, "If we find one that likes us and we like him, maybe we can."

Then they see a little black and white dog, who looks very sad because he doesn't have a home. Susie says, "Look, Mom, this one is just the right size for us!"

The dog wags his tail and barks. Billy says, "Yeah, he wants to come home with us!"

So they take the dog and give him a home. They name him ______________. *(Let kids decide on the name)*

Feelings Journals and Prayer Time

Give kids the feelings journals they started last week and let them "write" in them. While they work, conduct your prayer time as in weeks past. *Optional:* Have a variety of stickers available and let kids choose one to stick on their journal page.

Bible Time and Closing Prayer Huddle (15 Minutes)

Regathering

As in weeks past, assign one facilitator to lead the kids in songs or an activity as they come back together again.

"David Must Decide"

Present the Bible story (script is on page 69).

Memory Verse

Review Joshua 1:9 using only motions this week. Tell the kids they will say it for their parents during family night.

> **So don't be afraid. The Lord your God will be with you everywhere you go. Joshua 1:9 (*ICB*)**

Closing Prayer Huddle

Close the meeting as in weeks past. Use this prayer:

> **Dear God, thank You for loving me and giving me all my feelings! Amen!**

Snack and Quiet Games/Stories (15 Minutes)

Have ready a story book, short video, or coloring page to use after the snack and before parents arrive. The kids may enjoy coloring a picture or watching a video about the life of David.

Characters

- Marcy (a puppet) and a facilitator

The Bad Day

Facilitator	Hi, everyone! This is my friend Marcy, and she's not having a very fun day today. Marcy—
Marcy	*(Obviously angry)* Yeah? Whaddaya want?
Facilitator	Wow, you sound angry!
Marcy	I am not angry! Well, OK, yes I am.
Facilitator	What happened to make you so angry?
Marcy	I'm having a really bad day, OK? It's not fair to have so many bad things happen in one day!
Facilitator	What happened?
Marcy	Well, like when I got up this morning. I stubbed my toe on the dresser in my room—really hard! It hurt so much I yelled, "Ow, ow, ow!" and danced all around. I know I looked silly, but my dumb brother didn't need to laugh at me and call me a clumsy twerp! He's always calling me names like that and I wish he'd stop! It hurts to be called names.
Facilitator	So you hurt yourself and then you felt hurt. What happened next?
Marcy	Then when I got to preschool, I went to say good morning to Miss Molly and she was dead!
Facilitator	Good grief! Your teacher was dead?
Marcy	Not my teacher! Our goldfish! She was floating at the top of the bowl and nobody noticed except me!
Facilitator	So what did you feel then?

Marcy	I felt so sad, I cried! And then all the kids started laughing at me and making fun because I cried about Miss Molly. I felt all alone and a little scared.
Facilitator	Feeling all alone does feel scary. But how come you're so angry now?
Marcy	When my mom picked me up from preschool, she took me to get an ice cream cone. I got my favorite, chocolate cherry almond coconut banana caramel crunch! And just as we drove away, my ice cream fell off my cone and onto the car seat and my dog ate it! It's not fair! No little kid should have so many things happen all in one day!
Facilitator	I'm sorry, Marcy. Some days are just like that. I hope tomorrow will be a better day for you!
Marcy	*(Mumbles as they exit)* I think I'll just stay in bed all day tomorrow—

From

- 1 Samuel 26

Characters

- David, King Saul, and Abishai

Needed

- Biblical costumes for David, King Saul, and Abishai
- A spear
- A water jug

David Must Decide

David enters and stands center stage. Saul is off to the side, "sleeping" on the ground, with the spear and water jug next to him.

David Today I want to tell you about a time I felt lots of different feelings all in one day, like Marcy did in the skit. I was running away from King Saul, because he tried to kill me. I ran into the desert, thinking he would never follow me there! But I was wrong!

One day, I saw far off in the distance *(Puts hand over eyes as if looking in the distance)* King Saul and many, many of his toughest soldiers! They were looking for me. "Oh no," I thought to myself. "Won't King Saul ever leave me alone? I'm tired of running away and feeling scared that he will catch me and kill me. Maybe I will go and talk to him and ask him to leave me alone."

On the way to King Saul's camp I felt very scared! I prayed and asked God to keep me safe. And you know what God did? When I got close to the camp, it was totally quiet! No sounds at all—except snoring! *(King Saul snores)* Everyone was asleep. So I tiptoed into camp *(Tiptoe over to where Saul is "sleeping")* and found King Saul.

I couldn't believe what was happening! God was really keeping me safe. But then a friend who came with me picked up Saul's spear *(Abishai picks up spear and poises it over Saul's heart)* and said—

Abishai God has done this so you can kill Saul before he kills you! Let me kill him for you!

David I felt so many feelings just then. But I knew God would not want me to kill Saul. So I said, "No, let's just take his spear and water jug so he'll know we were here, and leave." So we did.

When Saul found out what happened, and that I could have killed him but didn't, he stopped chasing me for awhile, and I was safe. I felt happy that I had trusted God to keep me safe, and didn't kill Saul.

Hurting someone else is never a good way to handle your feelings.

Well, I havc to go. Remember to always ask God to help you when you are feeling scared or angry or confused, like I did. He'll help you, too—I promise! See you next week!

5

1

Goals

- Identify feelings that signal it is time to ask an adult for help
- Make a directory of specific people the kids can turn to for help
- Prepare the kids' memory verses for presentation at family night

Needed

- Supervised places around the room where kids can play
- A full-length mirror
- Happy/sad face masks
- *Optional:* Feelings faces poster
- Story puppets or props for skit
- Copies of "Who Can Help Me?" directory
- A telephone
- Feelings journals
- Prayer notebook or prayer boxes
- Children's praise music tape and/or other music items
- Items for "David Needs Help" Bible story
- Joshua 1:9 poster
- Snacks or drinks
- Items for quiet games
- Story book
- Other: ________________

Asking for Help

Preschool Session 6 Plan

Fill in the name of the person responsible for each activity and post this sheet in the room.

Time: ________________	*Arrival and Play Centers (20 Minutes)*
Greeter	________________
Center #1: Free Play	________________
Center #2: Mirrors	________________
Time: ________________	*Circle Time (15 Minutes)*
Group Rules and "How Are You Today?"	________________
"The Secret"	________________
Time: ________________	*Small Groups (25 Minutes)*
Talk About It	________________
"Who Can Help Me?" Directory	________________
Feelings Journals and Prayer Time	________________
Time: ________________	*Bible Time and Closing Prayer Huddle (15 Minutes)*
Regathering	________________
"David Needs Help"	________________
Memory Verse	________________
Closing Prayer Huddle	________________
Time: ________________	*Snack and Quiet Games/Stories (15 Minutes)*
Snack	________________
Quiet Games/Stories	________________

Asking for Help

Preschool Session 6

Opening Play Centers (20 Minutes)

Center #1: Free Play

As in weeks past, provide supervised, safe areas around the room for kids to play.

Center #2: Mirrors

Set up a full-length mirror where kids can see themselves easily. As kids arrive, have them look at themselves in the mirror as you suggest feelings words for them to act out. Ask them to watch what happens to their bodies as they express feelings like angry, happy, scared, etc. Then tell the kids that you are going to use an imaginary mirror to act out your feelings words. Place two kids together and ask one to be the "mirror." The "mirror's" job is to duplicate everything her partner does. Now give the other child a feelings word to act out, as the mirror "mirrors" his actions. Switch roles, so each child has a turn being the initiator and the mirror.

Circle Time (15 Minutes)

Group Rules

Display your group rules poster from last session and remind kids how the group rules and the time-out system work.

"How Are You Today?"

Invite kids to use the happy/sad face masks (or feelings faces poster) to tell you how they are feeling today. Pass them around the circle and let everyone have a turn.

"The Secret"

Introduce the story (script is on page 77).

Remember that in Confident Kids we are learning about our feelings. Some are fun to feel, and others are not. And sometimes, when we are feeling scared, or angry, or hurt, it's time to ask for help. Now let's watch a story about a boy who used his feelings to know when it was right to ask for help.

Small Groups (25 Minutes)

Talk About It

Use the following questions to discuss the story:

What was Myron's secret? *(He couldn't do a somersault)*

How did keeping his secret make him feel? *(Embarrassed, scared, sad, clumsy)*

How did he feel after he asked his grandma for help? *(Relieved, happy)*

Myron learned that it was better to ask for help with his problem than keep it all to himself. There are lots of times we need help from others—that's how God made us. We need parents to help us grow and give us what we need, teachers to teach us things, and friends to have fun with. Many times, others in our lives help us without our even having to ask for help. But sometimes they won't know we need help unless we ask for it.

"Who Can Help Me?" Directory

Distribute copies of the "Who Can Help Me?" Directory (page 80) and have kids begin coloring them. As they work, say:

Remember, whenever you feel scared or confused or lonely or sad, you can ask others to help. It is always smart to ask for help when you need it—especially if you feel scared or if you think you aren't safe. Always ask for help when you do not feel safe.

To use the activity sheet, ask each child to tell you their address and phone number. If they know it, write it on the sheet for them. If they can't say it, encourage them to ask a parent to help them learn it. Then help kids identify people in each of the categories they can ask for help. Write in names for them, and tell them to ask their parents to help them fill in phone numbers when they get home. Then point out the 911 in the center of the sheet, and be sure each child knows what it means.

End by placing a nonworking telephone in the center of the table and have the kids take turns dialing 911. If time permits, check to be sure each one knows how to read and dial a phone number—especially their own. They can practice on their papers.

Feelings Journals and Prayer Time

Give the kids their feelings journals and let them "write" in them. While they work, conduct this week's prayer time. End by letting them choose a sticker to paste in their journal.

Bible Time and Closing Prayer Huddle (15 Minutes)

Regathering

As in weeks past, assign one facilitator to lead the kids in songs or an activity as they come back together again.

"David Needs Help"

Present the Bible story (script is on page 78).

Memory Verse

Review Joshua 1:9 using the poster. Then practice the verse using the motions, reminding the kids that they will be performing it for their family on family night.

Closing Prayer Huddle

Close the meeting as in weeks past. Use this prayer:

> **Dear God, thank You for loving me and giving me all my feelings! Amen!**

Snack and Quiet Games/Stories (15 Minutes)

Have ready a story book, short video, or coloring page to use after the snack and before parents arrive. The kids may enjoy coloring a picture or watching a video about the life of David.

Characters

- Myron and his grandma

Needed

- If your room is not carpeted, you might want a mat or sleeping bag to use for protection when doing the somersault

The Secret

Myron is on center stage, awkwardly trying to do a somersault. He is obviously frustrated and ready to cry.

Grandma *(Enters)* Myron? Oh, here you are! Haven't you heard me calling you all this time? Come on, it's time to leave for school.

Myron No! I don't want to go today. I hate kindergarten and I don't ever want to go back.

Grandma Why? I thought you liked your class.

Myron I can't tell you. It's a secret.

Grandma Well, secrets can be funny things, Myron. Some are good, but others can hurt us. This secret looks like it is hurting you. When you are feeling hurt or scared, it is sometimes better to ask for help than keep your secret. Why don't you tell me what's wrong?

Myron No! I can't.

Grandma OK, but you know you can ask me for help whenever you need it. Now come on, or you will be late for school. *(Starts to walk away)*

Myron *(Looks thoughtful for a few moments)* Grandma?

Grandma *(Turns around)* Yes?

Myron Well, maybe I could use some help. The secret is—I can't do a somersault, and sometimes we go to the gym and everyone is supposed to do one. I feel really stupid and clumsy because I can't do it. *(Brightens)* Hey, Grandma! Do you know how to do a somersault?

Grandma Well now, I think I can help you with that! In my day I was quite a tumbler. I could do great somersaults—and cartwheels, too. When we get home from kindergarten today, I'll teach you how. It's easy, once you get the hang of it! Now let's go!

They exit.

From

- 1 Samuel 20

Characters

- David and Jonathan

Needed

- Biblical costumes for David and Jonathan

David Needs Help

David enters and greets kids. Jonathan is standing offstage.

David I really enjoyed today's lesson, especially the skit about Myron and his secret. It reminded me of a time I felt scared and tried to keep it a secret. I had to decide whether I should tell someone and ask for help. Let me tell you about it.

It all started when I was running away from King Saul because he hated me and was trying to kill me! Everywhere I would go, he or some of his men would find me. I was very frightened.

Now came my problem. What was I going to do? I wanted someone to help me, but who? What if no one believed me? What if the person I told went to King Saul and told him I was saying bad things about him? Pretty soon feeling scared and confused started to give me bad stomachaches and headaches. I knew I needed help! And so I picked a special friend to help me.

Jonathan *(Enters)* Hey, David, how are you? You're looking kind of funny lately. Are you OK?

David *(To kids)* This is Jonathan. He is my very best friend and King Saul is his dad! *(To Jonathan)* Actually, I don't feel well today. But I'm a little afraid to tell you my secret and ask for help.

Jonathan Why? We're best friends, aren't we?

David Yes, but you might not like what I have to say. You see, I believe your father is trying to kill me.

Jonathan *(Looks shocked)* What? You must be wrong! My father loves you!

David I don't think so. Let's go talk and I'll tell you all about it. *(The two of them walk a few steps to the side, pretending to be talking. Jonathan freezes in place there, and David comes back to center stage)*

Jonathan and I talked a long time that day, and finally we worked out a plan for him to help me stay safe from his father. I felt so much better, just having told my secret to my friend and asking for his help! Now I had someone to help me, and that made everything so much easier.

Well, I have to go. Just remember, when you feel scared, sad, confused, or lonely, be sure to find someone you can share your feelings with. You can always ask for help when you need it! And especially remember, you can always, always, count on God to help you when you ask Him. See you next week!

My name ____________________

My phone number ____________________

Family and friends

Church and school

My street address ____________________

My city and state ____________________

Huggers

Pets and stuffed animals

Goals

- Identify situations in which we can ask Jesus to help us
- Use Psalm 139 to assure kids of God's constant presence and care for them
- Participate in the story of David and Goliath as a further illustration of God's care

Needed

- Supervised places around the room where kids can play
- Invitations for Family Night
- Happy/sad face mask
- *Optional:* Feelings faces poster
- Story puppets or props for skit
- Copies of "Where Are You, God?" copied back to back and folded in half
- Feelings journals
- Prayer notebook or prayer boxes
- Children's praise music tape and/or other music items
- Items for "David Meets a Giant" Bible story
- Joshua 1:9 poster
- Snacks or drinks
- Items for quiet games
- Story book
- Copies of "Affirmation Balloons" and unit certificates from Appendix A, pages 377 and 379
- Other: ______________

Jesus Helps Me With My Feelings

Preschool Session 7 Plan

Fill in the name of the person responsible for each activity and post this sheet in the room.

Time: ______________ *Arrival and Play Centers (20 Minutes)*

Greeter ______________

Center #1: Free Play ______________

Center #2: Invitations for Family Night ______________

Time: ______________ *Circle Time (15 Minutes)*

Group Rules and "How Are You Today?" ______________

"Daddy" ______________

Time: ______________ *Small Groups (25 Minutes)*

Talk About It ______________

"Where Are You, God?" ______________

Feelings Journals and Prayer Time ______________

Time: ______________ *Bible Time and Closing Prayer Huddle (15 Minutes)*

Regathering ______________

"David Meets a Giant" ______________

Memory Verse ______________

Closing Prayer Huddle ______________

Time: ______________ *Snack and Quiet Games/Stories (15 Minutes)*

Snack ______________

Quiet Games/Stories ______________

Jesus Helps Me With My Feelings

Preschool Session 7

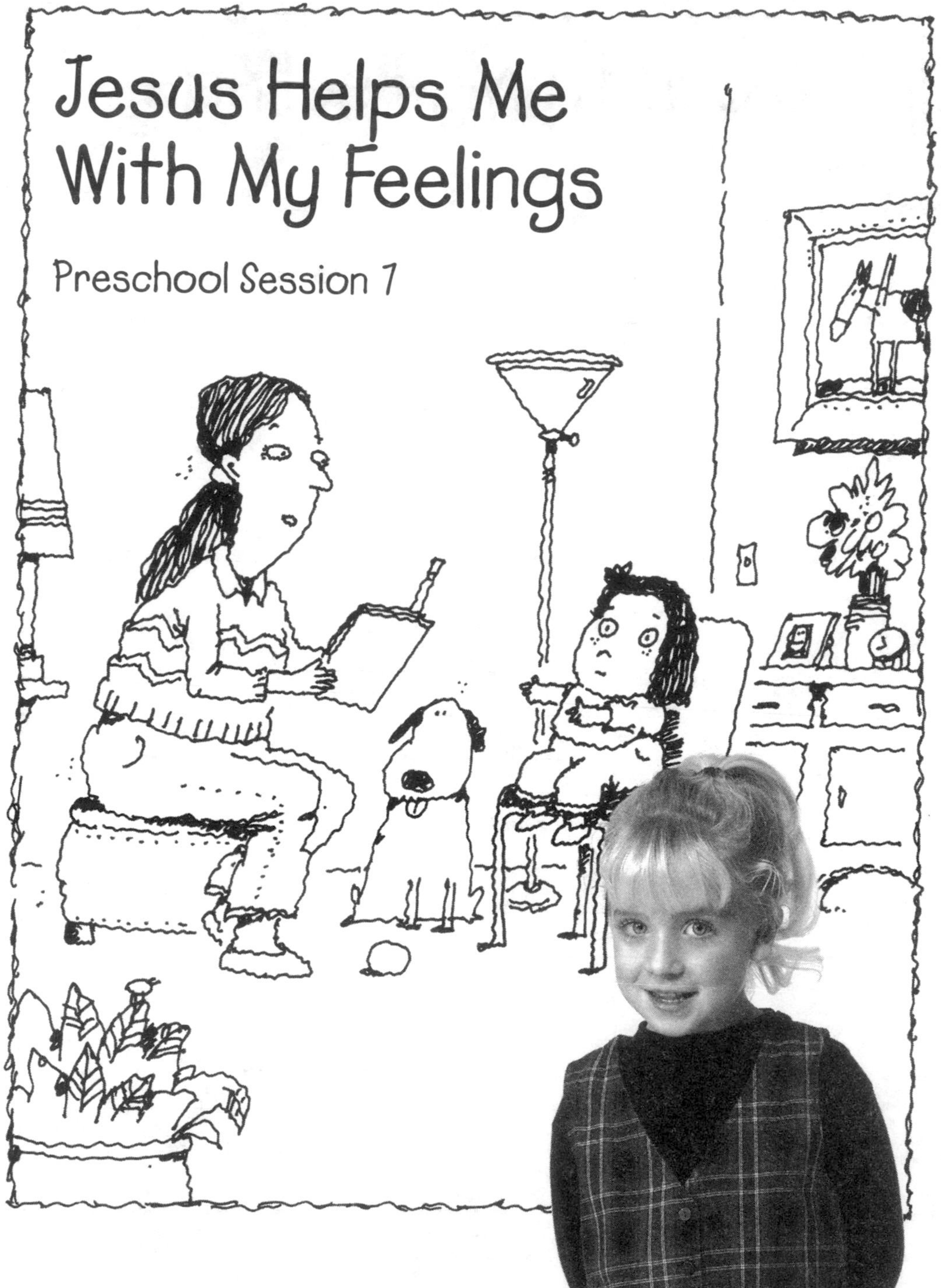

Opening Play Centers (20 Minutes)

Center #1: Free Play

As in weeks past, provide safe, supervised areas for children to play.

Center #2: Invitations for Family Night

As kids arrive, have them work on the invitations for Family Night (page 89). Explain that next week is the final session of this unit. There will be a party and they can invite their parent(s) to attend the party with them. Talk about the party enthusiastically so as to get the kids excited about sharing their group experience with their family. Read the invitations to the kids, and then let each child paste one to the center of a larger piece of paper and fill in the border with various designs.

Circle Time (15 Minutes)

Group Rules

Welcome everyone to the group, and greet them by name. Review the rules again, inviting kids to help you remember them.

"How Are You Today?"

As in weeks past, invite the kids to tell you how they are feeling today. Let everyone have a turn. (Facilitators should participate, too!)

"Daddy"

Introduce the story (script is on pages 85 and 86) by reminding the kids that we are learning about their feelings.

Some feelings are happy and fun to feel, and others are not fun to feel at all. When we have scary, sad, or lonely feelings, we can ask for help to face whatever is happening to us. Last week we talked about people who can help us. Today we are going to talk about the very best helper of all—Jesus! Here is a true story about a little girl who learned how to ask Jesus to help her during a scary time.

Small Groups (25 Minutes)

Talk About It

Use the following questions to discuss the story:

What was happening to Amy? *(Let kids respond)* **What feelings do you think she was feeling during the time her daddy was sick with cancer?** *(Help the kids verbalize feelings such as sad, angry, afraid)*

Who helped Amy during that scary time? *(Her mom and Jesus)*

When would be a good time for us to pray and ask Jesus to help us? *(Guide kids to verbalize different feelings words. For example, "Can we ask Jesus to help us when we feel afraid? Can you think of something that would make you feel afraid?" Give the kids ideas, then repeat, using other feelings)*

Remember, it is always OK to ask for help when we feel scared, sad, angry, or lonely. And the best helper we can have is God because He is always with us and always ready to listen to us and help us.

"Where Are You, God?"

Distribute the "Where Are You, God" coloring sheets, made by copying pages 90 and 91 back to back then folding the paper half. Let kids color them as you talk about the content, which is taken from Psalm 139. Point out that no matter where we are or what we are doing, God is always with us and ready to help us. *Alternate Idea:* You can also reinforce the same idea by providing any coloring sheet that presents the idea of God being with us all the time, always ready to answer our prayers.

Feelings Journals and Prayer Time

Distribute the feelings journals and let kids "write" in them. Let the kids choose a sticker for their entry. Conduct your prayer time as kids work.

Bible Time and Closing Prayer Huddle (15 Minutes)

Regathering

As in weeks past, assign one facilitator to lead the kids in songs or an activity as they come back together again.

"David Meets a Giant"

Present the Bible story (script is on pages 87 and 88).

Memory Verse

Review Joshua 1:9 using the poster. Then practice the verse using the motions. Remind the kids that they will be performing it for their family on Family Night.

Closing Prayer Huddle

Close the meeting as in weeks past, using this prayer:

> **Dear God, thank You for loving me and giving me all my feelings! Amen!**

Snack and Quiet Games/Stories (15 Minutes)

Have ready a story book, short video, or coloring page to use after the snack and before parents arrive. The kids may enjoy coloring a picture or watching a video about the life of David.

Note

Facilitators will need to take home copies of the "Affirmation Balloons" and the unit certificates from Appendix A (pages 377 and 379). Have them complete one for each child in their small group, so the balloons and certificates can be presented during next week's Family Night program.

Characters

- Narrator, Amy, and her mom

Needed

- Two chairs
- A notebook and pen

Daddy

Amy and her mom are sitting on the chairs, frozen in place while the narrator speaks. The notebook and pen are under Amy's mom's chair.

Narrator Our story today is a little different than our other Circle Time stories, because this one is true! It's about a little girl named Amy, who had something very sad and scary happen to her and her family. Let's watch.

Amy *(Hugs her mom)* Hi, Mom! I haven't seen you for such a long time. It seems like you're at the hospital with Daddy almost all the time. How is Daddy today?

Mom He's about the same, honey. But I want to talk to you about your birthday. It's next week and I want to know what kind of party you would like.

Amy *(Looks very sad)* I don't think I want a party this year. It would be too hard to have fun while Daddy's in the hospital with cancer. I'm really scared, Mom, that he's going to die. Then what would I do?

Mom I know. I'm scared, too. So, should we do some things together? First, let's pray and ask Jesus to help us. He will listen and help us—He always does! *(She takes the notebook and pen from under her chair)* And I bought you a present. I'd like you to write down all your feelings in this notebook. You can write to God, or write letters to Daddy, or me—or anything you want. I think doing those things will help us get through this hard time, OK?

Amy OK, Mom. *(Mom exits, and Amy opens her notebook and starts to write)*

Narrator So Amy did the things her Mom asked her to do. First she prayed and asked God to help her be OK, especially when she was thinking about her daddy. Then, she wrote lots and lots in her diary, about how she was feeling and how much she missed her daddy. Finally, after many weeks—past Christmas, past Easter, and through almost the whole summer—Amy's daddy finally came home from the hospital. Amy and her mom were very happy!

Mom	*(Enters)* Are you ready, Amy? We are going to the hospital to pick up Daddy very soon!
Amy	And this time he won't have to go back! *(They hug)* I'll be right there. There's just one thing I have to do first.
Mom	OK. But hurry. *(She exits)*
Amy	*(Puts her pen and notebook down and bows her head to pray)* Dear Jesus, thank You for helping me with all my feelings in this really hard time. Thank You for taking care of me and my mom when we felt lonely and afraid. Most of all, thank You that You won't stop taking care of me now, even though my daddy's coming home. I love You! Signed, Me—Amy! *(Runs offstage, calling out, "I'm coming, Mom!")*

From

- 1 Samuel 17

Characters

- David

Needed

- A spear
- A large coat or other "armor"
- A slingshot and five pebbles

David Meets a Giant

David enters and greets the kids.

David You know, it was really hard for me to choose what to share with you today. There are so many stories I could tell you about how God was a helper for me! But there is one story that is so special and so much fun to tell. It's my favorite. It's about the time God helped me kill the giant, Goliath. And this week, I'm going to need your help to tell it!

Choose volunteers to be David and King Saul. Ask your biggest facilitator to play Goliath. Give the spear to Goliath, the slingshot and stones to David, and place the coat on the floor within easy reach. Tell the rest of the kids they are the Israelites and their job is to cheer David and boo at Goliath. Then read the following script, prompting the characters to pantomime the action, and the "crowd" to cheer or boo at the appropriate places.

David When I was just a young boy, before all the trouble started with King Saul, there was a war going on between my people, the Israelites—*(Points to crowd)* that's you guys, cheer for yourselves—and the Philistines, the bad guys. The Philistines had a champion fighter named Goliath. He was taller than anyone who is alive today! *(Goliath stands on a chair, waves his spear, and growls at the kids. They boo in response)*

One day, Goliath shouted out a challenge to our people. He said, "I'm bigger and stronger than any man you have in your army! Send out your biggest, strongest guy and watch how I squash him flat!" *(Goliath growls and the kids boo)* But everyone was scared of Goliath. No one would fight him.

After many days, I stood up and said to my people, *(Prompt child playing David to stand up and face the other kids)* "Who will go and fight this bully? Somebody has to!" But no one did. So I went to see King Saul *(Saul stands in front of David)* and said, "King Saul, if no one else will go fight Goliath, I will. OK?" King Saul said, "OK, but first put on my armor to protect you, because you are so small and skinny." *(Saul hands the coat to David. David puts it on)*

As you can see, King Saul's armor was way too big for me. So I took it off again and said, "King Saul, I don't need this heavy armor. God will take care of me and help me beat the giant!"

So I went out and stood up to Goliath. *(David comes and stands in front of Goliath. The kids cheer for him. Goliath growls)* You know what? Even though I knew God would help me, I was really scared. I prayed harder than ever! Then Goliath started laughing at me! He said, "Is this the best you can do? This skinny little runt? I'll eat him for breakfast! Even your God can't protect him from me!" *(Kids boo)*

So I got out my sling and put a pebble in it. *(Prompt David to do this)* I prayed God would make it go to the right spot, and I fired it at Goliath. All of a sudden, the great giant put his hand to his forehead and growled one last time before he fell flat on his face! *(Goliath falls and the kids cheer)* I killed him with his own sword *(Prompt David to stab Goliath)* God had answered my prayers and helped me win against the bully.

Well, that's my story. And that's the last story I'm going to tell you. I feel sad about that! But just remember, it doesn't matter where you are or what is happening, you can always ask God to help you! Good-bye, my friends!

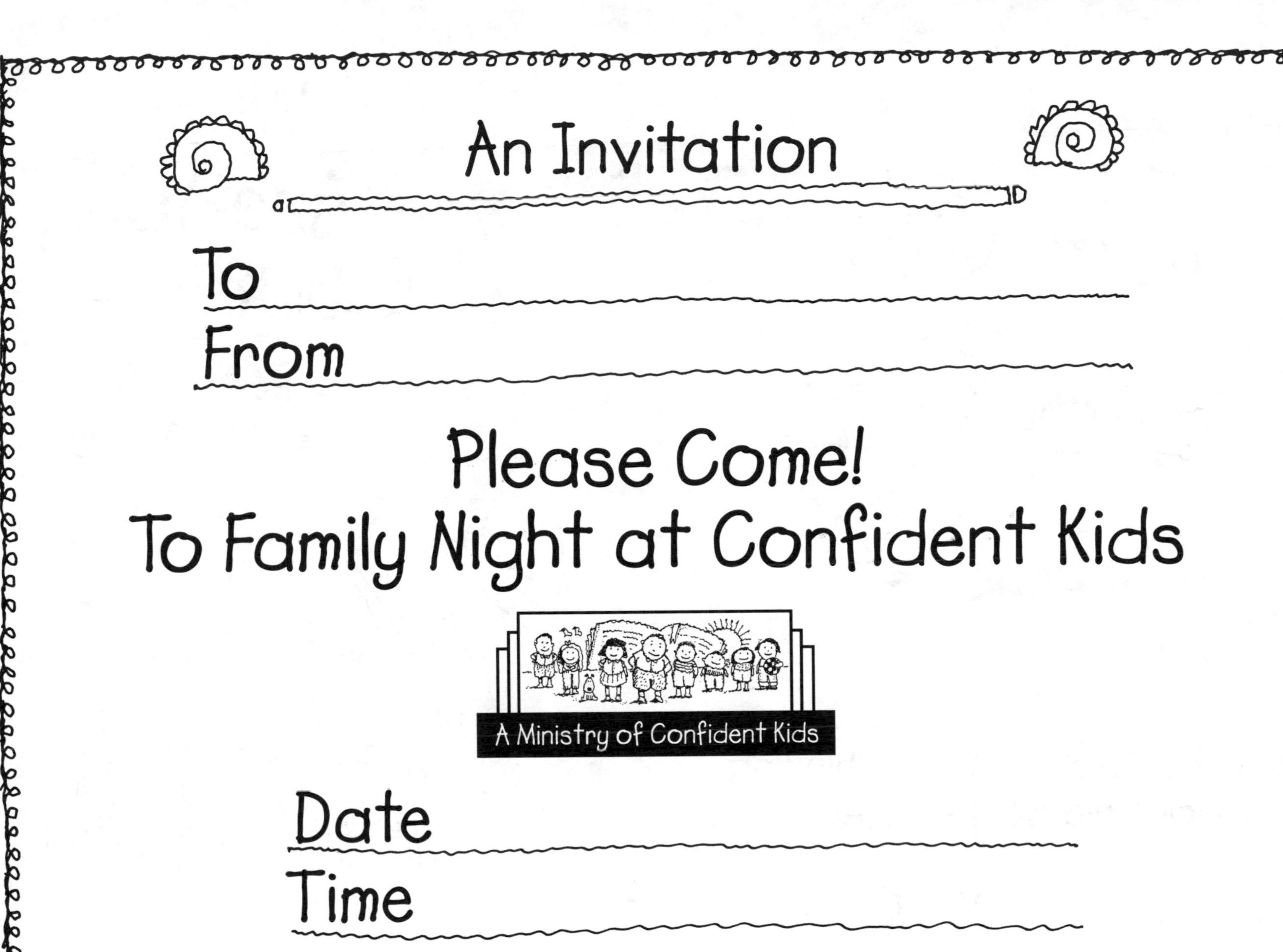
An Invitation
To
From
Please Come!
To Family Night at Confident Kids
A Ministry of Confident Kids
Date
Time

Thank You that You are thinking about me all the time!

That's how much You love me!

Where Are You, God?

Based on Psalm 139

You are with me everywhere I go!

In the day time, when it's light...

...and especially in the night when it's dark...

You are right with me!

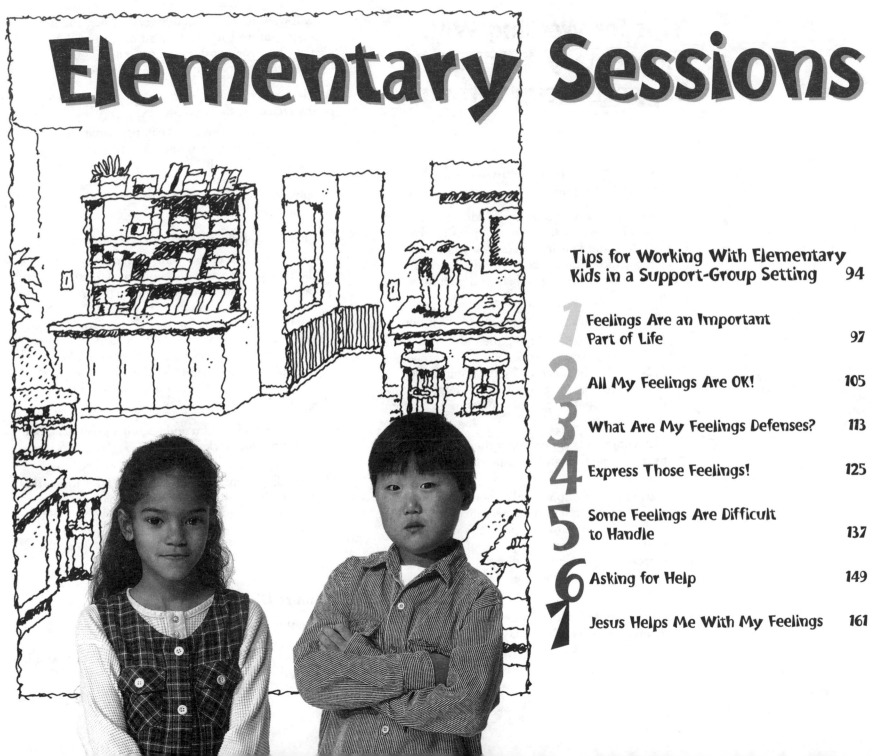

Elementary Sessions

Tips for Working With Elementary Kids in a Support-Group Setting

What to Expect From Elementary Kids in Confident Kids Groups

The following session plans are for kids in grades one through four. Because there are many differences between first and fourth graders, you will have to adapt this material to fit the grade level you are teaching. Here are a few key points to help you plan for your group:

- **Elementary kids value belonging to the group.**

  First graders are developing their ability to relate to each other in social settings. By fourth grade, the kids' need to be accepted by the group is well established. Having a best friend is important in these years, and there is peer pressure to conform to the group.

- **Elementary kids express their thoughts and feelings in short sentences and in response to direct questions.**

  Kids in your group will talk about their life circumstances, but don't expect them to ramble on and on about what is happening in their lives! Rather, listen for bits and pieces of their stories, especially as they answer direct questions. You'll also learn about them when you ask for prayer requests.

- **Elementary kids like to wiggle, act silly, and express themselves physically in play.**

  Expect lots of physical activity. These behaviors are more prevalent in high-stress kids. Boys, especially, will want to wrestle and hit each other, and girls may fight over who gets to sit next to you! Watch that this behavior does not get out of control and keep you from accomplishing group goals.

- **Elementary kids are increasingly aware of, and distracted by, the opposite sex.**

  First-grade boys and girls can participate in the same small group without many problems. From second grade on, however, coed small groups greatly decrease the kids' ability to focus on the subject at hand. Same-sex groups are most effective at this age.

- **Elementary kids still idealize their parents.**

  Kids at this age deeply want a relationship with their parents, no matter how their parents treat them. They cannot yet separate their parents' behavior from the childhood image of, "My dad (mom) is the best dad in the whole world!" When this discrepancy surfaces, help the child focus on her feelings and *do not attack the parent*. Say, for example, "It really hurts when dads break their promises, doesn't it? I can understand why you feel so sad."

- **Elementary kids learn and absorb a great deal, but offer little feedback.**

  New facilitators may fear they are not "getting through," or making a difference. Never forget that the positive feedback you are fortunate enough to receive is only the "tip of the iceberg." You will never know (except maybe in Heaven) the true extent to which you are influencing the kids' lives.

Minimize Discipline Problems

Because this age group is so physically active, controlling the meeting may be one of the greatest challenges you will have. You will be more successful if you heed the following suggestions:

- **Plan how you will use your physical space.**

  The kids' behavior is affected by their classroom. Before you begin your first session:
  - — *Limit the size of your area.* Too much space invites kids to run races rather than pay attention to you.
  - — *Remove or mark as "off limits" items that distract.* This includes stacks of extra chairs, boxes of toys, pianos, etc.
  - — *Use something physical to define boundaries.* Masking tape on the floor or an area rug can define where the kids are to sit for skits and Bible stories. A table or ring of chairs can establish the area for small groups.

- **Use activity sheets during small group discussions to keep the kids focused.**

  Elementary kids are not yet ready to sit in a circle and listen to one another share. Having something in front of them to work on will help them focus on the activity and lessen the temptation to look around the room or poke a neighbor.

- **Clearly state and consistently enforce rules.**

  All the facilitators in the room must work together to consistently remind the kids of the rules and enforce them. The kids must know that the adults in the room are in control of the meeting. If you give control to the kids, they will not respond to anything you say or try to do—guaranteed!

- **Recruit high schoolers, especially boys, to help in your room.**

  The presence of teens in the classroom has many advantages, but in terms of behavior issues, teens are invaluable. They can play games with the kids, wrestle with the boys at appropriate times, keep the physical energy focused, and help the kids settle down when it's time to listen.

- **Balance active and quiet activities according to the needs of your group.**

  If the kids get out of control because the opening activities are too active, start doing table activities! Or, if your kids can't focus on the Bible story after sitting for thirty-five minutes in small group time, use a few stretching exercises or a game of "Simon Says" as a regathering activity. In other words, learn to pay attention to the physical needs of your kids and do what works!

Skits and Bible Stories Are Key Learning Times

The elementary curriculum includes both an opening skit and an ending Bible story. These stories can be told in a variety of ways. Remember that kids today are highly visual and are used to seeing a lot of action in television shows, movies, and video games. Therefore, *be prepared to spend lots of time on the scripts each week to make them come alive.* Better yet, recruit a drama team to care for this part of the session!

- **Use puppets to tell the story.**

  Puppets take some practice and equipment, but the younger kids respond well to puppets.

- **Prerecord the skits on videotape.**

  Videotaped skits allow you the freedom to be creative with the skits and give the kids the familiar experience of watching a "movie" on video. Again, recruiting a team to produce the tapes would be ideal. High schoolers may really enjoy this "high-tech storytelling."

- **Do the skits yourselves.**

  The scripts are simple enough for your team to perform each week. Anything you can do to bring life to them—like adding extra props or characters—will make them more effective. Also, overdramatizing will help draw the kids into the action.

- **Involve the kids.**

  Some of the first and second graders, and most of the third and fourth graders are capable of taking roles in the skits. Assign these roles ahead of time, so the kids can look forward to participating and practicing. Also, all the kids can be recruited to act as a crowd or an army.

- **Use visual aids or videos to tell the Bible stories.**
  Pictures, flannelgraph figures, objects, and animated videos are excellent ways to help the kids focus on the story, especially the younger kids. If you use videos, be sure to have a facilitator summarize the story and apply it to your session theme. If you have an artist available to you, develop your own visual aids.

Have Basic Materials on Hand for All Sessions

Each session plan in the curriculum lists supplies unique to that session. However, before you begin any unit, be sure to set up your room with the following basic supplies. Adding the optional materials will further enhance the group's experience.

- **Basic Supplies**
  Confident Kids postcards and stamps
  Markers, pencils
  Colored drawing paper
  Tape, glue sticks, stapler
  Scissors
  Paper towels and other supplies for clean up
  Paper cups and napkins for snack time
  Extra snacks (in case someone forgets to return the snack tin)

- **Optional Supplies**
  Prop box for skits and role plays
  Glitter, lace doilies, scraps of fabric and ribbon
  Old magazines with lots of pictures
  Cassette tapes of songs for elementary kids
  A variety of stickers
  Elementary games and craft books to supplement the curriculum, if needed
  Books, puzzles, and craft items for first and second graders to fill extra time

Feelings Are an Important Part of Life

Elementary Session 1 Outline

Opening (30 Minutes)

"My Name Is ___ and I Feel ___"

Introduction of New Kids

Group Rules

"Two Kinds of Feelings"

Small Groups (35 Minutes)

Discussion of Session Theme

Feelings Alphabets

Prayer Time

Bible Time (20 Minutes)

Regathering

"Introducing David"

Memory Verse

Closing Prayer Huddle

Snack (5 Minutes)

The snack can be served during the Bible Time regathering.

Goals

- Introduce kids to the wide range of feelings God has placed within all of us
- Begin to develop a feelings vocabulary
- Assure kids that God understands and cares about their feelings

Needed

- Group rules poster
- Props for opening skit
- Sample "Feelings Word Poster"
- Notebook or boxes for prayer requests
- Materials for regathering activity
- Props for Bible story
- Memory verse (Joshua 1:9) printed out on poster board
- Snacks and snack tin

Feelings Are an Important Part of Life

Elementary Session 1

Opening (30 Minutes)

"My Name Is ___ and I Feel ___"

If you did not use the introductory session last week, have the kids make nametags as they arrive this session. Have tags, stickers, and markers available for kids to decorate their tags any way they wish. When all have arrived, proceed with the following game.

Ask the kids to stand in a circle. Have one facilitator say:

> **My name is** *[facilitator's name]* **and I feel** *[Fill in with a word that describes a feeling].*

The facilitator should use face and body movements to depict that feeling as the feeling word is said. Then have the whole group repeat the person's name and the motion. For example, the facilitator may say, "My name is Sue and I feel happy." *(Big smile)* The group should say, "This is Sue and she feels happy." *(Big smile)*

Continue around the circle until everyone has had a turn. Encourage kids to choose words that no one else has said yet. Be ready to suggest some if they can't think of a new word. *Note:* Third and fourth graders can choose a feeling word that starts with the same letter as their first name.

Introduction of New Kids

If you have done a Confident Kids unit before, you will likely have both returning kids and new kids in the group. Welcome the new ones by calling each one to the front of the room. Ask the new children to tell the others their name, grade, and one very unique thing about themselves. When they are finished, lead the group in yelling, "Welcome, *[child's name]!*" and give each one a round of applause.

Group Rules

If you did not use the introductory session, "Welcome to Confident Kids," last week, you will need to make a group rules poster. (See page 15 for complete directions on generating a list of rules for your group.) Spend some quality time doing this, as the group rules are crucial to the success of your support-group experience.

If you did use the introductory session, display the poster you made last week and review it. Be sure everyone understands the rules and the consequences for breaking them.

"Two Kinds of Feelings"

You will need to decide how the skits will be handled each week. (See "Tips for Working With Elementary Kids" on pages 94–96 for ideas.) This session's script is on pages 102 and 103. Dismiss to small groups after the skit.

Small Groups (35 Minutes)

Discussion of Session Theme

Use the following questions to discuss the session theme, "I have two kinds of feelings!"

What happened to make Clyde say that his heart hurt? *(Carol laughed and made fun of him)*

Have you ever felt that way? *(Ask kids to share specific examples)*

Do you agree that sometimes feeling hurt inside is worse than feeling hurt outside? *(Let kids respond)*

Everyone has two kinds of feelings. The first kind has to do with our physical sense of touching. We can feel things like heat or cold or someone touching us. This kind of touch does two things:

***It protects us.* Feeling heat through our fingertips keeps us from getting burned. Feeling cold tells us to put on a coat.**

***It gives us pleasure.* We feel pleasure when we get a big hug from someone we love!**

These feelings give us messages about things outside of us. But there is another kind of feeling that gives us messages about what is happening inside of us. We call these feelings *emotions* and they do the same things as our outside feelings:

***They protect us* by warning us that something is wrong or we need help, like when we see a stranger following us and feel scared.**

***They give us pleasure.* We feel good inside when we play with a special friend.**

Everyone has the same feelings—anger, sadness, happiness, love. Can you think of others? *(Let kids add more)* **Good! But not everyone expresses them in the same way.**

What do you think Carol meant when she talked about having a bandage for the inside feelings? *(Finding ways to make the inside hurt feel better)*

We are going to be learning healthy ways of expressing our feelings in Confident Kids in the next few weeks.

Feelings Alphabets

The first step in dealing with feelings is having the vocabulary to do so. To help kids build a feelings vocabulary, use the following activities.

I have two kinds of feelings!

Feelings Alphabet Race

Grades 3 and 4. Tell the kids you will have a race to sec how many feelings words they can name beginning with each letter of the alphabet. Put them in pairs and begin by having them write the letters of the alphabet down one side of a piece of paper. When everyone is ready, give them five minutes to fill in as many words as possible. Compare lists, and if you like, award small prizes to the winners.

Grades 1 and 2. Younger kids can work together or in pairs to list as many feelings words as they can think of. After five minutes, compare lists, or count the total number of words listed. If you like, you could award a small prize (such as one piece of candy) for each word they list.

Feelings Alphabet Posters

Grades 3 and 4. Prepare a feelings alphabet to decorate your room. Distribute paper and markers to the kids. Ask each child to choose a different feeling word for a poster. Tell the kids to write the word and decorate the paper in such a way that it depicts the meaning of the feeling word. They can use color, lines, symbols, pictures, or any other means to convey the meaning of the word. Here are some examples:

As the kids work, discuss the meaning of each word selected. Ask kids to share why they chose their word, the times and things that make them feel that way, etc.

Grades 1 and 2. As kids choose a word, write it for them in the middle of their poster. Then let them decorate the poster in any way they like to convey the meaning of the word. They may want to draw faces that depict the feeling or things that make them feel that feeling. *Optional:* You may want to have old magazine pictures available with pictures that depict feeling words.

Prayer Time

Each week you will spend the last seven or eight minutes of your group time in prayer. The purpose of this time is to help the kids learn that they can draw on God's presence and power as they face life's circumstances. Use a prayer notebook or other means to track the requests, and be sure to check back on them from time to time.

To begin your prayer journey for this unit, ask the kids for a few requests. Specifically ask them to think about any feelings they may be facing right now that seem difficult. Then pray for each child by name, thanking God that he chose to come to Confident Kids.

Bible Time (20 Minutes)

Regathering

Assign one facilitator each week to lead the kids in a favorite game, song, or activity (See Appendix B, "Resources," for ideas) as they come from their small groups to the Bible story area. This facilitator will have to finish her small group time a few minutes early to be ready to gather the kids as they dismiss from their groups. *Note:* Some groups prefer to serve the snacks at this time, with the rule that the snacks will be served as soon as everyone has arrived and is quiet.

"Introducing David"

As with the opening skit, you will have to decide how the Bible stories will be handled each week. This week's script is on page 104.

Memory Verse

Before the session, prepare a poster of Joshua 1:9, which will be introduced during the Bible story:

> **Be strong and courageous. Do not be terrified; do not be discouraged, for the Lord your God will be with you wherever you go. (*NIV*)**

Have the kids say the verse with you several times. Since it is an easy verse, turn the poster around and have kids say it from memory.

Closing Prayer Huddle

Each week the meetings will close in the same way. Gather all the kids into a tight circle and instruct them to stack their hands on top of each other in the middle of the circle. As they stand in this position, have them recite the following prayer together:

> **Dear God, thank You that You love me and understand all my feelings! Amen!**

Have them raise their hands out of the stack and over their heads as they yell, "Amen!"

Snack (5 Minutes)

The facilitators should bring the snack the first night. Before the kids leave, choose a child to take the snack tin home for next week. (See page 14 in "Getting Started" for more information about handling the snack.)

Characters

- Clyde and Carol

Needed

- A bandage for Clyde's hand

Two Kinds of Feelings

Clyde and Carol enter from different sides of the room and meet in the middle. Clyde has one hand bandaged, and he is groaning.

Carol	Hey, Clyde! What happened to you?
Clyde	Nothing!
Carol	What do you mean, "Nothing"? You didn't have that big bandage on this morning! What crazy thing did you do this time?
Clyde	It was just a little accident.
Carol	Oh boy, your accidents are great! Tell me more!
Clyde	Come on, Carol. Lay off. It was nothing.
Carol	No way! I'm not leaving you alone 'till you tell me what happened!
Clyde	I was just eating some soup, that's all.
Carol	How can you hurt your hand eating soup?
Clyde	Well, I dropped my spoon on the floor.
Carol	*(Looks puzzled)* Yeah, so?
Clyde	When I went to pick it up, I bumped the table.
Carol	That sounds like the good old Clyde I know! Then what?
Clyde	When I bumped the table, the bowl started to fall, and I tried to catch it. Only I missed and stuck my hand right into the boiling soup. Mom had just poured it into my bowl from the stove.
Carol	*(Laughs hysterically)* Boy, Clyde! You do more clumsy stuff than anyone I know! *(Stops laughing, noticing that Clyde looks hurt)* Ah, I guess it really hurt, though, huh?

Clyde Not as much as my heart hurts right now.

Carol Your heart? Are you having a heart attack, too? Gosh, Clyde, are you OK?

Clyde I don't mean my real heart. I mean my feelings heart. I know I get bumped around a lot, and sometimes it is pretty funny—

Carol Yeah, like the time you tripped in the school lunch line and spilled your meatloaf and carrots all over Mr. Roberts! Boy, the look on his face—

Clyde That's what I mean, Carol! Everyone laughed, but I felt stupid—like I wanted to die! I guess what I'm trying to say is that the hurt I feel on the inside when everyone laughs at me is worse than the hurt on the outside. *(Holds his bandaged hand up)* Even this burn doesn't hurt as much as my heart does when you make fun of me!

Carol I never thought about that. Hey, maybe we could find a bandage for your inside hurts, kind of like the bandage for your outside hurts! What do you think?

They exit.

From

- Various Psalms

Characters

- David

Needed

- A biblical costume for David
- A sling
- A shepherd's staff
- An autoharp
- A Bible
- A hymn or praise songbook
- A simple Psalm set to music that the kids can sing (use a children's praise music tape or an autoharp)

Introducing David

David enters carrying all the props.

David Hi! Uh—let's see. Did I find the right place? Is this the Confident Kids group? *(Let kids respond)* Good! I've been invited to be here with you each week to help you learn about feelings. That's because—by the way, do you know who I am? *(Engages the kids in conversation about his identity until they guess. Talks about each prop—except the songbook—and how it has meaning in David's life. If time permits, let volunteers use the sling)*

Now, as I was saying. We're going to be talking about feelings in the weeks ahead. I learned a long time ago that it is good to get your feelings out, and especially to tell them all to God! Does anyone here know how I express my feelings to God? *(Ask for responses. If they don't know, hold up the harp as a hint)* I learned early in my life to use music and poems to talk to God. I wrote them down, too. Do you know what they are? *(Show Bible and turn to Psalms. For older kids, ask a volunteer to find David's song and poems in the Bible before turning to Psalms in the Bible. Then show the kids the hymn book)* I guess you could say that my songs and poems became the first hymn book because people in my kingdom recited and sang them in their worship times for thousands of years! Even today people sing my Psalms as worship songs. *(Use the children's praise tape or the autoharp to lead the kids in a Psalm set to music)*

Why do you think people sing the Psalms, and other worship songs? *(Refer to the songbook. Let kids respond)* Because it helps them tell God what they are feeling. And there isn't anyone who understands our feelings more than God! And I'm going to be back every week to tell you more about how you can express all your feelings to God, too! But I'm out of time for today! See you next week! *(Exits)*

Goals

- Explore the fact that there are no "bad" feelings. All our feelings are important and necessary to living a healthy life
- Identify feelings the kids enjoy and ones they don't enjoy
- Affirm that all feelings are not only OK, but important to our lives
- Use a story about David to illustrate how he used God's presence to help him turn fear into something good

Needed

- "Feelings Words" charades cards
- Group rules poster
- Props for opening skit
- Length (approx. 4′) of butcher paper or shelf paper
- Many pictures from magazines, newspapers, old photos, etc. depicting feelings
- Prayer journals
- Materials for regathering activity
- Props for Bible story
- Joshua 1:9 poster from last session

All My Feelings Are OK!

Elementary Session 2 Outline

Opening (30 Minutes)

"Simon Says" or "Feelings Charades"

Group Rules

"Grandpa"

Small Groups (35 Minutes)

Discussion of Session Theme

"All My Feelings Are OK" Collage

Prayer Time

Bible Time (20 Minutes)

Regathering

"It's OK to Feel Afraid"

Memory Verse

Closing Prayer Huddle

Snack (5 Minutes)

The snack can be served during the Bible Time regathering.

All My Feelings Are OK!

Elementary Session 2

Opening (30 Minutes)

"Simon Says" or "Feelings Charades"

"Simon Says" (For First and Second Graders)

Begin when two or three kids arrive, and let others join the circle as they come into the room. Play in the same manner as traditional "Simon Says," except call for actions that express feelings:

Simon says look sad.

Simon says act excited.

Kids may express the feeling in any way they desire. Keep it moving quickly, and use a variety of feelings words. Let kids take turns being the leader.

Feelings Charades (For Third and Fourth Graders)

Before the session begins, make up a set of "Feelings Charades" cards by writing a feeling word on a 3" x 5" card. Make about ten cards. To play, ask for a volunteer to draw a card and act out the feeling word for the rest of the group. The rest of the group calls out guesses. After three incorrect guesses, the actor gives a hint by saying:

I feel this way when ___.

After the feeling has been guessed, allow any child in the group to volunteer an answer to the above statement. When all have shared, choose a new actor and repeat.

Group Rules

Use the group rules poster to review the rules again this week. Ask the kids how they are feeling about the rules, and how they are working.

Are there any that are not necessary? Are there some that should be added?

Use this time to allow the kids to negotiate and gain a sense of ownership about the way the group is going.

"Grandpa"

Use the script on page 109 to help kids begin thinking about the appropriateness of all their feelings. Dismiss to small groups after the skit is presented.

Small Groups (35 Minutes)

Discussion of Session Theme

Use the following questions to discuss the session theme, "All my feelings are important to me."

Why did Sally think she was bad? *(She thought feeling the way she did made her bad)*

What did Jeff mean when he told Sally that she needed to feel sad? *(He was trying to let her know that feeling sad is part of how we get over the hurt we feel when someone close to us dies)*

Have you ever felt like Sally? *(Ask kids to share. Be sure to affirm that even though they felt bad at the time, their feelings were not bad)*

Last week we talked about how feelings are a very important part of our lives. The next thing we need to think about is that some feelings feel better than others. We like to feel happy or excited or loved. We don't like to feel sad, embarrassed, or hurt. Because of that, it is easy to think that feelings we like are good feelings and feeling we don't like are bad feelings. But that is not true! All our feelings are important! Feeling sad may not be fun, but sometimes it is right for us to feel sad for awhile. God has created us with lots and lots of different kinds of feelings and all of them are important. So whenever you feel sad or angry or disappointed, remember that all your feelings are OK and there is nothing wrong with you because you feel them. Remember our slogan, "All My Feelings Are OK!" Let's say that together! *(Repeat a few times)*

All my feelings are important to me

"All My Feelings Are OK" Montage

You will need about a 4′ length of butcher paper or shelf paper with the words "All My Feelings Are OK!" lettered in the middle. Then designate two sections, one labeled *Feelings I Like to Feel* and the other *Feelings I Don't Like to Feel.* Leave lots of room around the letters for kids to paste or draw pictures. Place this on a wall or on the floor—wherever kids will have easy access to it. You will also need many pictures depicting feelings. These can be faces or scenes, and you can get them from magazines, newspapers, old posters, photo albums, or any other source you can think of. Just be sure you have a wide variety of feelings represented.

To make the collage, instruct kids that they can use pictures, drawings, or words to fill the spaces with depictions of feelings they like and don't like to feel. These can be overlapped, connected with lines—anything they want to do to create an art "masterpiece." When done, remind the kids that all our feelings are OK and important to us, even the ones we don't like to feel!

Prayer Time

Use your prayer notebooks or boxes to update your group's requests. Focus your prayers on asking God to help us accept all the feelings we have. Kids could be encouraged to share prayers of thanks for the things that brought happy feelings this week, and prayers of strength for dealing with the things that brought sad or difficult feelings.

Bible Time (20 Minutes)

Regathering

Have one facilitator lead the kids in a favorite game, song, or activity.

"It's OK to Feel Afraid"

Present the Bible story (script begins on page 111).

Memory Verse

Use the poster from last week to review Joshua 1:9.

Closing Prayer Huddle

Close the meeting as you did last week. Use this prayer:

> **Dear God, thank You that You love me and understand all my feelings! Amen!**

Snack (5 Minutes)

Distribute the snack the child brought. Before the kids leave, choose another child to take the snack tin home for next week.

Characters

- Sally and Jeff

Needed

- A chair

Grandpa

Sally is sitting in a chair, head hanging, feet swinging, looking sad.

Jeff *(Enters)* Hey, Sal! Did you get—hey, what's wrong? You look awful!

Sally I feel awful. I just found out my grandpa died. He had a heart attack and died. It was a big surprise! He wasn't sick or anything.

Jeff Wow! Your grandpa was neat! Is he really dead?

Sally Of course he's really dead! Do you think I'd look this terrible if something bad hadn't happened? This is awful! I've never had so many bad feelings all at once. What's wrong with me?

Jeff What do you mean?

Sally I mean, what's wrong with me that I'm feeling all this bad stuff?

Jeff That's silly, Sal. You're not feeling bad stuff.

Sally Well, I'm not feeling good stuff! I feel like someone stuck me in a blender and turned the switch on high! I feel so bad I just cry and cry and cry. And you know what's really bad? Sometimes I get really mad at Grandpa for dying! I hate feeling that way about him! It scares me!

Jeff Sally, I know it's not fun to feel those things, but there isn't anything wrong with you because you feel scared and sad and even mad! You aren't bad because you're feeling scared and sad and even mad!

Sally *(Gets up and starts pacing)* How can you say that? I feel very bad right now and I'd give anything to not feel afraid and sad! I just want to feel good again! Besides, how come you know so much about what I'm feeling?

Jeff I know because I felt the same way when my grandma died last year. Don't you remember how sad I was? My dad told me it was OK to feel sad. In fact, he wanted me to feel sad for awhile—it was important! And it's important for you, too. And you'll feel better again, I promise!

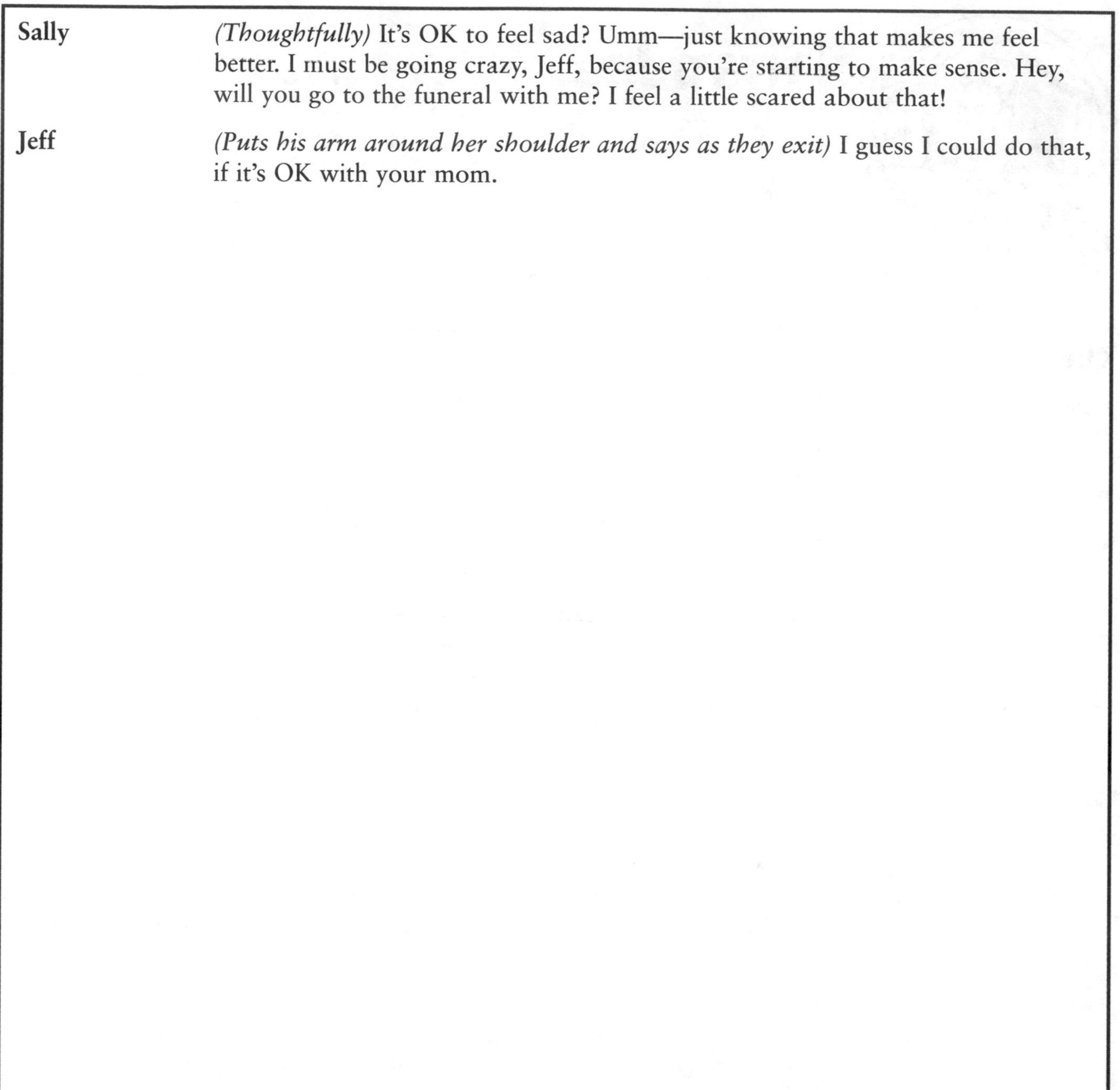

Sally	*(Thoughtfully)* It's OK to feel sad? Umm—just knowing that makes me feel better. I must be going crazy, Jeff, because you're starting to make sense. Hey, will you go to the funeral with me? I feel a little scared about that!
Jeff	*(Puts his arm around her shoulder and says as they exit)* I guess I could do that, if it's OK with your mom.

From

- 1 Samuel 17:1–51

Characters

- David

Needed

- A slingshot and small stones
- A Bible
- An adult-size heavy coat and boots or catcher's mask and chest pad

Suggested

- If it worked last session to sing a Psalm, be prepared to do so again this week

It's OK to Feel Afraid

David enters carrying all the props. He greets the kids.

David You know, we all have so many kinds of feelings that God has given us. And this week we're learning that all those feelings are important, even the ones we don't like to feel. So I thought I would tell you about the time that I felt afraid. No one likes to feel afraid, right? Well, I learned that even though I didn't like feeling afraid, it turned out to be just the right thing for me to feel.

Let's go way back now, to the time I was young and still living at home with my father and seven brothers. I was the youngest. How many of you are the youngest? *(Ask those who are the youngest to stand, and ask them to tell how they feel about being the youngest. What do they like the most? the least? Then have anyone with an older sibling stand. Ask them what things their older siblings get to do that they don't—like staying up later, going to games or parties, watching different TV shows or movies, etc. Then ask all the kids to name feelings words that describe being the youngest, such as fun, irritating, cheated, impatient to grow up, etc.)*

I remember something my brothers got to do that I didn't. They went off to fight with King Saul in a war. But I was too young and had to stay home to watch my father's sheep. I felt lots of the same things you just described. Then one day, my father asked me to take some things to my brothers in the field, and to find out how the battle was going while I was there. Remember, we didn't have TV in those days—we couldn't watch the news to see what was going on there like you guys do now. So I went. And that's when I first saw the man they called Goliath! While I was talking to my brothers, he came out to the middle of the field yelling insults at our people and our God! Now, I know many of you know this story well. So, let's review it together.

Invite kids to tell the basics from 1 Samuel 17. When you get to the part about Saul putting his armor on David, select a child from the group to come forward. Place the coat and boots or the catcher's equipment on him. Ask how it would feel to have to run a race wearing all this protective clothing. Emphasize that David decided to trust God and just be himself. Also, set up a target in the room and ask volunteers to try to hit it using the sling. Make the point of how God guided the stone to the center of Goliath's forehead.

David That was a big event in my life! But what I most want to say to you today is how I felt at the time. Do you think I felt afraid? Of course I did! But because I was afraid, I knew I needed to trust God to help me. And as you know, it was trusting God that brought the victory! So, when you feel afraid, you can just say to yourself: "When I'm afraid, I will trust the Lord to help me!" Say it with me. *(Have kids repeat it, with great enthusiasm, several times)* Optional: *At this time, you can lead the kids in singing a Psalm as a reinforcement of expressing their feelings to God, preferably one that expresses trusting God to help in times of trouble.*

That's it! I'm all out of time for today. See you next week! *(Exits)*

Goals

- Define feelings defenses as "feeling one way but acting another"
- List various feelings defenses
- Practice identifying various feelings defenses, including the kids' own
- Illustrate how David used a defense to avoid his feelings

Needed

- Paper plates, spinners, and brads
- Group rules poster
- Brown paper bag (grocery size) with a smiling face drawn on it for each facilitator
- Copies of "Defense Masks" activity sheet and six paper plates for everyone, including facilitators
- "Feelings Defense Situation Cards," cut apart and placed into a small basket
- Prayer journals
- Materials for regathering activity
- Props for Bible story
- Joshua 1:9, prepared according to the method you choose to review it

What Are My Feelings Defenses?

Elementary Session 3 Outline

Opening (30 Minutes)

Feelings Wheels

Group Rules

"I Don't Want to Hear This!"

Small Groups (35 Minutes)

Discussion of Session Theme

Defense Masks

Prayer Time

Bible Time (20 Minutes)

Regathering

"David Avoids His Feelings"

Memory Verse

Closing Prayer Huddle

Snack (5 Minutes)

The snack can be served during the Bible Time regathering.

What Are My Feelings Defenses?

Elementary Session 3

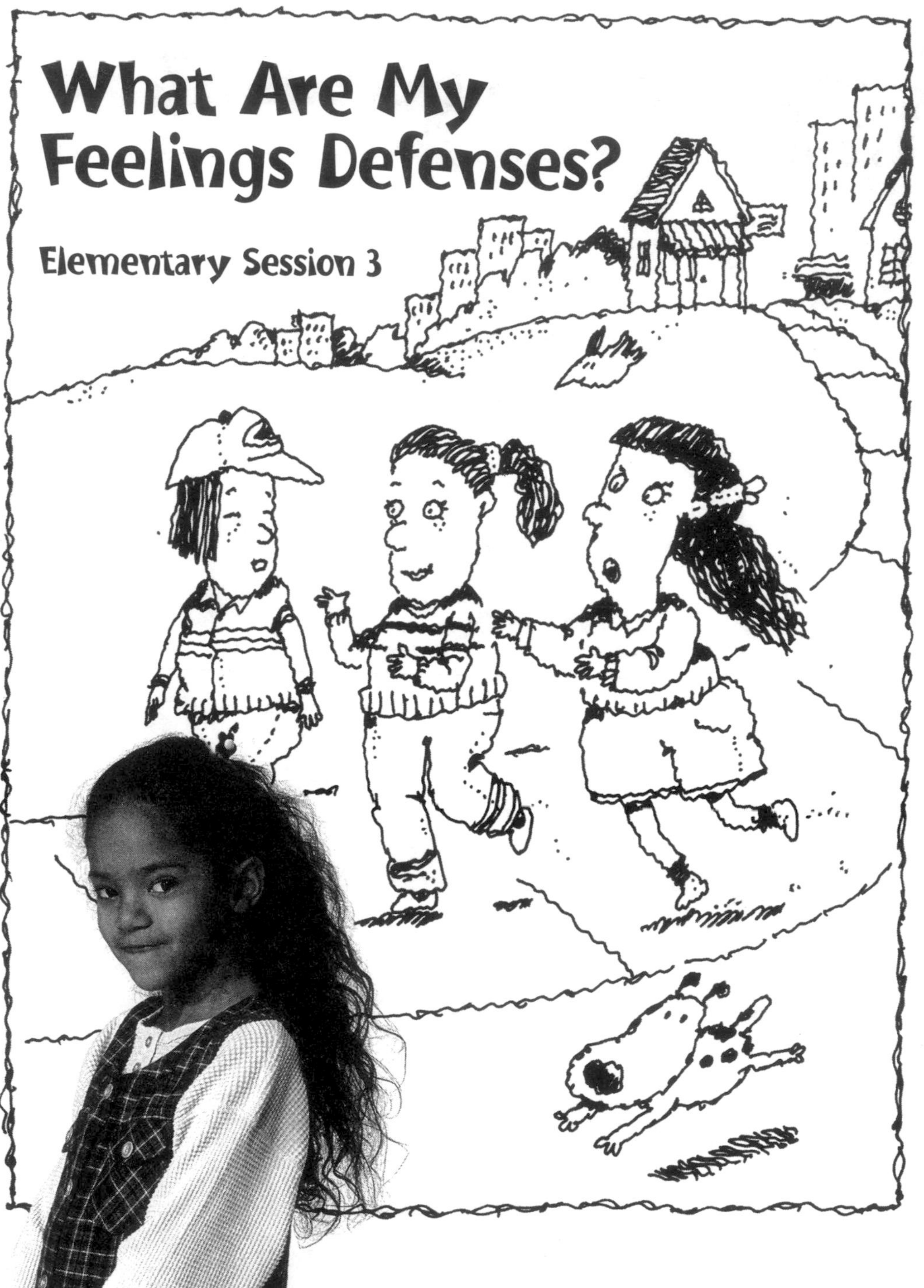

Opening (30 Minutes)

Feelings Wheels

Prepare for this activity in advance by dividing paper plates into six pie-wedge-shaped sections. In each section, write the following words: happy, sad, angry, depressed, loved, and other. (You may want to let third and fourth graders write the words themselves.) Cut spinners out of cardboard and have spinners and brads ready for the meeting. As kids arrive, give each a plate, spinner, and brad. Ask kids to color the sections with colors that remind them of that feeling. When they are finished, attach the spinner to the plate with the brad. To use the wheels, kids identify what they are feeling and point the spinner to that feeling.

Facilitators can either keep the wheels for use at the beginning of Confident Kids meetings, or send them home with instructions to post them in a prominent place in the house and keep the pointer on the feeling the kids are currently feeling. Other family members can make a wheel and keep them posted together.

Group Rules

Use the group rules poster to review the rules.

"I Don't Want to Hear This!"

Use the script on pages 117 and 118 to help kids begin thinking about how they may feel one way but act another. Dismiss to small groups after the skit.

Small Groups (35 Minutes)

Discussion of Session Theme

In advance, draw a smiling face on the outside of a brown grocery bag. While kids are gathering in the small group area, put the bag over your head. Ask children to tell you what they think you are feeling. After several responses, take the bag off and have an angry or sad look on your face. Say:

Did you know that I was really angry (or sad) on the inside, even though I was smiling on the outside? Everyone uses what we call feelings defenses from time to time. *A feelings defense is when we feel one way, but we act in a totally different way.* We use a defense mostly when we are feeling something that is uncomfortable and we want to pretend we are not feeling it; or we don't want anyone else to know what we are feeling.

How was Mary in the skit using a defense? *(She didn't want to feel bad about Jane's moving so she pretended it wasn't really happening)*

There are lots of feelings defenses we use. Let's think of some ways we act when we don't want to feel our feelings.

As you talk about each of the following defenses, prepare a defense mask by pasting the corresponding face from the "Defense Masks" activity sheets (pages 121–123) onto paper plates:

***Clowning*—We make jokes when we feel uncomfortable.**

***Pretending*—We keep from feeling hurt or disappointed by pretending the precipitating event didn't happen, or we use our imaginations to make up stories so we don't have to think about what really happened.**

***Silence*—We get quiet or we don't say anything, even if we feel angry or disappointed.**

***Getting Sick*—We get headaches and stomachaches when something we don't like happens, or we pretend to be sick to avoid facing scary or hurtful circumstances.**

***Blame*—We always make everything someone else's fault, especially when we're afraid we'll get into trouble.**

***Constant Talking*—We don't let anyone say anything, especially if we're afraid of what they have to say.**

Use the following questions to discuss the session theme, "Sometimes I feel one way but act another."

Which defense(s) did Mary use? *(Constant talking and pretending)*

How did the defense hurt her friendship with her best friend? *(Jane thought Mary didn't care about the fact that she was moving. She was hurt)*

How did using a defense hurt herself? *(She felt awful, her best friend was mad at her, she could have received comfort from both Jane and Cindy had she told them what she was really feeling)*

Everyone uses defenses sometimes. But when we *always* act in ways that make us look like we don't care about anything, or when we act in ways that make others not want to be around us, our defenses are actually hurting us rather than helping us. Therefore, learning how to lower our defenses is an important part of growing up healthy. *Lowering our defenses means we show on the outside what we are feeling on the inside and we use words to tell people we trust what we are really feeling.*

Sometimes I feel one way but act another

Defense Masks

Give everyone six paper plates and copies of the "Defense Masks" activity sheets (pages 121–123). Give kids time to cut out the faces and paste them onto the plates. They can add hair or other decorations, if they like. You can give older kids the option of drawing the faces on the plates themselves.

When the masks are ready, ask one child to pick a "Feelings Defense Situation Card" (page 124) from a basket and read it aloud. Then ask all the kids to choose a feeling word that describes how they would really feel if the situation happened to them, and one of the masks that shows what defense they might use to protect themselves from that feeling. On the back of the mask, have them draw a picture of what they are really feeling inside. Now ask kids to hold up the mask in front of their faces and look around.

> **Can you tell from the masks what everyone else is really feeling? What can you do to lower your masks?** *(Brainstorm ideas that relate to the situation on the card, such as apologize, tell a parent they are feeling afraid, hold a funeral for the pet, etc.)*

As time allows, draw new cards and repeat the activity.

Prayer Time

Use your prayer notebooks or boxes to update your group's requests. Then focus your prayer time by using a simple prayer litany. Sit in a circle and ask one volunteer to share a time when they felt alone, afraid, or very unhappy, as well as a defensive behavior they used, or might use in the future. Then ask the whole group to say to the person:

> ***[Child' name]*, God is with you when you feel *[feeling]*. You don't have to cover it with a feelings defense.**

For example, if Billy says he feels afraid when he has to take a math test, ask the whole group to say:

> **Billy, God is with you when you feel afraid. You don't have to cover your fear by getting a stomachache.**

Let as many share as want to. Close in prayer, thanking God for caring about how we really feel.

Bible Time (20 Minutes)

Regathering

Have one facilitator lead the kids in a favorite game, song, or activity.

"David Avoids His Feelings"

Present the Bible story (script is on pages 119 and 120).

Memory Verse

Choose a memory verse game from Appendix B, "Resources," to review Joshua 1:9.

Closing Prayer Huddle

Close your meeting as in weeks past.

Snack (5 Minutes)

Distribute the snack the child brought. Before the kids leave, choose another child to take the snack tin home for next week.

Characters

- Mary, Jane, and Cindy

"I Don't Want to Hear This!"

Mary and Jane enter. Mary is talking a "mile a minute" about nothing in particular. Jane is walking beside her, looking sad.

Jane	Mary, would you be quiet long enough for me to tell you something? I've been trying to get a word in edgewise for the last hour! *(Freezes)*
Mary	*(Steps away from Jane and addresses kids)* I noticed she was upset about something right away. I'm afraid of what she's going to say. It might be bad news, or worse yet, she might be mad at me! I don't want to hear anything bad, so I'm going to pretend everything is OK! *(Returns to Jane)* I just want to tell you one more thing! Did you hear that Mike Becker brought his frog to school yesterday and it got loose in the cafeteria? Mrs. Brooks—
Jane	Mary, be quiet! Everyone knows about that stupid frog! I'm trying to tell you something important!
Mary	OK! But what's more important than Mike Becker's frog?
Jane	*(Looks sad)* My dad told us last night that we have to move to Texas. He's got a different job and he starts next month. *(Freezes)*
Mary	*(Steps toward kids, looks anguished)* Oh, I knew it was something bad. I just knew it! Jane is my best friend in the whole world, and I don't think I can live without her! How could this happen? This hurts too much for me to face! I'm going to pretend she's just joking! *(Returns to Mary)* Hey, Texas! You'll look great in a cowboy hat! Are you going to have your own horse?
Jane	*(Looks shocked)* How can you be so cheerful? I thought you were my best friend! Don't you understand? We aren't going to be together anymore!
Mary	I heard! But I think Mike Becker's frog was more exciting! Did you hear it even got in the soup? Everyone—

Jane I thought you were my friend, but I guess I was wrong! You don't even care that I'm moving away or that we won't be together or that I feel hurt! You're just making a big joke out of this! I hate you! *(Runs out)*

Mary *(Stares after her, looks hurt and sad)* I feel awful! Now my best friend is not only moving away, but she hates me, too. I feel like I want to die! What am I going to do? I don't want to feel like this!

Cindy *(Enters)* Hi, Mary! What's new?

Mary *(Looks over her shoulder to where Jane exited, then back to Cindy and smiles)* Nothing much! Say, did you hear about Mike Becker bringing his frog to school yesterday?

Cindy Yeah! I was in the cafeteria when it got loose!

They exit, talking about the frog and laughing.

From

- 1 Samuel 16:1–13; 18:1–16; 19:1–10

Characters

- David and Jonathan

Needed

- An autoharp
- A spear
- Biblical costumes or headpieces for David and Jonathan

David Avoids His Feelings

David enters and greets the kids.

David I was listening to your conversation about feelings defenses. So I thought I would tell you about a time I avoided my true feelings for so long that I almost got *killed* because of it! It all started when a man named Samuel came to our house one day and told my dad that God had sent him there because someone in my family was going to become the next king! All seven of my older brothers got so excited! I was out taking care of the sheep at the time, so I didn't even know what was going on. Well, all my brothers went in one at a time to talk to Samuel, but none of them was the right one. Finally, my dad sent for me to come to the house. When I got there, Samuel fell down in front of me and told me that God had chosen me to be the next king!

From that moment on, my life changed. The king—his name was Saul—called me to visit him in the palace. Would you like to live in a palace? *(Let kids respond)* It was so beautiful, it took my breath away when I first saw it. I was—well, can you think of some feeling words that describe how I felt? *(Allow for responses)* While I was at the palace, I found out that King Saul often had terrible nightmares and fits of anger. One night he called for me to come and play my harp and sing. *(Strum and sing a few lines)* My songs made him feel better, and after that he called for me whenever he had a spell.

Things went along pretty well—for awhile. But then Saul's bad dreams got worse and even my music didn't help much. Finally, one night he took a spear *(Show spear)* and threw it at me! *(Throw spear)* He was a big, strong man, and it was only with God's help that I jumped out of the way in time. I was terrified! Now I was afraid of Saul, and very sad because he hated me. But you know what? I pretended I wasn't feeling those things. For a while, things got better. Saul sent me to the battlefield and I felt God's spirit with me, and we won many battles! Saul even talked me into marrying his daughter because, as *he* said, he was so pleased with me! And then one day:

Jonathan	*(Enters, looking worried)* David, you have to listen to me! My father hates you and wants to kill you, and everyone in the palace knows it—except you! You have to do something to stay safe!
David	*(Puts his arm around Jonathan and says to the kids)* This is my best friend, Jonathan. He is King Saul's son. *(To Jonathan)* Oh, come on, it can't be that bad.
Jonathan	What do you mean, "It can't be that bad!" He's tried to kill you almost every night for a month, and he's even talking to the servants about it!
David	Well, I'll admit it's been a little scary lately, but—
Jonathan	*(Agitated)* But what? Look, I love my father and all, but you're letting this situation get out of control. Wake up, my friend, or you'll be dead very soon! *(Exits, shaking his head)*
David	I have to admit, Jonathan's word upset me a bit. But then my friend talked to his father about the situation, and once again, things got better! So I let myself believe everything was all right. Until finally, one night when I was playing my harp for Saul, he once again flew into a terrible rage—for no reason I could see—and threw a spear at me. That night I couldn't ignore my true feelings any more. I had to face them. It was true. Saul wanted me dead! So I ran away! I was feeling so much inside—scared, sad, lonely, unsure of the future—but I felt better when I told my feelings to God and remembered that He would take care of me. Even though I didn't like those feelings, it was better than ignoring them! *(Sighs)* Well, there is so much more to tell you, but I have to wait until next week. But before I go, let's say our slogan together one more time *(Yell out together)*: "All My Feelings Are OK!" *(Exits)*

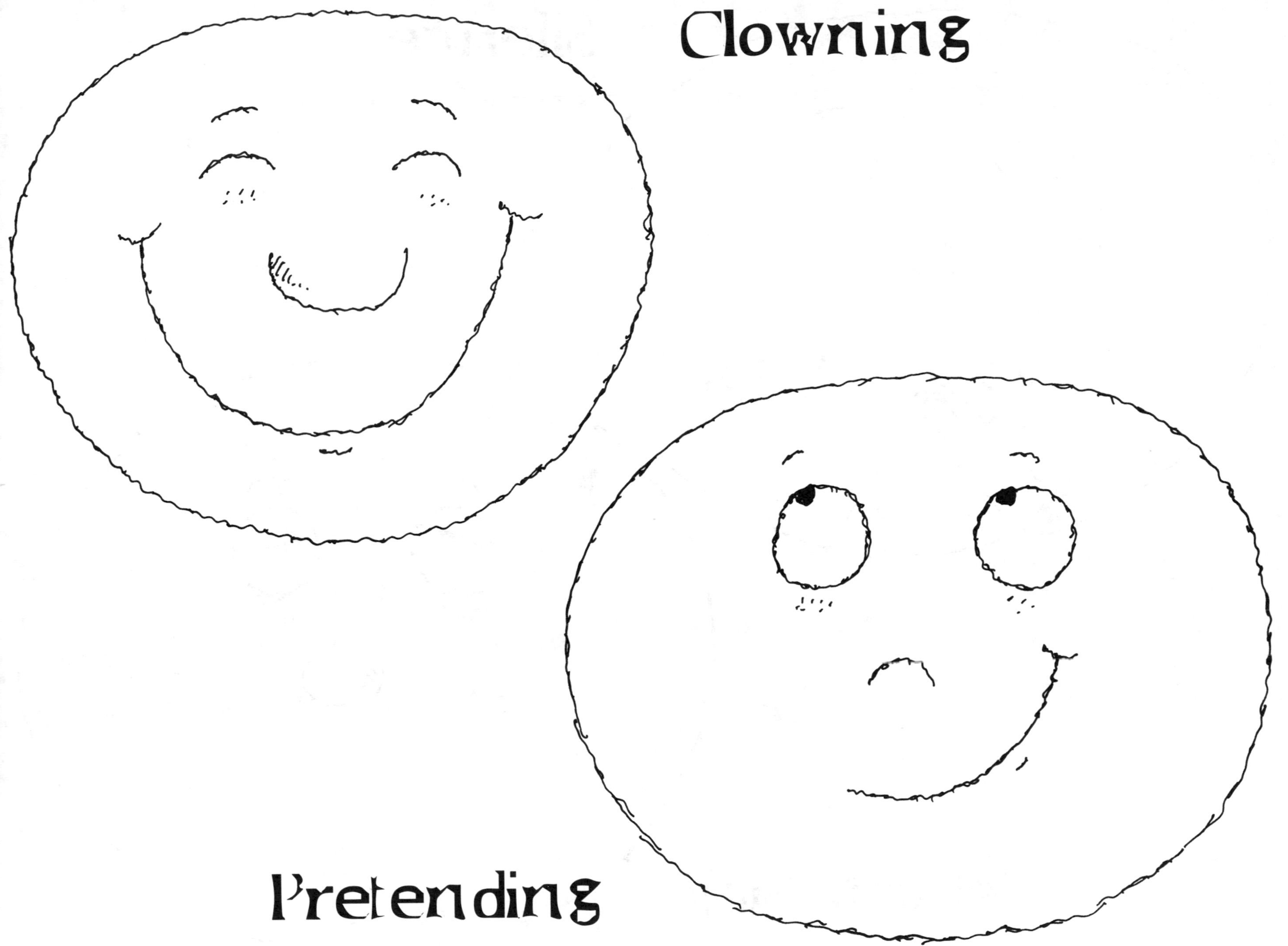
Clowning
Pretending

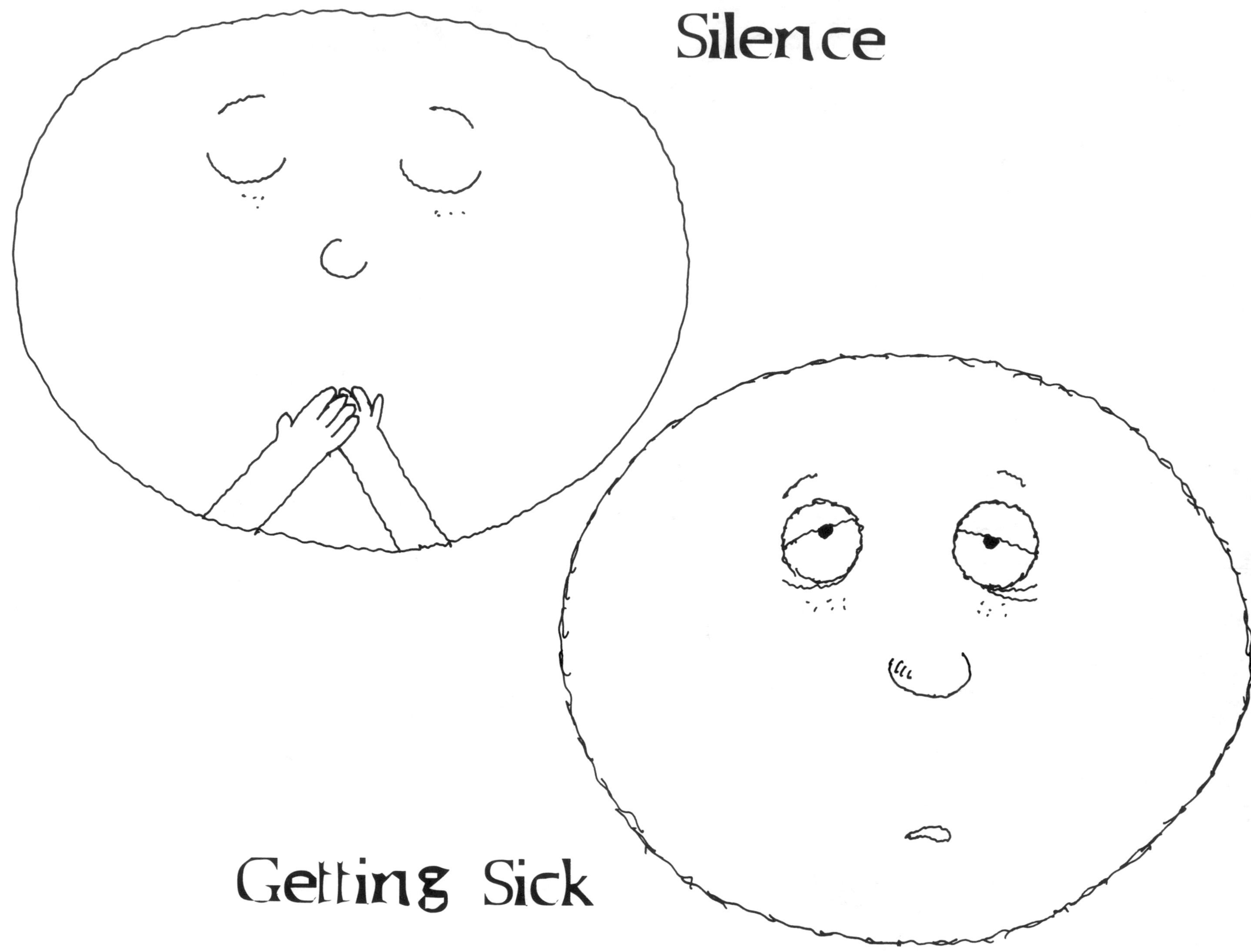
Silence
Getting Sick

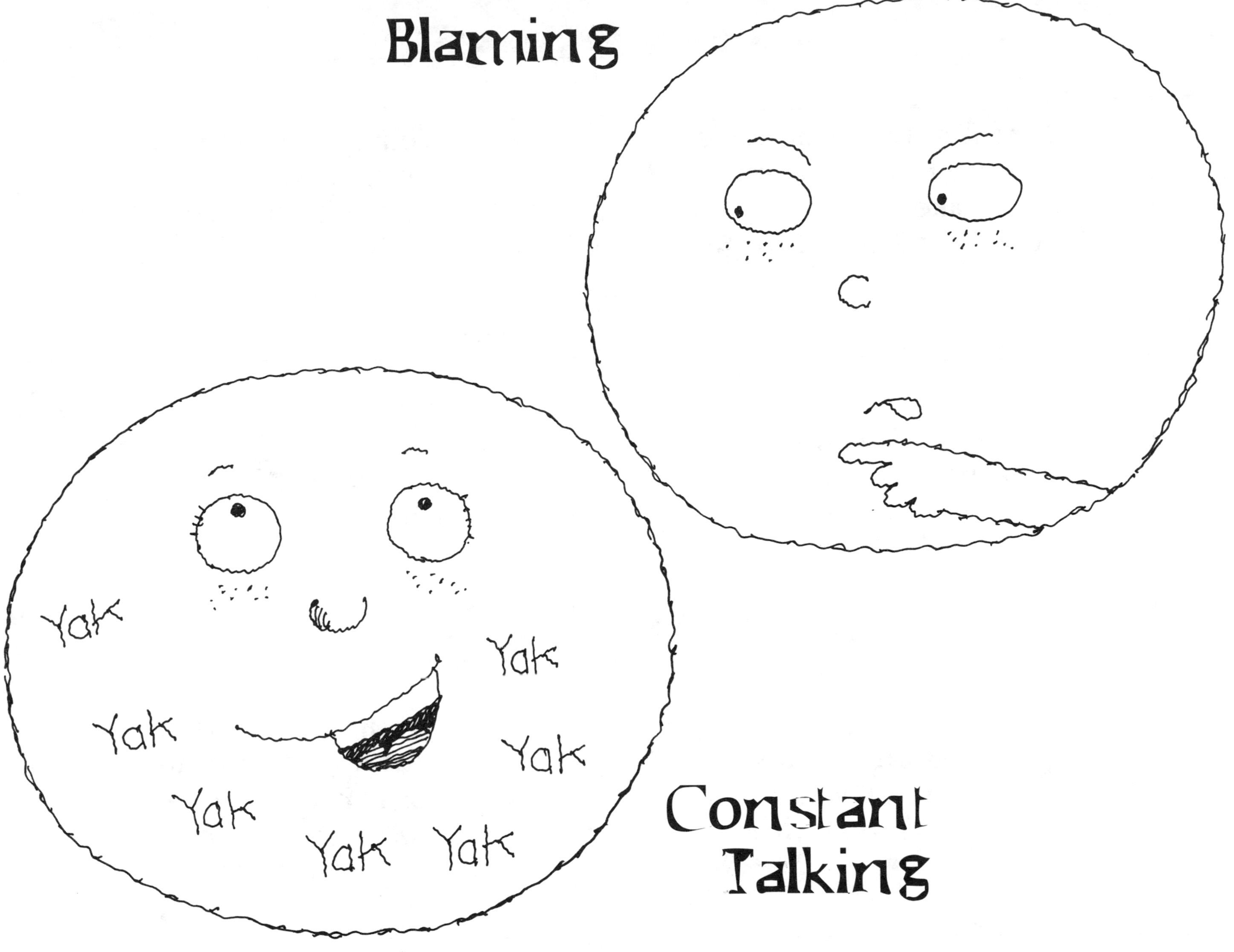
Blaming
Yak
Yak
Yak
Yak
Yak
Yak
Yak
Constant Talking

You feel uncomfortable
in a new situation
(like the first
Confident Kids meeting)

Your dad promises
to take you on a
camping trip and
then cancels.

You bring home
a bad report card
and your parents
yell at you.

Your dog gets
run over by a car.

Someone makes
fun of you
on the playground.

Your best friend
wants to go to the
school fair with someone
else from your class
instead of you.

Goals

- Introduce children to our need to express our feelings
- Distinguish between healthy and unhealthy ways of expressing our feelings
- Practice healthy ways of expressing our feelings
- Introduce a new verse (Philippians 4:6, 7)

Needed

- Group rules poster
- Props for opening skit
- A pillow, a telephone, a notebook, stationery and pen, drawing paper and crayons or markers, a pair of running shoes, a box of tissues, and a large red heart (one set per facilitator)
- "Feelings Defense Situation Cards" from last session
- "Feelings Logs" or a purchased blank journal (one per child)
- Prayer journal
- Items for regathering, if any
- Props for Bible story
- "Confident Kids Psalm 1" enlarged onto poster board or copied on an overhead transparency
- Philippians 4:6, 7 poster

Express Those Feelings!

Elementary Session 4 Outline

Opening (30 Minutes)

Knots

Group Rules

"Meet My Friends"

Small Groups (35 Minutes)

Discussion of Session Theme

Feelings Logs

Prayer Time

Bible Time (20 Minutes)

Regathering

"David Talks to God"

Memory Verse

Closing Prayer Huddle

Snack (5 Minutes)

The snack can be served during the Bible Time regathering.

Express Those Feelings!
Elementary Session 4

Opening (30 Minutes)

Knots

As soon as five or more children arrive, begin this activity. Ask kids to bunch up, standing as close together as possible. Have them put their arms straight up over their heads, reach across the "bunch," and take hands. The idea is to take hands randomly, so as to form a human knot. When all hands have connected, tell the group that their task is to untangle themselves. The only rule is that they may not let go of the hands they are holding. Allow the group to accomplish the task without your help. When the kids are done, or after the rest of the kids arrive, start again with everyone participating.

Group Rules

Review the group rules again, if necessary.

"Meet My Friends"

Use the script on pages 130 and 131 to introduce the importance of expressing our feelings.

Small Groups (35 Minutes)

Discussion of Session Theme

Use the following questions to discuss the session theme, "I can express my feelings in healthy ways."

> **What was the main character in the skit doing with her feelings?** *(Stuffing them inside)*
>
> **What upset her so much that she didn't want to feel her feelings?** *(Her dad came*

home drunk and she was hurt and embarrassed in front of her friends)

Did stuffing (avoiding) her feelings work? *(No)* **What happened?** *(She began to feel sick and her feelings exploded anyway)*

Have you ever stuffed your feelings inside, like you saw in the skit today? *(Let kids respond)*

Ignoring our feelings does not make them go away. Instead, it just stuffs them down inside of us where they will struggle to get out. The harder we try to ignore them, the harder they will struggle. Eventually they will come out, but it will probably be in hurtful ways.

What can happen when we try to ignore or hold our feelings inside? *(They can give us headaches and stomachaches, or they can work like a volcano and explode causing us to do or say things we don't really mean)*

But, we can avoid all that by remembering that "All Our Feelings Are OK," and by learning healthy ways to express them.

I can express my feelings in healthy ways

Have the kids sit in a circle on the floor and place the following objects in the middle: a pillow, a telephone, a notebook, stationery and pen, a pair of running shoes, drawing paper and crayons or markers, a box of tissues, and a large red heart.

Everyone has the same feelings but we don't express our feelings in the same way. For instance, when I feel happy, I ______________________.

(Finish this by telling the group what you do when you feel happy. Then ask kids to share different ways they express happiness. Repeat, using different feelings, like sad, angry, etc.) **There are many ways to express our feelings, and all of us need to find the ways that work best for us. But first, we have to know the rule about expressing our feelings:** ***I must never express my feelings by hurting another person, hurting myself, or breaking things. I can find a better way to handle my feelings!***

This rule must never be broken! Let's say it again together. *(Repeat rule several times)*

It is unhealthy to express our feelings by hurting another person or property. **Throwing or breaking things, and hitting or saying hurtful things to someone else are never OK!**

It is also unhealthy to express our feelings by hurting ourselves. **Using alcohol or drugs, getting physically sick, and thinking about harming ourselves are never good ways to handle feelings!**

Let's use these things I've brought today to find some healthy ways to express our feelings! *(Ask the kids to look at each object and decide how each one can help them express their feelings in positive ways)*

***Pillow*—Hit a pillow when you are angry, or cry into it when you are sad.**

***Telephone*—Call someone you trust and talk about your feelings.**

***Notebook*—Keep a diary or write a poem about your feelings.**

***Stationery and pen*—Write a letter about your feelings and give it to someone you trust.**

Drawing paper and crayons—Draw how you feel.

Box of tissues—Just cry about it!

Pair of running shoes—Do something physical.

Large red heart—Talk to someone you love, or ask for a hug.

Have kids take turns drawing a "Feelings Defense Situation Card" (page 124, from last session) and then choosing one of the objects that depicts how they would most want to express their feelings in that situation. Ask others to say what they would do in the same situation. Point out the differences in the ways group members choose to express their feelings. End by reminding the kids that everyone feels the same things, but we must each find the way that is best for us to express our feelings.

Feelings Logs

Give each child a "Confident Kids Feelings Log" (pages 133 and 134) consisting of the cover and three copies of the inside page assembled into a booklet. If you prefer, purchased blank journals can be used instead. Tell them:

> **This is your Confident Kids Feelings Log. You can use it all week long as a way to express your feelings. Write anything you want in it, and you don't have to share what you write with anyone else, unless you want to. If you bring your book back each week with at least one entry, you will receive a small prize. We won't read the entries unless you want us to.**

Prayer Time

Conduct your prayer time as in weeks past. Focus your prayers on asking God for courage to honestly face all our feelings, and not keep any stuffed inside. Thank Him for accepting all our feelings.

Bible Time (20 Minutes)

Regathering

Have one facilitator lead the kids in a favorite game, song, or activity.

"David Talks to God"

David helps the kids write a psalm to the Lord (script is on page 132). You will need to enlarge "Confident Kids Psalm 1" (pages 135 and 136) onto poster board or copy it onto an overhead transparency (in which case you will also need an overhead projector).

Memory Verse

This week's memory verse is Philippians 4:6, 7:

> **Do not be anxious about anything, but in everything, present your requests to God. And the peace of God will guard your hearts and your minds in Christ Jesus.** (*NIV*, condensed)

Introduce this verse by saying:

> **It is natural to feel worried and anxious about many things in our lives; all of us do. God knows that, and teaches us to come to Him with those feelings. Knowing that God will be with us and asking Him to help brings peace.**

Display a poster of the verse and have the kids repeat it several times.

Closing Prayer Huddle

Close the meeting as in weeks past.

Snack (5 Minutes)

Distribute the snack the child brought. Before the kids leave, choose another child to take the snack tin home for next week.

Characters:

- A female facilitator, Joy, and Anger

Needed

- A screen or blanket stretched across the front of the room, or some other means of hiding Joy and Anger

Meet My Friends

The facilitator enters with Anger and Joy on each side.

Facilitator Hi! I want you to meet my friends. This is Anger *(Puts arm around one)* and this is Joy. *(Puts arm around the other)* Say "hello" to the kids!

Anger *(Growls)* Hi.

Joy *(Brightly)* Hello! I'm so happy to be here! I've been looking forward to this all week! I feel so happy when I get to do stuff like this—

Facilitator OK, OK! *(To kids)* Joy would bubble on forever, if I let her! Anger, on the other hand, doesn't say much at first. But when he lets go, he really blows up!

Anger *(Looks at facilitator)* What are you talking about? I don't blow up! *(Increasingly agitated)* Are you trying to make me look bad in front of all these kids? I could get really upset if I thought you were trying to make me look bad—

Facilitator See what I mean? Well, as you can see, my two friends are very different. But they are both important to me! They help me know what I am feeling, and how to express my feelings to others. For instance, when something happens that makes me happy, Joy comes out and helps me share my good feelings with my friends.

Joy *(Bubbly)* Yeah, like the time that really cute boy sat next to you at lunch and you got all fluttery inside and you weren't going to tell anyone. But I came out and made you tell your mom and your brother and call Sally. *(To kids)* That's her best friend. Later on, you told me that sharing with all those people made you feel good!

Facilitator *(Glaring at Joy)* You're right. It's more fun to be happy with the people I love most than to keep it all to myself. But then there are other times, when things happen that make me mad and Anger comes out to help me get those feelings out—

Anger *(To kids)* If it weren't for me, she would never get mad about anything! Everyone needs to get good and angry once in a while!

Facilitator That's true! But sometimes things happen and I don't want anyone else to know how I'm feeling. In fact, sometimes I don't want to feel my own feelings! *(Takes Anger and Joy by the shoulders and pushes them behind the curtain)* So, I stuff them way down inside of me so I won't have to feel them! Once they are out of sight, I figure I'll stop feeling anything at all!

Anger and Joy begin yelling from behind the curtain. "Hey, let me out of here." "Why are you sticking me in this dark place?" "You can't do this to me." "Are you crazy?" "Let me out!" etc. Start out softly and as facilitator continues talking, build in intensity.

Facilitator *(Ignoring the voices)* Like the time my dad came home drunk when I had some friends over. I felt so scared and disappointed and embarrassed. I wanted to die! But instead, I pretended nothing happened and tried to go on playing as if I wasn't feeling anything!

(Looks at curtain and yells) Be quiet in there! I don't want to feel anything right now so go to sleep! *(Voices quiet for a moment, and then continue with increased intensity. Facilitator is now beginning to look irritated and upset and begins to hold her head and stomach. Anger and Joy start beating on the curtain. The more active they get behind the curtain, the more sick the facilitator becomes)*

Facilitator Unfortunately, stuffing my feelings out of sight doesn't get rid of them! It just makes me feel sick because my feelings are trying so hard to get out! The day my friends were over, I felt so sick one of them asked me if everything was OK. I said, "Sure," even though it was a lie! *(At that, Anger growls loudly from behind the curtain)* Well, I finally learned that stuffing my feelings doesn't get rid of them! After awhile—

Anger and Joy explode from behind the curtain, get on each side of the facilitator, and begin chastising him: "Why do you do that?" "You know you get sick when you keep us locked up!" "We're going to get out anyway, so knock it off, OK?"

Facilitator None of you ever do anything like stuffing your feelings, do you?

They exit.

Characters

- David

Needed

- "Confident Kids Psalm 1" enlarged onto poster board or copied onto an overhead transparency (in which case you will also need an overhead projector)
- "Confident Kids Feelings Log"

David Talks to God

David enters and greets the kids. He is looking through a "Confident Kids Feelings Log."

David Wow! This is really good stuff! Of course, writing is one of the ways I express my feelings. Whenever I'm feeling strong emotions, I write a new psalm to the Lord! And if that's not enough, I put it to music and sing it to Him! And, if that's still not enough, I dance before the Lord! One time when I came back from a really big battle, I actually led a whole parade through the streets. But enough about me. When I saw this log *(Holds up feelings log)* I had an idea. Today I'd like to help us all express our feelings to God by writing a psalm together. Do you know what a psalm is? *(Let kids respond)*

Display "Confident Kids Psalm 1." Ask the kids to think of words to fill in the blanks. Ask for several ideas for each blank, encouraging them to draw on their own experiences for possibilities. Try to keep the words concrete, avoiding general phrases such as, "You are my Lord and God." When all the blanks have been filled in, use the psalm as a choral reading. Proceed as follows:

1. *Read it through together until all can read it smoothly.*
2. *Read it through following the directions in the left margin.*
3. *Read it through again, adding expression and feeling.*
4. *Bow heads and read it together as a prayer.*

End by telling the kids that they will be sharing their psalm with their family on Family Night. Encourage them to write more psalms to the Lord in their feelings logs this week.

Official

Confident Kids

FEELINGS LOG

Name ____________________

Date: ____________________

A feeling I had today was:

____

What happened to make me feel that way? ____________________

____

____

____

I expressed my feeling by: ____________________

____

____

____

A new feeling word I learned this week is:

____

This is how it looks:

Dear God,

Confident Kids

Psalm 1

ALL: O Lord, You are my ______________ and ______________________________.

ALL: You understand all my feelings.

BOYS: When I feel ______________, You ______________________________.

GIRLS: When I feel ______________, You ______________________________.

ALL: There is nothing I can do that will ever stop You from loving me.

SOLO #1: Even when I ______________, You still love me.

SOLO #2: Even when I ______________, You still love me.

ALL: Thank you that You are always with me!

BOYS: When I ______________, You are with me.

GIRLS: When I ______________, You are with me.

ALL: O Lord, You are my ____________ and ____________. (repeat first line)

Goals

- Name feelings that are difficult to handle
- Identify circumstances that generate difficult feelings
- Learn and practice a three-step process to resolve difficult feelings
- Review Philippians 4:6, 7 and hear David tell about a time he had to handle the difficult feeling of revenge

Needed

- One copy per small group of "Stick Puppets Faces" activity and wide craft sticks
- Group rules poster
- A puppet for the opening skit
- One strip of butcher paper (about 3' long) per small group
- Stickers or other small prizes for feelings logs
- Prayer journals
- Items for regathering, if any
- Philippians 4:6, 7 poster from last week
- Items for Bible story

Some Feelings Are Difficult to Handle

Elementary Session 5 Outline

Opening (30 Minutes)

Stick Puppets

Group Rules

"The Spelling Test"

Small Groups (35 Minutes)

Discussion of Session Theme

Stick Puppet Role Plays

Feelings Logs

Prayer Time

Bible Time (20 Minutes)

Regathering

"David Feels Revenge"

Memory Verse

Closing Prayer Huddle

Snack (5 Minutes)

The snack can be served during the Bible Time regathering.

Some Feelings Are Difficult to Handle

Elementary Session 5

Opening (30 Minutes)

Stick Puppets

Begin your session by making the stick puppets you will need during the small group time. Each small group will need one set of the "Stick Puppet Faces" (pages 146 and 147). Kids can make the puppets by coloring each face, cutting it out, and gluing it to a wide craft stick. Be sure each facilitator gets a completed set of puppets for use during small group time.

Group Rules

Review the rules and the consequences for breaking them.

"The Spelling Test"

Use the puppet script on pages 141 and 142 to introduce a three-step process for handling difficult feelings. Dismiss to small groups after the skit is presented.

Small Groups (35 Minutes)

Discussion of Session Theme

Use the following questions to discuss the session theme, "I can handle all my feelings!"

> **In today's skit, Skip wasn't feeling good. What was the problem?** *(He had gotten a bad grade on his spelling test and he felt stupid)*
>
> **In the conversation, he learned three steps to handle his feelings. What are they?** *(Name the Feeling, Stop and Think, and Work It Out. Older kids can also recount*

how Skip used each step to resolve his feelings)

It would be nice if the things that happened in our lives were always good things that gave us pleasant feelings. But life is not like that. Things happen in everyone's life that are not pleasant. Even kids have to learn to accept being hurt and disappointed sometimes.

What are some unpleasant—or difficult—feelings? *(Anger, resentment, jealousy, sadness, etc.)*

What are some things that happen to cause those feelings? *(Encourage kids to name events from their own lives. For example, a sibling breaks a favorite toy and they feel angry, their pet dies and they feel sad and lonely, thunderstorms frighten them, etc.)*

It is hard to know what to do when we feel hurt, disappointed, lonely, or jealous. It's hard for everyone. Because it is hard, we try to find ways not to feel those feelings. But, as we have learned before, it is not bad or wrong to feel these things and sometimes it is even the right thing to do. Remember: "All My Feelings Are OK!"

Place a strip of butcher paper in the middle of your table. Divide it into three sections and gather the kids around it so they can write on it with you. Then say:

Last week we talked about some ways we can express our feelings, both pleasant and unpleasant ones. Today we are learning three steps to handle feelings that are especially difficult to feel. Let's review those steps. *(As you talk about each step, print it out in the middle of one of the sections. Then ask kids to add words or pictures to illustrate the step)*

Step 1: Name the Feeling—The first step is to give what we are feeling the right name. *(Draw faces that show difficult feelings on your mural)*

Step 2: Stop and Think—Once I know what I'm feeling, I need to think about why I'm feeling it. I can ask questions like: Did something happen? Did someone say something to me? *(Draw a stop sign, question mark, someone thinking, a lightbulb, etc.)*

Step 3: Work It Out—When we know what we are feeling, and stop and think about what's really going on, then we can make a healthy choice about what to do next. Answer this question: "What is the *best* thing to do right now?" *(Add pictures of the items discussed last week as healthy ways to express their feelings [e.g., pillow, telephone, running shoes, letter paper]. They can draw a picture of Skip studying his spelling words)*

Stick Puppet Role Plays

Place the stick puppets made earlier in the middle of your group. Ask kids to say what feeling they think each face represents. Using one of the following situations, ask kids to design a short puppet play depicting how to use the three steps to resolve the situation. Work together as a group to choose the right puppets, and discuss the action for each step. Third and fourth graders can work in pairs to design their own play and present them for each other. Here are some ideas:

Your parents tell you they are getting a divorce

Your dog gets hit by a car while you are at school

I can handle all my feelings

Someone in your class calls you a name

Your mom is too busy and too tired to talk to you

Your best friend must move to a different state

Feelings Logs

Reward kids who brought their feelings logs back this week by giving them a sticker to put inside their log, or another small prize they would enjoy. Encourage kids who did not bring or write in their books to do so next week. Ask if any of the kids would like to share an entry.

Note: Don't be alarmed if no child brings the log back. By offering an incentive and asking about them each week, you are reinforcing the need to express their feelings on a consistent basis. That reinforcement will have meaning, even if they don't follow through at this time!

Prayer Time

Use your prayer notebooks or boxes to update your group's requests. Focus your prayer time by asking kids to share any difficult feelings they may be struggling with this week. Encourage each one to express their feeling to God in a sentence prayer.

Bible Time (20 Minutes)

Regathering

Have one facilitator lead the kids in a favorite game, song, or activity.

"David Feels Revenge"

Present the Bible story (script is on pages 144 and 145).

Memory Verse

Review Philippians 4:6, 7, emphasizing how God tells us to pray about the things that worry us most, and to trust Him to help us. That is another way we handle our difficult feelings!

Closing Prayer Huddle

Close your session as in weeks past.

Snack (5 Minutes)

Distribute the snack the child brought. Before the kids leave, choose another child to take the snack tin home for next week.

Characters

- A facilitator and Skip (a puppet)

Needed

- Any kind of puppet stage
- A spelling test

The Spelling Test

Skip is holding a spelling test. He is shaking his head and pacing back and forth across the puppet stage.

Skip	Oh dear! Woe is me! *(Big sigh)*
Facilitator	*(Enters, says brightly)* Hey, Skip! How are ya, my man? *(Notices Skip is upset)* What's wrong, guy? Are you OK?
Skip	Me? I'm fine. *(Hangs head, sighs. He's obviously not "fine.")*
Facilitator	You could have fooled me! Are you feeling sick or something?
Skip	Well, yeah, I guess so. I feel yucky. But I'm not gonna throw up or anything like that.
Facilitator	Well, it's certainly not fun to feel "yucky." Let's see if I can help. I was just getting ready to teach the kids some steps to help them handle their unpleasant feelings. And since you look about as unpleasant as anyone else around here today, can I practice on you?
Skip	I guess so. I don't care, I guess. Can't hurt. I mean I feel so bad now even you couldn't make me feel worse!
Facilitator	OK! The first step is to Name the Feeling. Think about all the feelings words we've learned in the past few weeks. Can you think of one that describes what you are feeling right now? Besides "yucky," that is.
Skip	Well, let's see. There's "the pits," "icky," or "totally bummed." How's that? Am I getting close?
Facilitator	Not really. Be more specific.
Skip	Well, I'm sad. Yeah, that's it! Uh, well, maybe that's not it exactly. *(Brightens)* I feel depressed! No, no, that's not quite it, either. I guess I feel mostly—stupid. Yeah, that's it! I feel stupid!

Facilitator	Great! You feel stupid!
Skip	*(Looks hurt)* Hey—
Facilitator	*(Embarrassed, stumbling)* I don't mean great that you're stupid—I mean, feel stupid! I mean great that you know you're stupid—I mean know that you feel stupid! Wait! I didn't mean—
Skip	If this is supposed to be cheering me up, well, all I can say is you're a rotten cheerer-upper!
Facilitator	Never mind. Let's just go on to Step 2, which is to Stop and Think. Can you think back and remember what happened today that caused you to feel stupid? Did you do something, or did someone say something to you?
Skip	Nothing happened! I just did the usual dumb stuff. School was sort of boring. *(Pauses, hangs head)*
Facilitator	Uh-oh. Something happened at school today.
Skip	Well, I kind of got a "not-so-hot" grade on my spelling test.
Facilitator	Like, how "not-so-hot"?
Skip	Like, I missed eight words.
Facilitator	Eight! How many were on the test?
Skip	Eight.
Facilitator	Uh-huh! Well, I can see how you might be feeling stupid because of that. Now let's think some more. Were the words too hard for you?
Skip	*(Brightens)* Yeah, that must be it! *(Hangs head again)* Or maybe I just didn't study.
Facilitator	So, you're feeling stupid because you didn't do well on your spelling test today because you didn't study the words well enough. Good! Now you're ready for Step 3.

Skip	Which is?
Facilitator	Work It Out. What can you do about this feeling?
Skip	*(Sighs)* I guess I could go to my room and cry.
Facilitator	You could. Is that how you want to work it out?
Skip	No. *(Thinking)* Maybe I could pray and ask God to make me smarter!
Facilitator	You could. Do you think you need to be smarter?
Skip	Sure! Well, maybe not smarter. My teacher says I'm pretty smart when I "'apply" myself.
Facilitator	I think you're plenty smart, Skip. So, what can you do about this feeling?
Skip	I suppose I could study my spelling words.
Facilitator	Sounds like a good idea to me! *(They look at each other for a few moments)*
Skip	*(Realizes the next move is his)* Right! OK, I'm outta here! *(Exits, mumbling)* Now where did I leave my spelling book?

From

- 1 Samuel 26

Characters

- David, Saul, and Abishai

Needed

- A spear
- A canteen or water bottle
- Biblical costumes for David, Saul, and Abishai

David Feels Revenge

David enters and greets the kids.

David You have been talking about a very important subject today! Knowing what to do when you feel unpleasant feelings is really hard—even for King David! Let me tell you about one of the hardest feelings I ever had to handle! I'll never forget it! I was running for my life! King Saul wanted to kill me. In fact, he was obsessed with killing me! It seemed as though there was nowhere I could run to get away from him! So, I went into the desert, hoping that Saul would not look for me there. But, sure enough, one day—

Abishai *(Runs in, excited)* David! Come quick! Saul is coming! And I figure he's got about 3,000 of his toughest soldiers with him!

David *(With great feeling)* Not again! Why is he doing this to me? I never did anything to deserve this! I can't keep living on the run like this! *(Paces back and forth)* What can I do about this, my friend? This has to stop! *(Gets idea)* Maybe if I try and reason with Saul, he will listen.

Abishai You must be kidding! You know the man is half mad—especially when it comes to killing you!

David You're right. But still, I have to do something. Will you come with me? I want to go to Saul's camp.

Abishai *(Shocked)* Now *you're* going mad, too! No way, David. That would be suicide!

David All right, I understand. Say a prayer for me, OK? *(Exits)*

Abishai *(Shakes his head)* Oh, all right! David, wait up! *(Runs after him)* Great, now *I'm* going mad, too!

Saul	*(Enters, carrying a spear and canteen. He is confused and scared)* What is happening in my camp? Some sort of strange disease, or what? *(Looks around)* What's happening to all of you? All my men are sleeping! This isn't natural! Oh, my! I can't stand up. I feel so tired all of a sudden! *(Lies down with his spear and canteen near his head and starts to snore softly)*
David	*(Enters with Abishai)* What's going on here? These men—they're all asleep!
Abishai	David! Don't you see what's happening? God has put all these men to sleep just to protect you! He has delivered your enemy into your hand this day! Look! *(Picks up Saul's spear and holds it over Saul's heart)* I can pin him to the ground right now with just one thrust of this spear! Just say the word and you'll be free from Saul forever!
David	*(To kids)* What a moment that was! I wanted to say, "Go for it!" but something didn't feel right. So I did what you learned about today: First, I named my feelings. I was feeling so many things, but mostly I was feeling revenge. I wanted to get back at Saul for all he had put me through! But then I stopped to think about what I was feeling. I wanted to get back at Saul for all he had done to me, but I also knew God didn't want me to kill Saul. Finally, I thought about ways I could work it out. What would be the best thing to do in this situation? I asked God for wisdom and strength, and then said to my friend— *(To Abishai)* No! Killing is wrong. But take his spear and water bottle and let's go.
Abishai	*(Looks disappointed)* Well, OK. *(Takes items and exits)*
David	Later on, I had a chance to tell Saul what had happened. He almost fainted when he heard how I could have killed him, but didn't. And even King Saul had to respect that. So, he left me alone—for awhile, at least. Oh! I'm out of time for today! I'll have to wait to tell you more! See you next week!

David and Saul exit.

S

Z

Yuck!

Goals

- Identify feelings and symptoms that signal it's time to ask an adult for help
- Identify safe people the kids can turn to for help
- Introduce the kids to other people in the Bible who expressed their feelings to God through poetry and music

Needed

- Group rules poster
- Props for skit
- Copies of "Where Do I Feel It?" activity
- Copies of "Who Can Help Me?" Directories
- Stickers or other small prizes for feelings logs
- Items for regathering, if any
- Props for Bible story
- Joshua 1:9 and Philippians 4:6, 7 posters
- Items for memory verse review games

Asking for Help

Elementary Session 6 Outline

Opening (30 Minutes)

Mirrors

Group Rules

"The Secret"

Small Groups (35 Minutes)

Discussion of Session Theme

"Who Can Help Me?" Directories

Feelings Logs

Prayer Time

Bible Time (20 Minutes)

Regathering

"David Asks for Help"

Memory Verses

Closing Prayer Huddle

Snack (5 Minutes)

The snack can be served during the Bible Time regathering.

Asking for Help

Elementary Session 6

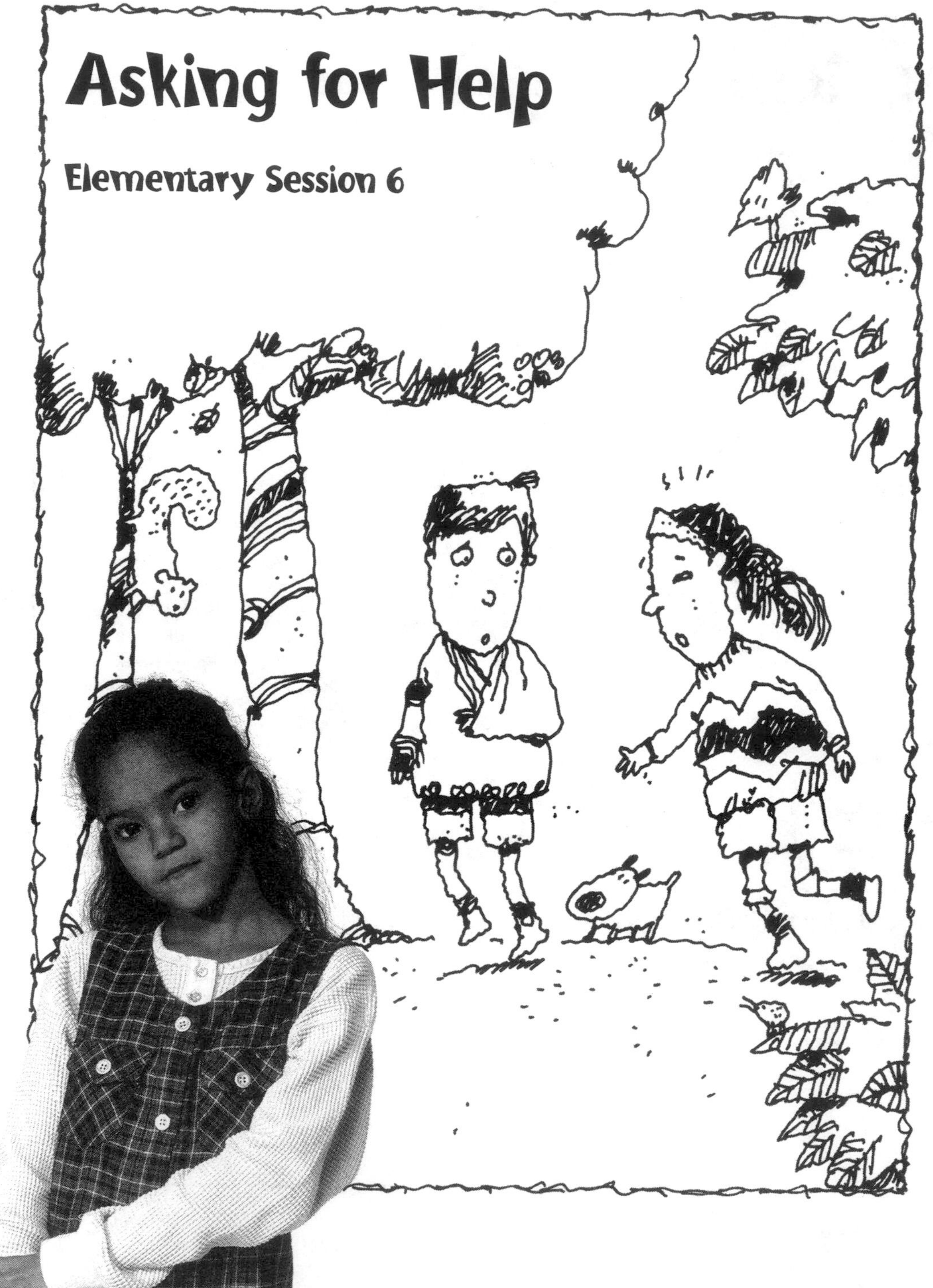

Opening (30 Minutes)

Mirrors

As kids arrive, put them in pairs to play this game. Instruct one person to be the leader, and the other to be the mirror. Have the kids face their partners as you call out a feeling word. The leader in each pair must then assume a facial expression and body position that depict that feeling. The mirror must duplicate the leader exactly. They must do this without talking, and freeze in the position until you give the word to relax. Then, have the partners switch roles and repeat the process when you call out a new feeling word. Switch partners as new kids arrive.

Group Rules

Review the group rules, if necessary.

"The Secret"

Use the script on pages 153 and 154 to introduce the subject of asking for help. Dismiss to small groups after the skit is performed.

Small Groups (35 Minutes)

Discussion of Session Theme

Use the following questions to discuss the session theme, "It's always OK to ask for help!"

> **Our theme today is about asking for help. In the skit, who needed help?** *(Both David and Lisa needed help)*
>
> **What were the signs that David and Lisa needed help from someone?** *(David*

couldn't even look at his best friend and Lisa couldn't sleep)

Do you think Lisa should tell her mom about David? Why or why not? *(Guide kids to see that Lisa should talk to her mom about David. It is always right to get help when someone we know is being hurt)*

God has designed people to need each other. We need parents to take care of us, teachers to teach us how to read, friends to have fun with, etc. *(Kids can add more)* **But sometimes we need people to help us more than at other times. At those times, the people in our lives may not even know that we need help. When we are hurting inside, no one will know unless we tell someone what we are feeling and ask for help.**

What are some times you may need help but no one will know unless you tell them? *(When the kids don't understand something, are afraid, need a hug, etc.)*

Learning to ask for help is an important part of growing up. If you cannot let others know when you need help now, you probably won't when you grow up, either. A good rule is that we need to ask for help whenever something inside feels uncomfortable.

It's always OK to ask for help!

Distribute copies of the "Where Do I Feel It?" activity (page 158). Discuss how listening to our bodies can let us know when it is time to ask for help. Ask them to think about places on or in their bodies that show they feel certain feelings. When they think of one, have them write that feeling on that part of the body on the sheet. For example, *anger* could be written on the fist; *sadness* or *love* on the heart, *fear* or *guilt* on the head and stomach, *fear* on the knees, etc. Younger children can use pictures, such as drawing butterflies in the stomach, a hammer in the head (headache), or a question mark over the head (confused). Older kids might write the word in a color that represents it (e.g., *anger* in red, *fear* in yellow, or *jealousy* in green). Encourage kids to be creative.

Summarize by reminding kids that things like headaches, stomachaches, tears, wobbly knees, etc., may signal them that they need to ask for help.

"Who Can Help Me?" Directories

Introduce the activity:

> **We each need to know of others in our lives who can help us. Sometimes we just need to talk about what we are feeling. Sometimes we need advice as to what to do next. Today we are going to help you identify safe people in your life who can help you when you need it.**

Distribute copies of the "Who Can Help Me?" Directory (pages 159 and 160), copied back-to-back and folded in half. You will need to help younger kids fill them out. As the kids work, encourage them to think carefully about the names they select in each category. Instruct them to fill in phone numbers when they get home and keep this list in a convenient place so they can use it when they need help.

Feelings Logs

Reward kids who brought their feelings logs back this week with a sticker to put inside their log, or another small prize they would enjoy. Keep encouraging kids to write in and bring their logs each week. Ask if any child would like to share an entry.

Prayer Time

Use your prayer notebooks or boxes as in weeks past. Focus on prayer as a way of asking God for help. Say:

Just as you can go to the people on your worksheets for help, you can also ask God for help.

Bible Time (20 Minutes)

Regathering

Have one facilitator lead the kids in a favorite game, song, or activity.

"David Asks for Help"

Present the Bible story (script is on page 155).

Memory Verses

Use the Joshua 1:9 and Philippians 4:6, 7 posters to review the unit verses. As time allows, review them further using one or two memory verse review games from Appendix B, "Resources."

Closing Prayer Huddle

Close the meeting as in weeks past.

Snack (5 Minutes)

Distribute the snack the child brought. Before the kids leave, choose another child to take the snack tin home for next week.

Characters

- Lisa, David, and Lisa's mom

Needed

- Makeup to give David a black eye (or an arm sling)
- A sleeping bag

The Secret

Scene 1

David and Lisa enter from opposite sides of the room. David has a black eye (or one of his arms in a sling).

Lisa Hi, David! Hey—what happened to you?

David *(Looking down)* Nothing.

Lisa What do you mean, nothing? That's the biggest black eye I've ever seen!

David is silent and avoids making eye contact. Lisa moves around to establish eye contact, but David keeps moving away.

Lisa Come on, David. I'm your best friend! If you can't tell me, who can you tell?

David *(Slowly)* Well—if I tell you, you have to swear to me on your life that you won't tell anyone else. Ever!

Lisa Hey, lighten up, will you?

David OK, just forget it. *(Starts to walk away)*

Lisa Wait! OK, I swear! Now, what happened?

David It's my mom, Lisa. She doesn't mean to, but sometimes she just loses control. But you can't tell anyone because she's a great mom and she'll get in trouble if you tell!

Lisa I swore on my life, didn't I? I won't tell, David. But does this mean that all those other times—like when you said you tripped on the steps and ran into the door and wiped out on your bike—were those all from your mom, too?

David Yeah. I'm getting pretty good at making up stories. Except I really did wipe out on my bike.

They exit.

Scene 2

Lisa is in the sleeping bag, tossing and turning, unable to sleep. Finally, she sits up.

Lisa	I feel awful! All I can think about is David. He needs help, but he won't get it. I swore I wouldn't tell, but I can't just let him get hurt like that all the time! I don't know what to do! *(Gets up and paces)* I could tell my mom. What am I saying? I swore on my life I wouldn't tell! But I'll never sleep again if I don't do something! *(Groans, sighs, holds stomach)* Mom! Mom! *(Yells)* Mom!
Mom	*(Enters, looking sleepy and concerned)* Lisa, what is it? What's wrong? Are you sick?
Lisa	No—well, not like you mean. But I do feel sort of sick inside.
Mom	*(Sits on bed)* OK, let's have it. What's bothering you?
Lisa	Mom, what do you do when someone tells you a secret, and you swear on your life that you won't tell anyone, but then you can't sleep because you really want to tell someone?
Mom	What?
Lisa	I mean, I think one of my friends is in bad trouble, and I don't know what to do.

From

- Various Scripture passages

Characters

- David, Hannah, Solomon, Mary, and Paul

Needed

- Simple costume and a prop for each character: David, Bible; Hannah, doll wrapped in a blanket; Solomon, rolled up scroll; Paul, a children's praise songbook and tape
- A Confident Kids Feelings Log

Suggested

- If have not been using a drama team for the Bible stories, invite some guests to be with you today to play these roles
- Read the verses indicated from the *International Children's Bible*

David Asks for Help

David enters with a Bible.

David Hi, everyone! Today I want to tell you about some people in the Bible—besides me—who expressed their feelings to God through poetry and music. In fact, I've brought some of them with me today. Here is my first guest.

Hannah *(Enters, carrying a baby)* Hello!

David This is Hannah. Do you remember several weeks ago when I told you about the time the prophet Samuel came to my house and anointed me as the next king? Well, Hannah is Samuel's mother! Her story is told in the Old Testament in the same book that tells about me—1 Samuel. Hannah, you wrote a psalm of thanksgiving to the Lord. Why did you write it?

Hannah Because for many years I had prayed and prayed to the Lord to let me have a baby. My husband wanted children, but I could not get pregnant. I was very hurt by that!

David And then one day, you prayed for help.

Hannah Yes! One day when I was praying in the temple, the priest Eli heard me and prayed with me that God would answer my prayer. And the next time I saw him, I had a beautiful son!

David And you wrote a psalm to thank the Lord?

Hannah I couldn't think of any other way to tell God how happy I was. So I wrote: *(Takes Bible from David and reads 1 Samuel 2:1, 2)*

David Thank you, Hannah! *(She steps to the side)*
The next person is *my* own son—Solomon!

Solomon	*(Enters, carrying a scroll)* Hi!
David	Solomon wrote many psalms and poems and wise sayings called proverbs. You can find them in the Bible right after my psalms.
Solomon	From the time I was very small, my dad taught me how to express my feelings to God with poetry and music. I did it all my life. Maybe my most famous piece goes like this: *(Opens scroll and reads Ecclesiastes 3:1, 2a, 4a, 5b, 7b, 11b)*
David	Thank you, my son! *(Solomon steps to the side, with Hannah)* Let's see, who else is here today?
Mary	I'm here!
David	Oh, yes! This is a very special guest! This is Mary, the mother of Jesus! You hear her story every Christmas and probably know it very well! But did you know that Mary wrote a beautiful psalm to the Lord?
Mary	You can imagine how many feelings I had when I found out God had chosen me to be the mother of Jesus! I was terrified and happy all at the same time! I had to get those feelings out, so I wrote: *(Takes Bible from David and reads Luke 1:46-49)* You can read the rest of it in the New Testament in the book of Luke. It's part of the Christmas story.
David	Thank you, Mary. *(She joins Hannah and Solomon)* I have one more person I want you to meet.
Paul	*(Enters, with a children's praise songbook and tape)* That must be me.
David	This is Paul, the great missionary. You may have heard many stories about Paul's travels around the world. His stories are also in the New Testament.
Paul	I had many adventures trusting God and seeing Him do miracles!
David	You wrote letters to Christians in the places you visited, right?
Paul	Yes. I wanted to teach them how to live as God's children.
David	In one letter you wrote, you said, "Sing psalms, hymns, and spiritual songs with thankfulness in your hearts to God."

Paul	Right! I taught everyone to sing to the Lord! God loves to hear us tell Him our deepest feelings and music and poetry are some of the best ways to do that.
David	And Christians today still sing psalms and hymns and spiritual songs to the Lord. In fact, we can sing to the Lord right now!

Paul and David show the praise songbook and tape, then use the tape to lead the kids in singing a song of praise.

David	Well, it's time for us to go.
Paul	*(Shows* Confident Kids *Feelings Log)* We all hope you'll use your feelings logs to write your feelings in psalms and songs to the Lord—just like we did!
David	I'll see you next week!

All wave good-bye and exit.

"Where Do I Feel It?"

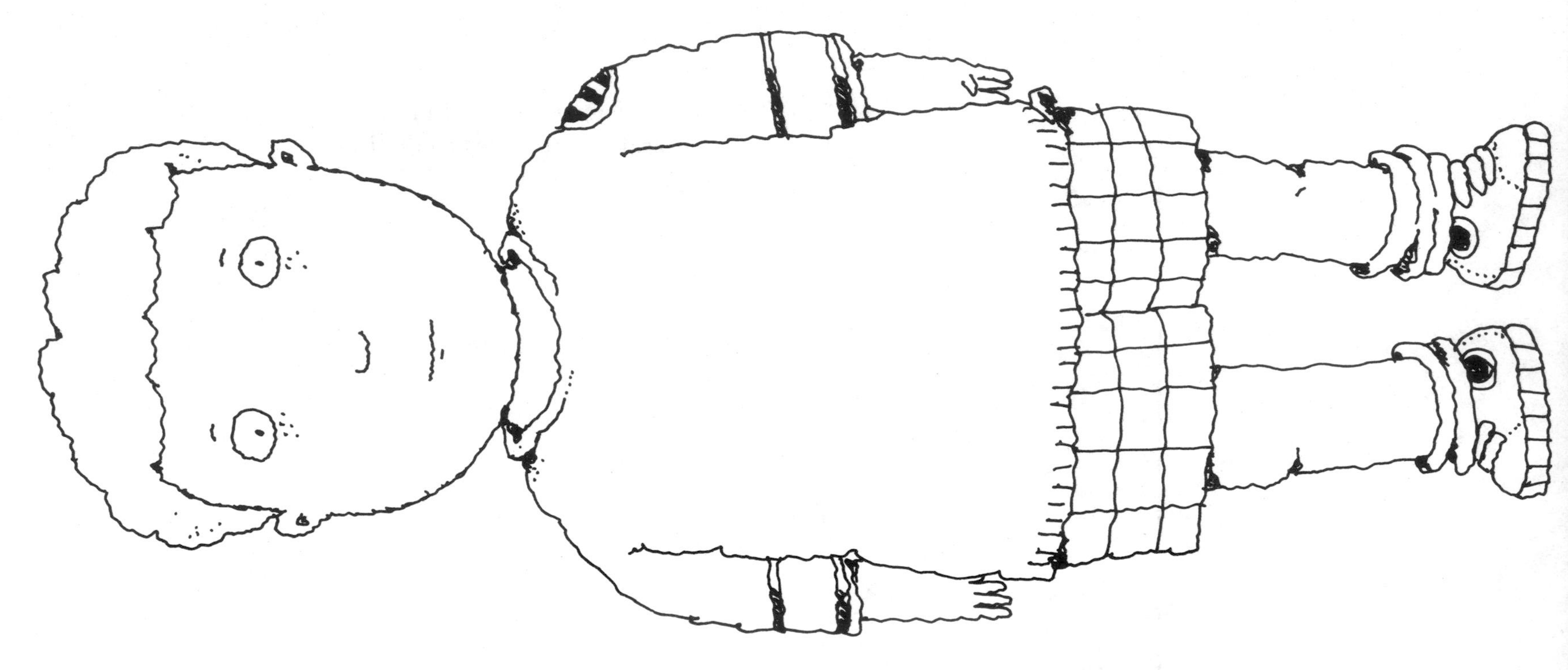

Pets, stuffed animals I can "talk to"

Who Can Help Me? Directory

Everyone needs help sometimes! It's always **OK** to ask for help.

When I need help, I can ask...

Family members
People at my church
People at my school
The best hugger I know is:

Goals

- Present Psalm 139 as an assurance of God's great care and presence with us in all parts of our lives
- Do an activity to reinforce the concept of God being with us
- Give kids an opportunity to ask Jesus to come into their lives

Needed

- Invitations for Family Night
- "Daddy" letters
- Copies of "Where Are You, God?" copied back to back and folded in half
- Paper lunch bags (one per child)
- Copies of "Inside Me" activity
- Copies of "Jesus" activity copied onto red paper and cut apart so each child has one "Jesus" heart
- Stickers or other small prizes for feelings logs
- Props for Bible story
- Copies of "David and Goliath" activity
- Confident Kids Psalm 1 poster or transparency from Session 4
- Copies of "Affirmation Balloons" and unit certificates from Appendix A (pages 377 and 379)

Jesus Helps Me With My Feelings

Elementary Session 7 Outline

Opening (30 Minutes)

Family Night Invitations

Group Rules

"Daddy Letters"

Small Groups (35 Minutes)

Discussion of Session Theme

Jesus Bags

Feelings Logs

Prayer Time

Bible Time (20 Minutes)

Regathering

"Prepare for Family Night"

Memory Verses

Closing Prayer Huddle

Snack (5 Minutes)

The snack can be served during the Bible Time regathering.

Jesus Helps Me With My Feelings

Elementary Session 7

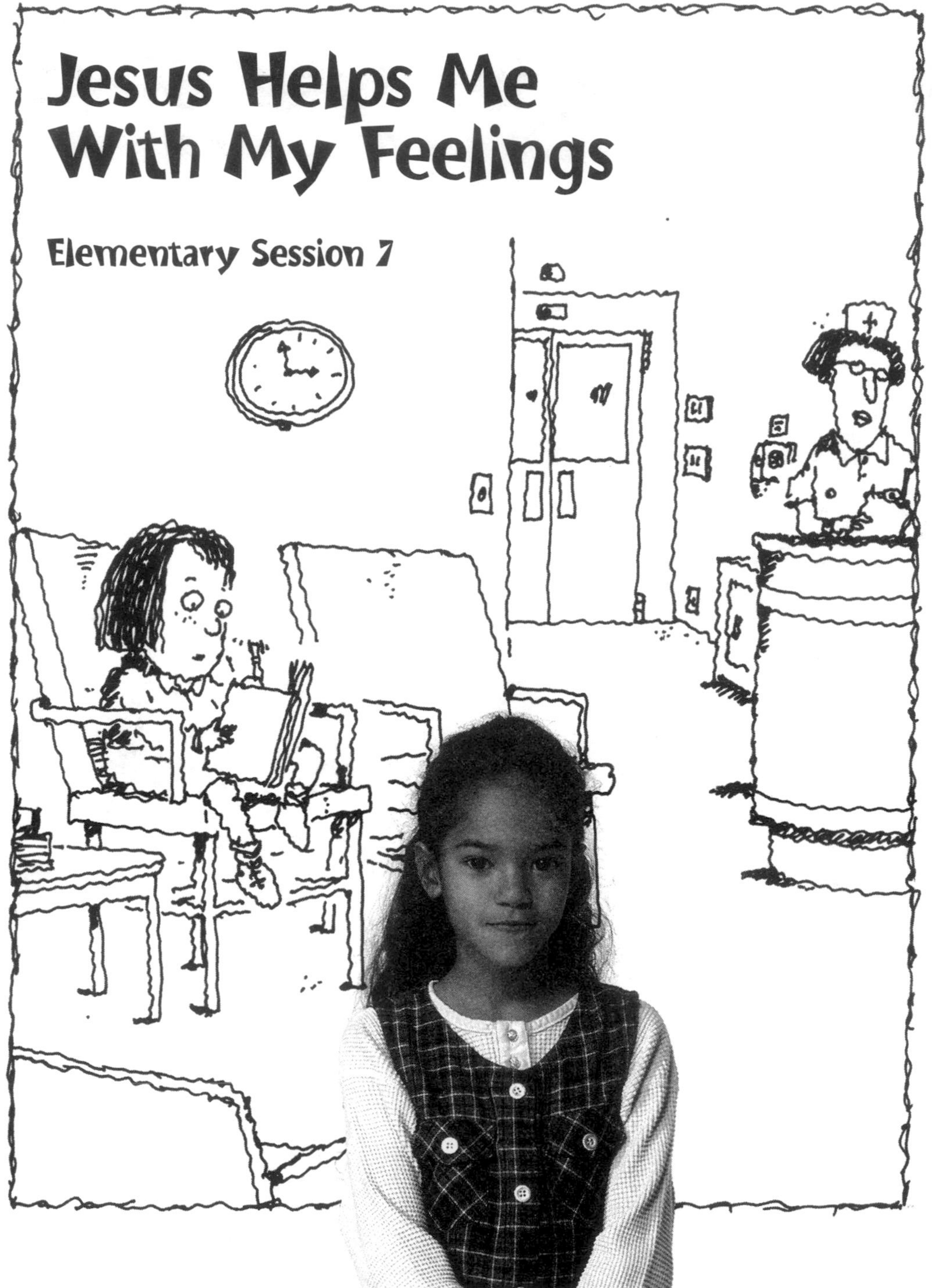

Opening (30 Minutes)

Family Night Invitations

Next week is the final session of this unit, which is Family Night. Tell the kids that next week you will host a party, and they can invite their parents to come with them. Talk about the party enthusiastically to build a sense of excitement for sharing the group with their parents. Have the kids make invitations (page 176) or use purchased party invitations.

Group Rules

Review the group rules again this week, if necessary.

"Daddy" Letters

The "Daddy" letters (pages 166–173) are a collection of letters written by Amy, an eleven-year-old girl, during the months her father was being treated for cancer. She never showed these letters to anyone until after her father recovered. They were Amy's secret journal, her way of handling her feelings through a difficult period of her life. Read them to the kids with expression, highlighting places where she talks about prayer.

Small Groups (35 Minutes)

Discussion of Session Theme

Use the following questions to discuss the session theme, "Where are You, God?"

> **Have you ever had anything happen in your life that made you feel like Amy?** *(Let kids respond)* **What were some of her feelings?** *(Let kids respond)*

Amy talks about praying for her daddy. In the first letter she says, "I've been praying that you don't (have cancer), but sometimes that doesn't matter." What do you think she meant by that? *(Let kids respond)*

Do you think Amy ever wondered if God was answering her prayers? *(Let kids respond)*

Have you ever asked God, "Why is this happening to me?" as Amy did? *(Let kids respond)* Have you ever been angry with God for what was happening in your life? *(Let kids respond)*

During the hardest times of our lives, it is only natural to ask, "Where are You, God?" God can be a great help to us, but sometimes it is hard to know that when we can't see or touch Him. The Bible talks about that. In fact, one of the Psalms written by David talks about that. Let's look at it.

Distribute copies of the "Where Are You, God?" activity sheets, made by copying pages 177 and 178 back to back and folding it in half. Read through it, emphasizing how this Psalm (139) teaches us how special we are to God.

No matter where we are, or what is happening to us, God is always with us. He knows us inside and out, and cares deeply about everything that happens to us. But even though God may not answer our prayers in just the way we asked Him to (parents get divorced anyway, grandparents die), that doesn't mean that God is not there or that He does not care! Remember Amy's last letter, in which she says:

"I should have listened to Mom when she told me that God does listen but He does things His way not ours!"

The fact that God is always with you makes Him the best helper you can have. Sometimes people will not be able to help you when you need it most, but God promises to be with you all the time! And you can count on that!

Jesus Bags

This activity is designed to do two things. First, it will reinforce Psalm 139 and the concept that God knows and cares about everything in our lives. Also, it will give you an opportunity to make a salvation presentation, guiding the kids to understand that accepting Jesus as Savior is the beginning point of having God in their lives. Pass out paper lunch bags and the "Inside Me" activity (pages 179 and 180). Proceed as follows:

Each of us has an inside and an outside life. Our *outside* lives are that part of us that everyone can see. What might that include? *(What we look like, what we are good at, what we like or don't like, who our friends are, our families, etc.)* Our *inside* lives contain all the private things no one knows unless we choose to tell them. *(Our feelings and reactions to situations; our fears, likes, and dislikes we never talk about; our hopes and dreams; etc.)*

Pretend this paper bag is you. It has an outside and an inside. Spend a few minutes decorating the outside of this bag to make it like you. Write or draw the things about you that are known to everyone. *(Allow time for this)* Now use the "Inside Me" activity sheets to write about some things that are part of your inside life. Put these private things inside your paper bag.

Psalm 139 tells us that God knows not only the outside part of our lives, but the

"Where are You, God?"

inside as well. **And no matter what is inside your heart, He cares about those things and loves you very much. In fact, there is no living person who knows you as well as God, or loves you as much. That is why you can come to God in prayer about anything in your life.**

Jesus wants to live in the inside place of our lives. **I want to give you one more piece to put inside your bags.** *(Pass out one "Jesus" heart from page 181 to everyone)* **The Bible teaches us that if we ask Him to, Jesus will come to live in our inside lives and be there with us forever. And, one day when we die, God will take us to His home in Heaven because Jesus is in our inside lives.** *(Place "Jesus" piece inside the bag. Staple the bag shut to symbolize that once Jesus is in our hearts, He will never leave us)*

You can invite Jesus into your inside lives right now. **God wants to live inside each of you, but He will only do so if you ask Him. I hope each of you has already made a decision to live for Jesus, but if you have not done so, you can do so right now.**

Optional: If you have pamphlets describing how kids can give their lives to Jesus, distribute them at this time. The children's ministry department of your church will most likely have such a resource. If not, check with your local Christian bookstore for material consistent with your beliefs.

Lead in a simple prayer. Ask any kids who have never invited Jesus to be a part of their lives and would like to do so now to pray with you. To avoid peer pressure, ask kids to pray silently and invite them to tell you what they prayed when the group is dismissed.

Feelings Logs

Reward the kids who brought their feelings logs back this week by giving them a sticker or other small prize. Although this is the last week they will bring their logs with them, encourage them to keep writing in them, especially when they are feeling difficult feelings. Remind the kids how Amy wrote letters to her Dad to help her deal with her feelings.

Prayer Time

Since this is your last prayer time together, review all requests and celebrate what God has done throughout the unit. Pray again for all requests that are still on the kids' hearts today.

Bible Time (20 Minutes)

Regathering

Have one facilitator lead the kids in a favorite game, song, or activity.

"Prepare for Family Night"

Next week, during Family Night, all kids will present something from the Confident Kids meetings for their families. First through fourth graders will do one or both of the presentations on page 165, depending on the size of your group, the amount of time available, and the kids' level of enthusiasm. Your options are:

1. Have all kids do one of the presentations.
2. Have all kids do both presentations
3. If your group is fairly large, divide into two groups and assign each group one of the presentations.

Presentation 1: David and Kids Present the Story of David and Goliath

Have "David" enter and greet the kids. He should say:

> **Today we are going to do something a little different. We are going to get ready for our Family Night next week by preparing a little presentation to tell them some of the things we've been learning about God. As I was thinking about today's theme of Jesus helping us with our feelings, I decided to choose the one story from my life that illustrates how God is our helper more than any other. So we are going to prepare the story of how God helped me fight Goliath.**

Organize the kids to act out the story (script is on pages 174 and 175) in a simple pantomime. David can act as narrator. Proceed as follows:

1. Assign parts to all kids: Goliath (use your largest facilitator), David, Saul, and David's three brothers. Divide the rest of the group into Philistines and Israelites.
2. Distribute copies of the narration and read it together. Talk it through with the kids, helping them think of what they can do to depict the action. Ask:

   > **What can you do to help those watching understand this part of the story?** *(Let all contribute ideas)*

3. Practice! When all the actions have been established, practice the story until the kids are comfortable with their parts.

Presentation 2: David and Kids Present Confident Kids Psalm 1

Distribute copies of Confident Kids Psalm 1 (Session 4) or project the psalm using an overhead projector. Have David prepare the kids to read the psalm as a choral reading, following the directions in the margins. Practice until it can be said smoothly and with feeling. *Note:* If this is the only presentation you are making, you might want to help the kids write a new psalm to share with their parents.

Memory Verses

Review Joshua 1:9 and Philippians 4:6, 7 one last time.

Closing Prayer Huddle

Close the meeting as in weeks past.

Snack (5 Minutes)

Distribute the snack. Thank all of the children who brought snacks during this unit.

Note

Facilitators will need to take home copies of the "Affirmation Balloons" and the unit certificates from Appendix A (pages 377 and 379). Have them complete one for each child in their small group, so the balloons and certificates can be presented during next week's Family Night program.

"Daddy" letters are used by permission.

Characters

- Amy, an eleven-year-old child (Choose a child or an adult who will read these letters with expression)

Needed

- A loose-leaf or spiralbound notebook

Daddy Letters

Amy is seated, reading these letters from a notebook.

Amy Have you ever thought something bad would happen and then it did? I always wondered how I would live if one of my parents got really sick or died. Well, I didn't have to wait long because when I was eleven years old, my dad got very sick! We didn't know what was wrong, but I was bound and determined to find out so he could get better and be normal again. Will he get well and if so will he be like himself again? To find out the end to this exciting story read my letters to Daddy.

#1 FEBRUARY 5, 1988

Daddy,

Where are you? Will you ever be here with me again? I miss you so much!

Why were you in the operating room so long? The doctors said your surgery should only take about a half an hour; instead we waited about five terrible hours till you came out of the operating room and then you went straight into intensive care so I couldn't see you! Why did you do that?

The doctors say you'll be all right but they don't know if you have cancer or not. I've been praying that you don't but sometimes that doesn't matter!

I wish you were here. I want to talk to someone, but everyone has their own problems. Why would they want to listen to mine? You always listen to me no matter how stupid my problem is!

Daddy, I have to go, but next time I write you I will try to have more information. I love you! Get well really fast!

Love, Amy

#2 FEBRUARY 6, 1988

Daddy,

How are you? Mom told me that you had a rough night, but you will be out of intensive care today! I am really glad because now I can see you and talk with you.

I talked to Mom last night and she said that the reason you were in the operating room so long was because the doctors had a lot of complications. They started out fine until they hit one of your arteries trying to get at the tumor next to your heart. She said the doctors told her they almost lost you. Thank goodness I was praying for you. Miracles do happen!

Guess what? I won the Speech Meet. I was so excited! I won it for you, Daddy! It was really a challenge. I was up against Joy Stewart. She is really wonderful! You gave me the will to win, and I won. The district meet is in April sometime. I hope you will be all over your sickness by then, so you can come watch me.

Since Mom has been at the hospital with you, we had to stay at the Migliorini's last night. I was scared to be there alone! I hope you can come home soon. Then I won't have to stay with other people and impose on them anymore!

I have to go. Get well soon!

Love, Amy

#3 FEBRUARY 9, 1988

Daddy,

I have some good and bad news! I will tell you the bad news first. The doctors still don't know what is wrong with you. I don't want to say this, but I think you have cancer. The doctors would have probably already told you if you didn't have cancer! I'm praying you don't, but I'm just preparing myself for the worst. Well, let's not dwell on the bad. Now for the good news! Do you remember in my last letter how I said that I didn't want to impose on other people by having to stay with them? Well, I don't have to worry about that anymore because Michele is going to move in with us. She will share my room with me and take care of us when Mom has to be with you. In case you are trying to remember who Michele is, I will try to describe her to you. She is 18 years old, goes to our church, and most important she loves us!

It is about time to start softball. Next Saturday I have to go to John Marshall Park to sign up and try out. I hope I get on Tony Bank's team. He is really good! Maybe you could help coach his team. That would be fun!

Dad, I have to go but I will come see you as soon as possible. I love you!

Love, Amy

#4 FEBRUARY 12, 1988

Daddy,

Today was the worst day of my life! I can't believe you have cancer! One day you were as healthy as could be, then the next time I looked at you, you're in the hospital with cancer. How could this happen to us?

I almost couldn't come see you today. I have a really bad sore throat. Now I wish I wouldn't have been able to come see you because I hate to cry in front of you. It is not your fault you have cancer. I don't want you to feel bad! I just don't want you to die. I couldn't and wouldn't live without you.

Daddy, the doctors don't know what kind of cancer you have but they are still trying to find out. I hope they find out soon so they can treat you correctly.

I have to go to bed but I promise to write you tomorrow. I love you!

Love, Amy

#5 FEBRUARY 15, 1988

Daddy,

The doctors have finally narrowed your cancer down to a type called lymphoma. At first they said there was a possibility of lung cancer! This type of cancer does not respond to treatment that well. They took the tissue they got during your biopsy and sent it to the City of Hope. The City of Hope is a place that specializes in all types of cancer! There they figured out that you have lymphoma. This type of cancer responds very well to chemotherapy. Chemotherapy is a treatment that uses drugs to kill the cancer cells. It also kills good cells like hair cells but at least you will be alive, and your hair will grow back. The doctors don't know which type of lymphoma you have. They couldn't tell from the sample they took, so they will treat you for many different types of lymphoma. That way they will make sure they stop it completely!

I will be praying for you. I have to remember to ask Mom when you're going to start your treatment. The sooner you start your treatment the sooner you will be well again! I love you!

Love, Amy

#6 APRIL 23, 1988

Daddy,

How are you? I know life's been pretty rough lately for you. Chemotherapy has been really hard on all of us. I never would have expected it to be so tough! You seem so far away! You walk by me and seem to be trying to tell me something but you can't. Instead you just go past me as if you were in your own little world! Mom says it's just the drugs and I believe her but it's hard not to be able to touch you because I am afraid I will hurt you. You are so weak and so thin. I can't believe you are the same person who won the state championships in the javelin! I ask the Lord every night if he will heal you. I think it is working. You only have a couple of weeks left of chemotherapy and the doctors said the worst part is over with. You have already lost most of your hair, your teeth are as sensitive as they can be, your fingernails have deteriorated, and your body is so weak you can barely move. If it makes you well then that's fine but if it doesn't I am going to be really mad!

Anyway, today was the district Speech Meet for school. I won a blue ribbon for scoring a superior. I really tried my best and I won! I also got on Tony Bank's team. He thinks I'm pretty good! I'm playing catcher, my favorite position. I have to go.

I love you!

Amy

#7 JUNE 18, 1988

Daddy,

Guess what? I got out of school today, and I am so excited! Now I can spend more time with you.

Now that the doctors said you have to have radiation I can go with you and keep you company. It's going to be rough if it is anything like chemotherapy. We went through it once so I guess we can go through it again!

I love you and would do anything for you! It hurts me so much when you come to watch me at my softball games and you just sit there and you look like you are hurting so badly. It also makes me feel so special that you love me enough to suffer!

My friends have been a really great support, Dad. They are all praying for you, and me. It was hard on me. Wherever I went, I had this thought haunting me in the back of my mind. I was out playing while my dad was at home suffering, maybe even dying! I tried to overcome that thought because even if I was at home you wouldn't really know, and I am not some miracle doctor. I couldn't make you any better if I was with you!

I have to go. I love you!

Love, Amy

#8 AUGUST 5, 1988

Daddy,

Happy Birthday! Congratulations! You made it another year. That is quite an accomplishment considering the past year. I'm so proud of you! You're starting to look more like yourself again. You're building up your strength and I am so glad because for awhile there, I was starting to worry that you would never get well! The Lord blessed you. I guess praying does help. I should have listened to Mom when she told me that God does listen but He does things His way, not ours.

Your hair is growing back curly. The doctors told you that your hair may grow back a different color but so far your hair is still brown, maybe a shade darker, though.

What did your doctor say about the fluid around your lung? I hope there is nothing seriously wrong. I don't want to go through another year like last year!

I love you and I am so glad you're well. The doctors said you are in remission. That means the cancer is really gone! Thank goodness.

I think this will be my last letter because I can talk to you and you will understand me again! During your cancer I had to get my feelings out and I couldn't talk about it out loud. Thanks for listening.

Love, Amy

From

- 1 Samuel 17

Characters

- David, Goliath (your biggest facilitator), and kids to act as David, Saul, three of David's brothers, and Philistines and Israelites

Needed

- Biblical costumes for David and Goliath
- A slingshot and five stones
- A sword
- Biblical headdresses for the other characters

David and Goliath

David narrates the scene from the side of the stage. The other actors portray the scene as David describes it.

Scene 1: Goliath Challenges the Israelites

David Two armies were ready for war. On one hill was the Philistine army, and on another was the Israelite army. Between them was a valley. The Philistines had a champion fighter named Goliath. He was a giant, standing 9 feet, 4 inches tall. He wore heavy armor weighing 125 pounds!

The armies stood on their hills staring at each other for a time. Finally, Goliath went down into the valley and shouted to the Israelite army:

Goliath Choose a man to fight me. If he can kill me, all the Philistines will become your servants. But, if I kill him, you will all become our servants! I dare the armies of Israel to send someone out to fight me!

David Saul and his men stood on their hill listening to Goliath, and they were afraid. No one would go out to fight him!

Scene 2: David Brings Lunch to His Brothers

David Right about this time, my father Jesse sent me to take some food to my three brothers, who were with the Israelite army. I was excited to go to the battle-front, and I ran all the way! I found them and gave them their food. Just then, Goliath came out again and started taunting the Israelites. Like the other times, the men in the army began to shake with fear. But I looked around and said:

Child David	Why is everyone afraid? Goliath may be big, but he is a Philistine! He is no match for the armies of the living God! If you won't go out and fight him, then, with God's help, I will!
David	One of my brothers tried to tell me to be quiet, but King Saul had heard what I had said. He said:
King Saul	No one else has volunteered to take on Goliath. If you are willing, go, and may God be with you.

Scene 3: David Fights Goliath

David	So I took my slingshot and five perfectly smooth stones. With these as my weapons, I went to fight the giant. I was afraid, but I knew in my heart that God was with me and would be my helper. When Goliath saw little, scrawny old me, he laughed a big belly laugh and said:
Goliath	Come closer and I will feed your body to the birds and the wild animals!
David	I moved closer and said:
Child David	Today I will feed you to the birds and animals. And everyone here will know that the Lord does not need swords or spears to save His people. The battle is not mine, but God's!
David	Then I put a stone in my sling, and we started to run toward each other. I prayed as I slung the stone right toward Goliath. And God sunk that stone right into Goliath's forehead. The giant never knew what hit him as he fell to the ground! I killed Goliath with his own sword! When the Philistines saw what happened, they turned and ran away. King Saul and the army of Israel praised the Lord for the great thing He had done, and for being my helper!

An Invitation

To

From

Please Come!
To Family Night at Confident Kids

Date

Time

praise You because You made my whole being in an amazing and wonderful way.

And because You never stop thinking about me! That's how much You love ME!

Where Are You, God?

Based on Psalm 139

O Lord, You know all about me...

You are all around me—in front and in back.
You have put Your hand on me.
There is no where I can go where
You would not be with me.

If I go up to the skies, You are there.
If I rise with the sun in the east
and ride with it all the way to the west—
even there You would guide me.
With Your right hand You would hold me.

Even the dark cannot
hide me from You.
The dark and the light
are the same to You;

You are with me in the darkest place!

Something I fear...
Something I think about a lot...

Something for which I need to be forgiven...
Something I wish for...

Jesus

Jesus

Jesus

Preteen Sessions

Tips for Working With Preteens in a Support-Group Setting

What to Expect From Preteens in *Confident Kids* Groups

Preteens are at a much different developmental level than younger elementary kids, and function in and respond to the support-group experience uniquely. Here are a few key points to help you plan for your group:

- **Preteens are developing skills of abstract and cause-and-effect thinking and therefore will have less difficulty with the process-oriented concepts in the *Confident Kids* material.**

  Dealing with issues such as feelings, grief, and evaluating the results of choices are well within the range of preteens' emerging thinking capabilities. Take advantage of this, but don't be alarmed if the kids don't understand everything perfectly.

- **Preteens are letting go of "magical thinking."**

  About the age of ten, kids' perspectives broaden beyond the restrictions of their own home environments. Until this time, their home and parents—regardless of how good or bad things actually are—were magically interpreted by the child to be the "best in the world." But now, they begin to see that there are other families and other parents who are different—maybe even better—than their own. If there are problems in the family, this can be a particularly agonizing time for kids as they let go of their idealized view of the parent and begin to see reality. You will see kids in your group struggling with these issues. Be patient if they bounce back and forth between realism and magical thinking!

- **Preteens are entering puberty.**

  Be prepared for the accompanying effects of puberty: emotional upheaval; "love/hate" attraction to, but awkwardness around, the opposite sex; and many complaints about things being "babyish." Although the curriculum does not address the issues connected to puberty directly, you are likely to get into discussions in your small groups about the many changes that are taking place. Sixth graders may be particularly curious.

- **Preteens have defense mechanisms that are deeply internalized and mostly subconscious.**

  By this age, the behaviors kids have developed to defend themselves from emotional pain will significantly affect the way they relate to the world at large. In addition, many of them will enter your groups feeling "too cool" to open up about the painful points of their lives. You may have to work hard to establish trust with your kids, and wait patiently for them to feel safe enough to lower their defenses with you. Once the kids do, however, you will be rewarded with the opportunity for extended conversations on healthy ways to deal with the emotional stress points in their lives.

Skits and Bible Stories Are Key Learning Times

Fifth and sixth graders *love* the skits! Invest a lot of energy in these parts of the session. Here are a few tips to help you do so:

- **Be prepared.**

  Be sure to read each skit at least a week in advance so you can prepare adequately. You can also recruit a drama team to manage this part of the program to free you to focus on building relationships with the kids.

- **Give the kids adequate time to prepare for skits in which they will participate.**

  When the scripts call for the kids to participate, they need time to get ready! Prepare them by having them practice during the gathering activity, or better yet, choose skit participants a week in advance and send scripts home with them to study. Also, if you recruit a drama team, be sure the kids are involved as much as possible! It is one of the most important ways the kids bond with the group!

- **Use adults to be the main Bible story characters.**

  We recommend that the same adults play the main Bible characters each week. This ensures consistency, and allows the adults to properly emphasize the biblical concepts written into the stories. Do not assign kids to these roles.

- **Add as many props and visuals as possible.**

  Remember that today's kids are highly visual! The more you put into the skits, the more effective a communication tool they will be!

Competition, Projects, and Outings Motivate Preteens

Competition, projects, and outings help you keep your preteens involved with the group. Here are some tips for using these three motivators with your kids.

Competition

Kids at this age *love* to compete. But competition can be motivating *or* destructive to the participants, depending on how it is handled. Be sure to:

1. Play down the competition by not making a big deal over who wins and who loses. Simply move on to the next activity.
2. Be sure everyone wins sometimes.
3. Do not give big prizes to winners. If you want to use prizes, be sure they are small and that over the course of the unit, all of the kids receive prizes at one time or another.
4. Recognize when some of your kids can't handle the competition, and stop using it!

Projects

Preteens can be motivated to work together on projects, especially when the projects accomplish a specific goal. Kids this age enjoy working together on community service projects, or preparing a program or teaching materials for the younger kids. You can also have them start working on a skit or other presentation for the Family Night program early in the unit.

Outings

Plan an end-of-the-unit outing for the kids. Early in the unit, set a group goal that if the kids work hard each week, they will have a party, overnight retreat, or other outing to enjoy. Maximize this motivator by having the kids spend a few minutes each week making plans for their special outing. They can vote on what they would like to do, and then plan a few details each week.

Adapt the Session Plans to Fit Your Kids

There is more material in each of the preteen session plans than you can probably do in one session! As you get to know the kids in your group, you will begin to see what works with them and what elicits the best response. Find your own comfort level with the material and prioritize the things you most want to accomplish each week. Also, there is nothing magical about this material. Make whatever changes are necessary for you to most effectively connect to your kids, in your setting.

Have Basic Materials on Hand for All Sessions

Each session plan in the preteen curriculum lists supplies unique to that session. However, before you begin any unit, be sure to set up your room with the following basic supplies. Adding the optional materials will further enhance the group's experience.

- **Basic Supplies**

  Confident Kids postcards and stamps
  Markers, pencils
  Colored drawing paper
  Tape, glue sticks, stapler
  Scissors
  Paper towels and other supplies for clean up
  Paper cups and napkins for snack time
  Extra snacks (in case someone forgets to return the snack tin)

- **Optional Supplies**

  Prop box for skits and role plays
  Small prizes
  Cassette tapes of songs for preteens
  Preteen games and craft books to supplement the curriculum, if needed

Goals

- Introduce the unit theme
- Develop a feelings vocabulary
- Introduce "Flatfoot Freddy," who will host the Bible stories each week

Needed

- Many sheets of paper or a long strip of butcher paper
- Group rules poster
- Three copies of each of the "Three Families of Feelers" scripts plus props
- "True/False Cards" (one copy per child)
- "Feelings Alphabet Race" (one copy per child)
- Prayer journal for each small group
- Items for regathering, if any
- Props for the "Fabulous Freddy" Bible skit
- Joshua 1:9 poster
- Snacks and snack tin

Feelings Are an Important Part of Life

Preteen Session 1 Outline

Opening (25 Minutes)

"Feelings Words" Posters

Introduction of New Kids

Group Rules

"Three Families of Feelers"

Small Groups (40 Minutes)

Discussion of Session Theme

Feelings Alphabet Race

Prayer Time

Bible Focus (20 Minutes)

Regathering

Feelings Alphabet Race Tally

"Fabulous Freddy, the Famous Feelings Finder Flatfoot, Finds David"

Memory Verse

Closing Prayer Huddle

Snack (5 Minutes)

The snack can be served during the Bible Focus regathering.

Feelings Are an Important Part of Life

Preteen Session 1

Opening (25 Minutes)

"Feelings Words" Posters

You will need sheets of paper with a variety of feelings words written on them, one word per sheet. The letters should be open-faced so they can be colored in. *Optional:* Instead of sheets of paper, you could make a mural by printing the feelings words in large, open-faced letters on a long strip of butcher paper. As kids arrive, have them choose a word to color and decorate in such a way that it depicts the meaning of the feeling. They can use symbolic colors (e.g., red for *anger*; green for *jealous*), lines, pictures, etc. Display the finished posters in the room.

Introduction of New Kids

If you have done a Confident Kids unit before, you will likely have both returning kids and new kids in the group. Welcome the new ones by calling them to the front of the room. Ask them to tell their name, grade, and one very unique thing about themselves. After each child is finished, lead the group in yelling, "Welcome, *[child's name]*!" and give him a round of applause.

Group Rules

If you did not use the introductory session, "Welcome to Confident Kids," last week, you will need to make a group rules poster. (See page 15 in the "Getting Started" section for complete directions on generating a list of rules for your group.) Spend some quality time doing this, as the group rules are crucial to the success of your support-group experience.

If you did use the introductory session, display the poster you made last week and review it. Be sure everyone understands the rules and the consequences for breaking them.

Feelings are an important part of life

"Three Families of Feelers"

At this time, divide the kids into three groups. Give each small group copies of one of the skits (pages 192–195) and give them time to prepare to present them. If necessary, add or delete characters or change the sex of characters so everyone is included. Encourage the kids to put some thought into their skits and to overexaggerate the kind of "feeler" they are representing. Introduce the skits with the following information, and then let each group present its skit.

This unit is about getting to know our feelings. That may sound easy, but it's really not! As you will see in the weeks ahead, feelings can be complicated, scary, fun, or hurtful and sorting them out can be really confusing. But there's one thing about feelings that *is* easy—we all have them! Like it or not, we are full of many feelings and growing up means learning how to handle them in ways that will help us live a healthy life. So, let's begin by taking a look at different ways people handle their feelings.

Small Groups (40 Minutes)

Discussion of Session Theme

The families in the skits illustrated different ways people express their feelings. Use the following questions to discuss the session theme, "Feelings are an important part of my life."

How did those in the Robot family handle their feelings? *(They ignored them, stuffed them inside, refused to admit they had any)*

How did those in the Happy family handle their feelings? *(They only let* *themselves feel happy feelings; they would not let themselves ever feel or express sad or angry feelings)*

How did those in the Gusher family handle their feelings? *(They let their feelings "gush" out; they overreacted to everything and had no idea how to handle their feelings appropriately)*

Which family handles their feelings in a healthy way? *(None of them. Although there is no one way to handle our feelings, each family is headed for trouble)*

Which family in the skits is most like your family—handles their feelings like your family does? *(Let kids respond)*

In this unit, we are going to learn how to live comfortably with all the many feelings we have. Unfortunately, most people have a lot of trouble learning how to handle them well. Let's see if we can learn some things about feelings.

Give each child one "True" and one "False" voting card (page 199). Have each child lay their cards face down on the table. Then read each of the statements below, asking kids to use their cards to vote as to whether the statement is true or false. They should choose their card, but not turn it over until everyone is ready. At your signal, have them turn their cards over. Compare answers and have kids explain why they voted as they did, especially if their votes differed from those listed below.

Big boys don't cry. *(False)*

Girls have more feelings than boys. *(False)*

Everyone has the same feelings. *(True)*

Everyone expresses their feelings in the same way. *(False)*

Feelings like happy, excited, proud, and love are OK to feel. *(True)*

Feelings like sad, angry, hate, and jealousy are not OK to feel. *(False)*

It's OK to have feelings, but you should never let anyone know what they are. *(False)*

Only "scaredy cats" and "sissies" are afraid. *(False)*

It's OK to be angry, as long as you don't hurt anyone or break anything when you are. *(True)*

Kids who can feel all their feelings and express them in good ways are healthier kids than those who don't express their feelings. *(True)*

God has given each of us an incredible number of feelings. Some of them are fun and we like to feel them, and others are scary and difficult and we will do anything we can to keep from feeling them. In this unit, we are going to learn that all our feelings are OK—and every single feeling is very important!

Feelings Alphabet Race

Distribute copies of the "Feelings Alphabet Race" (page 200). Give the kids five minutes to work alone to come up with one feeling word for each letter of the alphabet. Then compare the lists and make a master copy of all the different words the kids came up with. Count the total and write it at the top of the sheet. Take this sheet with you to the Bible Focus large group gathering.

Prayer Time

Each week you will spend the last seven or eight minutes of your group time in prayer. The purpose of this time is to help the kids learn that they can draw on God's presence and power as they face life's circumstances. To make this time tangible, set up a prayer notebook for your group to keep track of requests and answers. Review the requests each week and talk about what God has done in response to each one. Write your answers in the notebook.

Bible Focus (20 Minutes)

Regathering

Assign one facilitator each week to lead the kids in a favorite game, song, or activity (see resource listing for ideas) as they come from their small groups to the Bible story area. This facilitator will have to finish her small group time a few minutes early to be ready to gather the kids as they dismiss from their groups.

Note: Some groups prefer to serve the snacks at this time, with the rule that the snacks will be served as soon as everyone has arrived and is quiet. *Optional:* Because this unit discusses feelings and the main character is David, you might consider using praise tapes to teach the kids some Psalms set to music.

Feelings Alphabet Race Tally

Before going on to the Bible skit, ask each small group to report how many feelings words they thought of during the Feelings Alphabet Race. Give a round of applause (or even a small prize) to the group that came up with the most words.

"Fabulous Freddy, the Famous Feelings Finder Flatfoot, Finds David"

As with the opening skit, you will have to decide how the Bible stories will be handled each week. This week's script begins on page 196.

Memory Verse

Before the session, prepare a poster of Joshua 1:9.

> **Be strong and courageous. Do not be terrified; do not be discouraged, for the Lord your God will be with you wherever you go.** (*NIV*)

Introduce the verse today by having the kids say it with you a few times. Since this is an easy verse, take the poster away after reading it together once or twice.

Closing Prayer Huddle

Each week the meetings will close in the same way. Gather all the kids into a tight circle and instruct them to stack their hands on top of each other in the middle of the circle. As they stand in this position, ask a volunteer to lead in a short closing prayer. When the prayer is finished, have them raise their hands out of the stack and over their heads as they yell, "Amen!"

Snack (5 Minutes)

The facilitators should bring the snack the first night. Before the kids leave, choose a child to take the snack tin home for next week. (See page 14 in the "Getting Started" section for more information about handling the snack.)

Characters

- Robert, the father; Roberta, the mother; and Robby, the son

Needed

- A table set with dinner dishes
- Three chairs
- The sound of brakes squealing and a crash

Feelings Expression

- The members of this family handle their feelings by pretending they do not have any at all. They are like robots, doing whatever needs to be done but never allowing themselves to feel anything. As you act out this skit, be sure to maintain a totally blank expression and flat tone of voice. Do not smile, frown, etc.

Three Families of Feelers

Script 1: The Robot Family

The family is seated around the table eating dinner.

Father *(Said without expression)* Hello. We are the Robot family. I am the father, Robert Robot. This is my wife, Roberta Robot *(She looks up from her plate and says "Hello" with no expression, then continues eating)* And this is my son, Robby Robot *(Robby responds as his mother just did)* Ahem. Well, family, how was your day?

Mother *(Said without expression)* Fine. I broke a window and tore my best dress and burned up the chicken. Oh, and I won $10,000 in that big contest down at the store.

Robby *(Said without expression)* Fine. I got suspended from school for the next three days, and someone stole my bike from the rack so I had to walk home.

Father Yes, it sounds like a fine day. I, too, had a fine day. I got fired from my job this afternoon. *(From offstage comes the sound of brakes squealing and a crash. The family looks offstage, with no expression.)* Well, perhaps we should go see what that was all about. *(They get up and move "outside")*

Mother *(Without expression)* Oh, my. It's our little dog, Robo. He's been hit by a car.

Father And the driver hit our house and put a big hole in it, and then just drove away.

Robby Oh, well, we can get another dog, right?

Father Of course. First thing tomorrow.

Mother And the insurance will cover the hole in the house, right?

Father Very good thought, Mother. So, now that that's all settled, let's go finish dinner.

All Fine. *(They walk back to the table and start eating again, staring expressionless at their plates)*

Script 2: The Happy Family

The family is seated around the table eating dinner. They are laughing and talking together.

Father	*(Laughing)* Hi there! Welcome to our happy home! We are the Happy family. I'm the father, Hap Happy, and these are my children. This is Very Happy, my daughter, who just turned five years old last week.
Very	*(Giggles)* Yeah! I had the happiest birthday party of my whole life! *(Everyone laughs and says, "You bet, Very, it was great")*
Father	And this is her older brother, Always Happy. I'm so proud of him! He's a great kid. Say a few words, Always.
Always	*(Smiles brightly)* Gee, thanks, Dad! We have the best family! It's so much fun to live here!
Father	Well, gang, how was your day?
Very	Oh, it was such a happy day! In preschool we saw a movie about a spider who wanted to eat a fly who got caught in his web, but then they learned how to be best friends instead! Isn't that a happy story?
Always	*(Stops smiling)* What? Spiders are supposed to eat flies. What would he live on if he didn't? He'd starve to death. I think it's a dumb story.
Very	*(Starts to cry)* It was not! It was a happy story!
Father	*(Smiles)* Hey, that's enough from you two! Remember, no crying in this family! We're the Happy family! So, let's see those big smiles!
Very and Happy	*(Big smiles)* OK, Dad! *(From offstage comes the sound of brakes squealing and a crash. The family looks offstage, with happy expressions)*
Always	Wow! What was that? *(They all get up and move "outside")*
Very	*(Looks horrified)* Oh, no. It's our little dog, Smiles! He's been hit by a car!

Characters

- Hap, the father; Very, the daughter (about five years old); and Always, the son (about ten years old)

Needed

- A table set with dinner dishes
- Three chairs
- The sound of brakes squealing and a crash

Feelings Expression

- This family handles their feelings by always being happy. Any feeling is okay as long as it is a happy feeling (e.g., excitement, love, pride). Any sad feelings that come along are immediately cut off. As you present this skit, over-exaggerate the happy feelings by smiling all the time, laughing, etc.

Characters

- Gertie, the mother; and her twins—Gus, a boy, and Gail, a girl (about ten years old)

Needed

- A table set with dinner dishes
- Three chairs
- The sound of brakes squealing and a crash

Feelings Expression

- This family handles their feelings by letting them "all hang out." They don't know how to control their feelings or express them appropriately. They just act on whatever they feel. As you present this skit, overexaggerate all the feelings involved. When you are happy, jump up and down, laugh, etc. When you are mad, scream and yell, and when you are sad, "weep and wail."

Always *(Looks anxious and worried)* And the driver hit our house and put a big hole in it, and then just drove away. What are we going to do, Dad?

Father *(Looks sad and worried for a minute)* I—I don't know— *(Pauses, then brightens and smiles again)* Hey, wait a minute! It's not so bad! We'll have a nice funeral for Smiles and then go to the pound and get a new dog, OK? And as for this house, well, it's a happy thing! With the insurance money we'll be able to fix it up better than it was! Where are all those big smiles? Remember, we're the Happy family and we can handle anything with a happy face!

Very *(Smiles)* Yeah! I'll invite all the kids for the funeral and make cookies for us!

Always *(Smiles)* Yeah! And we'll probably find an even better dog at the pound!

Father That's the spirit! OK, let's go finish dinner! *(They walk back to the table and start eating again, laughing and talking together)*

Script 3: The Gusher Family

The family is seated around the table eating dinner. They are all in a pleasant mood.

Mother *(Pleasantly)* Hello, and welcome to our home! We are the Gusher family. I am the mother, Gertie Gusher, and these are my twins, Gus Gusher *(He says "Hi" with a big smile and continues eating)* and Gail Gusher. *(She responds in the same way as her brother)* We were just about to check in with each other. *(Turns to kids)* So, kids, how was your day?

Gus It was OK. Except for lunch time. I had a little accident at lunch.

Gail *(Giggles)* A little accident! He tripped in line and spilled his food all over the floor! He turned bright red in front of everyone— *(Says in a taunting way)* especially in front of Carla, his girlfriend!

Gus *(Gets very angry)* Shut up! You just shut up, OK! I don't have a girlfriend and if you say one more word I'll punch your lights out! *(Makes a fist and shoves it in her face)*

Gail	*(Starts to pull away and is angry, too)* OK! OK! Get out of my face, will you! You touch me and you die!
Mother	*(She is angry, too, but is trying to control it)* Stop it, you two! Is this any way to act in front of all this company? Now cool it before I get mad or you'll be sorry! *(Pauses, as she composes herself)* Now, Gail, how was your day?
Gail	*(Suddenly looks sad)* It was OK. Only I didn't get the part in the school play.
Mother	*(Said with great feeling and concern)* Oh, no! Gail, you poor dear! You must feel so disappointed! I know you wanted that part so much!
Gail	Gosh, Mom! I really did! I'm so disappointed! I don't think I've ever been this disappointed in my whole life! *(Starts crying)*
Gus	*(Looks disappointed for his sister)* Wow, Sis, tough break. *(From offstage comes the sound of brakes squealing and a crash)* Wow! What was that? *(The family immediately gets up and moves "outside")*
Mother	*(Looks horrified)* Oh, no. It's our little dog, Geyser! He's been hit by a car!

Gus and Gail carry on with great grief, crying and hugging each other and saying things like, "How could this happen?" "Poor Geyser!" "I can't live without him," etc.

Mother	*(Looks anxious and worried)* And the driver hit our house and put a big hole in it, and then just drove away.
Gail	*(Worried, wringing her hands)* Oh no, not our house! What are we going to do, Mom? Where will we live? We'll be homeless!
Gus	*(Frightened)* And burglars will come in through the hole and steal our stuff—
Gail	And kill us in our sleep because Geyser's not here to protect us!
Together	*(Look shocked and sad)* Oh, no! *(They cry for a few minutes, clinging to each other)*
Mother	Now, now, children. We'll get by somehow. Let's go inside and figure out what to do.

They exit.

From

- Psalm 56 (*ICB*)

Characters:

- Fabulous Freddy (a detective) and King David

Needed

- A detective outfit for Freddy (e.g., a trench coat, hat, and sunglasses)
- A royal biblical costume for King David
- A small notebook

Suggested

- A large magnifying glass
- A recording of the theme from "Mission Impossible" or other appropriate detective/spy music

Fabulous Freddy, the Famous Feelings Finder Flatfoot, Finds David

The stage is empty; the music recording starts to play. Freddy enters, sneakily, with his coat collar turned up, his hat low on his forehead and wearing sunglasses. He is looking for something, and takes a few moments to search while the music plays.

Freddy *(Sees the kids and addresses them)* Oh, there you are! I thought someone was supposed to meet me for this caper. *(Takes off his sunglasses and pushes his hat back on his head)* Actually, I'm glad for the company on this one! Can't say that I've ever had a tougher case! *(Pauses)* Aww—perhaps I should introduce myself. I'm Fabulous Freddy, the Famous Feelings Finder Flatfoot, and I'm on a mission! My job is to find feelings in places no one else would think to look for them.

(Pauses) Why, you ask me? *(Speaks with a "tough guy" tone of voice)* I'll tell you why! Because an awful lot of people in this world got the crazy idea that feelings are for sissies! You wouldn't believe the wackos I come across in this job! Like, guys who think they can only be tough; grown-ups who stuff all their feelings and pretend they don't have any! And you know what else I see in this crazy world? Kids—like all of you—who just let their feelings run away with them! Why? Because they don't understand how important feelings are in their lives! So, I'm on the job to seek out feelings in unlikely places—and to take them back to all those people who are all messed up about their own feelings!

But, enough about me! Let me tell you about this caper! This one is a real lulu! I'm supposed to find feelings in the Bible! *(Looks puzzled)* Now how am I supposed to do that? I'm sure glad all of you are here to help me with this one!

King David	*(Reads from his notebook as he walks onstage. He reads loudly and with much feeling)* God, be merciful to me because people are chasing me. The battle has pressed me all day long. My enemies have chased me all day.
Freddy	*(To the kids)* Wow! Who is this guy? He sure looks like he knows something about the Bible, and he's definitely upset about something! Let's check it out! *(To David)* Excuse me, sir, can you help me?
David	What? Who are you, and why are you dressed so funny?
Freddy	My name is Fabulous Freddy, the Famous Feelings Finder Flatfoot, and I'm on a mission.
David	*(Puzzled)* Famous Freddy the Flatfoot Feeler—no—ah—whatever! You say you're on a mission? What kind of mission?
Freddy	I'm supposed to find feelings in the Bible. Can you help me, sir?
David	*(Brightens)* Can I help you? What kind of a question is that? Don't you know who I am?
Freddy	*(Embarrassed)* Well—ah—no! I can't say that I do.
David	Son, I am King David! Surely you know me from everything you've read about me in the Bible!
Freddy	Well, actually, sir—ah, King sir, that is—I've never read the Bible.
David	*(Shocked)* Never read the Bible? Well, then, I can help you. Give me your Bible and I'll be glad to help you find feelings in it. The Bible is full of feelings! Especially in my favorite book, Psalms!
Freddy	I don't have a Bible. And what are Psalms?
David	*(Sighs)* Looks like we're going to have to do this the hard way. Tell you what, son, meet me back here next week at this same time, and I'll get you started finding all sorts of fabulous feelings in the Bible! Right now, I have to be on my way. Oh, and don't forget to bring a Bible! *(Exits, reading loudly from his notebook)* When I am afraid, I will trust you. I trust God. So I am not afraid. What can human beings do to me?

Freddy	*(Stares after him)* Wow! What a lead! This guy just might help us crack this case wide open! *(Theme music comes back on. Freddy pulls his collar up, pushes his hat down, and dons his sunglasses)* Hey, I guess that's all we can do for today. I'll go find a Bible and meet you all back here next week. Don't be late, OK? See you then! *(Exits, as music plays)*

TRUE	FALSE
TRUE	FALSE
TRUE	FALSE

Feelings Alphabet Race

Think of feelings words that begin with each letter of the alphabet.
You will have five minutes to think of as many as you can.

A -

B -

C -

D -

E -

F -

G -

H -

I -

J -

K -

L -

M -

N -

O -

P -

Q -

R -

S -

T -

U -

V -

W -

X -

Y -

Z -

Goals

- Discover that there are no "bad" feelings. All our feelings are important and necessary to living a healthy life
- Identify how feelings affect different parts of our bodies
- Practice identifying different feelings and the important information they communicate to us
- Affirm through the story of David that God understands all our feelings and we must express them to Him

Needed

- Large strip of butcher or shelf paper and water-based markers
- "Feelings Charades" cards
- Group rules poster
- Props for opening skit
- "Feelings Cards" (one set per small group)
- "Feelings Scenarios" (one set per small group)
- Items for regathering activity, if any
- Props for "Freddy" Bible skit
- Joshua 1:9 poster

All My Feelings Are OK!

Preteen Session 2 Outline

***Opening** (25 Minutes)*

Graffiti Board and Feelings Charades

Group Rules

"You're Supposed to Feel That Way!"

***Small Groups** (40 Minutes)*

Discussion of Session Theme

Where Do I Feel It? and Feelings Scenarios

Prayer Time

***Bible Focus** (20 Minutes)*

Regathering

"Fabulous Freddy, the Famous Feelings Finder Flatfoot, Learns David's Story"

Memory Verse

Closing Prayer Huddle

***Snack** (5 Minutes)*

The snack can be served during the Bible Focus regathering.

All My Feelings Are OK!
Preteen Session 2

Opening (25 Minutes)

Graffiti Board

Before the kids arrive, divide a large piece of butcher or shelf paper into two sections, one labeled *Good Feelings* and the other *Bad Feelings*. Tape it to the wall. As kids arrive, have them use words and pictures to depict what they consider to be good and bad feelings on each side of the graffiti board. (Be sure kids use water-based markers to write on the board, so they don't bleed through onto the wall.) *Note:* If the kids have already been instructed that there are no good or bad feelings, ask them to think of better words to use in the headings, and change the words at this time. If they don't catch this, wait until later to address this issue.

Feelings Charades

When kids have finished adding feelings words to the graffiti board, have them play a few rounds of feelings charades. In advance, prepare slips of paper with feelings words written on them. Use this as an opportunity to expand the kids' feelings words vocabularies by choosing words they may not be familiar with. If they have trouble guessing the correct word, the child acting out the charade can give a hint by saying, "I feel this way when _________."

Group Rules

Use the group rules poster to review the rules again this week. Ask the kids how they feel about the rules, and if they think the rules are working. Are there any that are not necessary? Are there some that should be added? Use this time to allow the kids to negotiate and gain a sense of ownership about the way the group is going.

"You're Supposed to Feel That Way!"

Introduce the skit by referring to the graffiti board. Review the words written on each side, and ask kids if they all agree that the words are accurately labeled *good* or *bad*. Then make the point that you see one problem with the board. Ask the kids to see if they can discover what it is, as they watch the skit. When the skit is finished, refer back to the graffiti board.

> **Can anyone see what is wrong with the graffiti board?** *(The words "Good" and "Bad")* **Last week we talked about how many different kinds of feelings there are and that feelings are a very important part of our lives. The next thing we need to think about is that some feelings feel better than others. We *like* to feel happy, excited, or loved. We *don't like* to feel sad, embarrassed, or hurt. Because of that, it is easy to say that there are *good* feelings and *bad* feelings. But that is not true! It is important for us to learn that *all* our feelings are OK, and each one does something important for us.**

Ask the kids to suggest more appropriate words to use in the headings of the graffiti board (e.g., *fun/not fun* or pleasant/unpleasant). Change the words on the board and then dismiss kids to small groups.

Our feelings give us important information

Small Groups (40 Minutes)

Discussion of Session Theme

Use the following questions to discuss the session theme, "Our feelings give us important information."

> **In the skit, why did Roscoe think he was doing something wrong?** *(He equated feeling bad with doing something bad or wrong)*
>
> **What do you think Buddy meant when he said, "Right now, your feelings are telling you something important, something you should pay attention to"?** *(Let kids respond)*
>
> **Do you agree that there are no bad feelings? Why or why not?** *(Let kids respond)*
>
> **Our feelings are not just something we have to put up with, or try to ignore. God gave us every one of our feelings for a special reason. Buddy was right when he said that Roscoe's feelings were telling him something very important. All feelings give us messages, and when we can learn to understand them properly, they help us in many ways!**

Place the "Feelings Cards" (page 211), cut apart, in a pile face down on the table. Ask one child to draw a card and suggest a message that feeling could be communicating. Then ask the whole group to think of as many other messages connected to that feeling as possible. Write these down so you can review them later. Then have the next child draw a card, and repeat the process. Here are some possibilities:

> **Anger—Someone did something to us (e.g., broke a promise, took something of ours, told a lie about us). We need to do something to protect ourselves from getting hurt again (a motivation to action). We may be in danger of doing something destructive (like striking out to get even).**
>
> **Guilt—We did something wrong and need to do something to make it right (e.g., apologize, pay back something we stole, confess).**

Love—This person (or pet, or other object of our love) is important to us, and we care about having a good relationship.

Lonely—We have been alone too much and need to be with someone we love, or we need to make some new friends.

Proud—We did a good job at something. There is something we know we do well.

Hate—We have been deeply hurt by someone, often someone we love very much. (Hate is a strong emotion and is not stirred up by people or situations we don't care about.)

Fear—We are in danger and need to take precautions to stay safe. We are facing something that could hurt us (like failing a test) and we have to work hard at succeeding. We are facing something new and unexpected but not necessarily dangerous.

Excited—Something good has happened or will be happening soon. We need to find someone to share our news with as soon as possible!

Where Do I Feel It?

Make the point that feelings are also tied to our physical health; they affect our bodies. Stand in a circle and read one of the feeling words below. Ask someone to pantomime how that feeling affects our bodies. Then have everyone say the word together and do the pantomime together. Go through the list below. Here are some ways the words may be expressed:

Afraid—Hold stomach (stomachache); knees wobble

Sad—Tears from our eyes; mouth turned down; body slumped

Angry—Teeth gritted; fists tight; eyes slit

Worried—Hold head (headache); hold eyes open (can't sleep); hold stomach (stomachache)

Loved—Hands over heart; big smile

Surprised—Eyes wide; heart pounding; jump (involuntary reaction)

Depressed—Whole body slumped

Proud—Big smile; chest out

When you are done, have the group sit down and ask the kids:

Can you stop your body from reacting to feelings? *(No, the feelings are stronger)*

If you try to *resist* a feeling, what will happen? *(You will make yourself sick; the feelings are stronger and eventually will gain control of your body)*

Feelings Scenarios

Distribute two copies of "Feelings Scenario #1" (pages 212–214) to two of your kids. Ask them to perform it for the group as a skit. Then have them ask the group to answer each of the questions printed on the bottom of the sheet. *Note:* Be sure the actors get a few answers from the other group members *before* they read the suggested answers on the bottom of the sheet. Do "Feelings Scenarios #2, 3" if time allows.

Prayer Time

Ask kids to think about any messages their feelings may be trying to communicate to them. Do their feelings suggest any prayer requests? (For example, "I have been unable to sleep because I am so worried about my math test next week. Pray that I'll do well.")

Bible Focus (20 Minutes)

Regathering

Have one facilitator lead the kids in a favorite game, song, or activity.

"Fabulous Freddy, the Famous Feelings Finder Flatfoot, Learns David's Story"

Present the skit as you did last session. The script is on pages 208–210.

Memory Verse

Use the poster to review Joshua 1:9 again this week, or choose another memory verse game (see Appendix B, "Resources" for ideas).

Closing Prayer Huddle

Close the meeting with the prayer huddle, as you did last week.

Snack (5 Minutes)

Distribute the snack the child brought. Before the kids leave, choose another child to take the snack tin home for next week.

Characters

- Roscoe and Buddy

Needed

- A picture of a grandfather

"You're Supposed to Feel That Way!"

Roscoe is sitting on his front porch, holding the picture and looking very sad.

Buddy *(Enters)* Hey, Roscoe, I heard about your grandpa. I came right over.

Roscoe Yeah, well, it's no big deal. Everybody has to die sometime, right?

Buddy Did he die? I thought he had a heart attack and is in the hospital.

Roscoe But he's gonna die! Mom says he may not live through the night.

Buddy Wow! I'm really sorry, Roscoe. Can I see his picture?

Roscoe Sure. It's the last one he had taken. *(Hands picture to Buddy. They sit in silence for a few moments while Buddy looks at it.)*

Buddy Your grandpa was the neatest man!

Roscoe *(Angrily)* Was? He's not dead yet, Buddy!

Buddy OK, OK! I'm sorry. So, I guess you'll be going to the hospital to see him, huh?

Roscoe And let grandpa see me like this? No way, man!

Buddy *(Confused)* Like what? You look fine to me.

Roscoe Like a sissy! Look at me, Buddy! I'm being a wimp about this! I should be strong!

Buddy Says who?

Roscoe Says everybody! What would the guys say if they knew I was crying? I feel like I'm not me anymore!

Buddy Hey, man! Your grandpa is dying! You're supposed to feel sad and hurt.

Roscoe	So what? If I was strong, I wouldn't feel like this! I feel so awful inside; I just know I'm doing something really wrong! It's better that I don't let grandpa see me like this. He's better off without me!
Buddy	Roscoe, there's nothing wrong with you! Just because you feel awful doesn't mean you're doing anything wrong! You're feeling just what you're supposed to be feeling.
Roscoe	You keep saying that. But how can I be having all these bad feelings if I'm not doing something wrong?
Buddy	Look, numb-brain, don't you know that there are no bad feelings? All your feelings are OK! And right now, your feelings are telling you something important, something you should pay attention to.
Roscoe	*(Stands up and starts to pace)* Buddy, you're crazy! What can *feeling like I'm falling apart* and *crying* tell me that's so important? Except maybe that I'm being a sissy!
Buddy	Well, I know what your feelings are telling me. They're saying you love your grandpa very, very much. If you didn't care about him, you wouldn't be feeling so hurt about losing him.
Roscoe	*(Looks surprised)* I never thought about it like that—
Buddy	*(Stands up and puts an arm around Roscoe's shoulders)* So what's so terrible about loving someone that much? Trust me, man! You're supposed to feel this way! I'd be worried about you if you didn't!
Roscoe	*(Looks at the picture, relieved)* I do want to go to the hospital, but I'm scared. Will you come with me?
Buddy	OK. Let's go find your mom.

They exit, Buddy's arm around Roscoe's shoulders.

From

- Psalm 23 (*ICB*, modified) and 1 Samuel 17

Characters

- Fabulous Freddy (a detective), King David, and young David

Needed

- Detective outfit and a Bible for Freddy
- A royal biblical costume for King David
- A biblical costume for young David including a shepherd's staff, slingshot, and five small stones in a pouch

Suggested

- A recording of the theme from "Mission Impossible" or other appropriate music

Fabulous Freddy, the Famous Feelings Finder Flatfoot, Learns David's Story

The stage is empty; the music recording starts to play. Freddy enters, sneakily, with his coat collar turned up, his hat low on his forehead, wearing his sunglasses, and carrying a Bible.

Freddy *(Sees the kids and addresses them)* All right! You guys came back, and right on time, too! Good, because we need to get moving on this finding feelings caper! *(Holds his Bible up, looks around)* Now, if we can just spot that King David guy—

King David *(Enters)* I'm here, Fergie. Did you bring a Bible this time?

Freddy It's Freddy, sir, and I have a Bible right here.

King David Good. Now open it to the middle.

Freddy The middle? OK. *(Opens Bible)* Let's see, this says Pa-salms.

King David Not "Pa-salms"—just "Salms." The "P" is silent.

Freddy Oh, yeah, I knew that. So, what am I looking at here?

King David What you have there, Fido, is a book of poems and songs that I wrote specifically to express my feelings to God. In these pages, you will find every feeling you can ever imagine!

Freddy *(Irritated)* My name is *Freddy*! Hey, this is a lot of stuff!

King David I've been expressing my feelings to God since I was a young boy. *(Young David enters with all items and sits on the other side of the stage)* I was a shepherd boy in those days. It all started one day, when I was out on the hillside taking care of my sheep, and I felt overwhelmed when I realized that just as I take care of my sheep, *God takes care of me*! So I wrote a song to God …

Young David	*(Takes shepherd's staff and walks around the stage as he says, with great feeling)* The Lord is my shepherd! He gives me everything I need! He gives me rest in green pastures and leads me to calm water. Even if I walk through a very dark valley, I will not be afraid because You are with me. You give me more than I can hold. Surely Your goodness and love will be with me all my life! *(Freeze)*
Freddy	Wow! You were feeling safe, and secure, and happy and—
King David	And it was all because I knew God was taking care of me!
Freddy	So, according to this, you were never afraid of anything.
King David	Not true! I've had many, many adventures in my life and have felt every feeling you can name! In fact, it wasn't too long after I wrote the shepherd psalm that I took on Goliath, the giant!
Freddy	Gol—who?
King David	Ah, now that was an adventure! We were at war, but I was too young to fight. I remember that all my older brothers enlisted, but I stayed with my father's sheep.
Young David	*(Puts shepherd staff down and picks up the slingshot and pouch; looks wistful)* Why am I the one who has to stay with the sheep? Just because I'm the youngest? I'm as powerful a fighter as anyone! I wish I could just *see* what's going on at the battlefield! *(Freezes)*
King David	And then one day I heard news from the front. There was a giant man—over nine feet tall—who was challenging our troops. "Send out your best fighter! If he kills me, you win the war!" Then he would laugh, because no one from our side would fight him! So, I went to King Saul, and begged for permission to fight.
Young David	*(Looks as though he is talking to someone)* Please, Your Majesty, let me fight Goliath! I'm the best there is! *(Pauses)* Yes, sir. I know I'm just a kid, and small for my age. But I'm fast! And, besides, no one else is willing to do it! Are we going to let this barbarian win by default? *(Pauses)* Oh, thank you, sir! You won't be sorry! *(Freezes)*

Freddy	So, you went to fight a nine-foot giant? And you weren't scared?
King David	I was terrified! The night before the battle, I almost threw up! I prayed long and hard, asking God to calm me and give me success. And God answered my prayers.
Young David	*(Looks a little scared, but confident; takes a stone and puts it his sling. Speaks loudly, and with authority.)* Goliath, you have mocked us and our God one time to many! Today, God will fight you, and He will win! Prepare to die! *(Freezes)*
Freddy	You mean, you said that to a nine-foot giant who wanted to kill you?
King David	*(Laughs)* I did! And God answered my prayer. I had picked five perfect stones from the river but I only needed one. And when it was over, I felt—
Freddy	Relieved! And proud! This is great stuff, your kingship! *(Starts to look through the Bible)* What other feelings are in here?
King David	Many more than I can tell you about today. But I'll come back next week, if you like. Now, I must be on my way. *(Both Davids exit)*
Freddy	*(Stares after him)* Wow! This is great stuff! *(Theme music comes back on; he pulls his collar up, pushes his hat down, and puts his sunglasses on)* But, that's all we can do for today. Meet you all back here next week. See you then! *(Exits, as music plays)*

Anger
Guilt
Hate
Fear
Love
Excited
Lonely
Proud

Feelings Scenario #1

Charlene *(You are very upset; be sure to show this in your face and how you hold your body. What do you look like and do when you are upset?)* Josephine is so stupid! I hate her!

Mother Josephine is your best friend.

Charlene Not any more! You know what she did? She said she won't come to my pajama party on Friday because Robin—that new girl—asked her to go to the mountains with her and her family! How could she do that to me? She's supposed to be my best friend!

Questions

1. What is Charlene feeling?
2. What messages are those feelings telling her?
3. What must she be careful about right now?
4. What is one healthy thing she can do in response to her feelings?

Answers

1. Jealousy, betrayal, anger
2. She cares about her friend very much (if she didn't care about this friend, she would *not* have such strong feelings about her not coming to the party). Also, she has been wronged (violated) and needs to think carefully about how to take care of herself.
3. She must be careful to not strike back in anger or seek revenge.
4. She can call her friend or write her a letter and tell her how she feels betrayed.

Feelings Scenario #2

Gary	Hey, Leo! Let's go over and check out that place where they're tearing down the building. I'll bet we can find lots of neat stuff over there.
Leo	Didn't you listen the last time we were there? The man said it was really dangerous and he'd have us arrested if he ever caught us there again!
Gary	You didn't believe that stuff about getting us arrested, did you? He was just trying to scare us! Hey, man! The danger is half the fun! Nothing's gonna happen to us! Let's go.
Leo	*(Hesitant and scared. Be sure to show this in your face and your body)* Gary, I think something could happen to us over there! Remember Albert Bishop? He broke his leg there. And they would too have us arrested!
Gary	*(Taunting)* What's the matter, Leo? You *chicken*?

Questions

1. What is Leo feeling?
2. What messages are those feelings telling him?
3. What must he be careful about right now?
4. What is one healthy thing he can do in response to his feelings?

Answers

1. Fear, guilt (about having been there before and possibly doing something he knows is wrong)
2. There is danger involved in what his friend is asking him to do; this is a very real danger.
3. He must be careful to not let his friend taunt him into doing something he feels is dangerous and wrong.
4. He can walk away.

Feelings Scenario #3

Brian	Hey, Marjorie! Look at this! My drawing for art class was chosen to be on display at the kids' exhibit in the art museum! They only chose 200 pictures from over 6,000 that were entered, and mine was one of them!
Marjorie	Big deal!
Brian	*(Looks hurt)* What do you mean? It *is* a big deal!
Marjorie	Maybe to you it is, but who cares about art, anyway? I think the art museum is boring. Now, if you were the first kid astronaut going to the moon, or something cool like that, maybe I'd be impressed.
Brian	You're just jealous!
Marjorie	Who, me? No way! *You* just have a big head!

Questions

1. What is Brian feeling?
2. What messages are those feelings telling him?
3. What must he be careful about right now?
4. What is one healthy thing he can do in response to his feelings?

Answers

1. Proud (about his artwork); hurt (that his friend is not happy for him, too)
2. He is a good artist; he has done something well and can enjoy being honored for it.
3. He must be careful to not let his friend's jealousy stop him from enjoying his honor and taking his art seriously.
4. He can find other friends, teachers, and family members who will be happy with him.

Goals

- Define feelings defenses (feeling one way, acting another)
- Brainstorm a list of possible defensive behaviors
- Practice identifying various defenses, including the kids' own
- Continue exploring feelings in the Bible with Freddy and David

Needed

- "Joshua 1:9" poster activity (one copy per child)
- Group rules poster
- Props for opening skits
- A large paper grocery bag with a smiling face drawn on it
- Five Styrofoam cups per child, plus eight extra per small group, and markers for writing on them
- "Safe People List" (one copy per child)
- Prayer journals
- Items for regathering, if any
- Props for the "Freddy" Bible skit
- Joshua 1:9 memory verse poster, and a number of small prizes

What Are My Feelings Defenses?

Preteen Session 3 Outline

Opening (25 Minutes)

Joshua 1:9 Posters

Group Rules

"The Clown" and "The Bully"

Small Groups (40 Minutes)

Discussion of Session Theme

Defense Cups

Prayer Time

Bible Focus (20 Minutes)

Regathering

"Fabulous Freddy, the Famous Feelings Finder Flatfoot, Learns More From David"

Memory Verse

Closing Prayer Huddle

Snack (5 Minutes)

The snack can be served during the Bible Focus regathering.

What Are My Feelings Defenses?

Preteen Session 3

Opening (25 Minutes)

Joshua 1:9 Posters

As kids arrive, have copies of the "Joshua 1:9" posters (page 227) and fine-line markers available. Talk with kids about the different things in the world today that frighten or terrify them, and have them make pictures of these things in the space around the verse. They can color the words of the verse, and decorate the poster any way they choose. Keep the posters handy for use during today's prayer time. If kids have trouble thinking of things, suggest one or two items to get them started. Possibilities include: guns/violence, war, parents' divorce, environmental concerns, school, or drugs/alcohol.

Group Rules

Review the rules again, and the consequences for breaking them.

"The Clown" and "The Bully"

These two skits are designed to help kids understand the concept of hiding from our feelings by using defensive behavior. If you choose to have kids help with these skits, be sure to practice with them so they can effectively communicate the nature of the defensive behavior. Introduce the skits as follows:

> *(Facilitator enters with a paper grocery bag with a smiling face drawn on it, over his head)* **Who can tell me what I'm feeling?** *(Allow for responses, then take the bag off and reveal a sad or angry face)* **Last week we talked about how there are a lot of feelings that are uncomfortable. This week we are going to see that when we feel these feelings, we often protect ourselves by pretending we aren't feeling**

them. That's called using a feelings defense. Let's see how it works. *(Present skits)*

Small Groups (40 Minutes)

Discussion of Session Theme

Use the following questions to discuss the session theme, "Sometimes I feel one way, but act another."

Skit 1: The Clown

What was Mary really feeling? *(Fear, anxiety, sadness)*

What did she do about her feelings? *(She pushed them aside; she protected herself from them by using a feelings defense)*

What defense did she use? *(Clowning)*

What did Jane think Mary was feeling? *(Happy; didn't care that she was moving away)*

Skit 2: The Bully

What was Andy really feeling? *(Sad, lonely)*

What did he do with his feelings? *(Said he didn't care; turned them into anger and fighting)*

What defense did he use? *(Bullying)*

Did the other kids know what Andy was really feeling? *(No)* **Why not?** *(Because he never let them see what he was feeling)*

Everyone uses feelings defenses from time to time. We use them mostly when we are feeling something that is uncomfortable and we want to pretend we are not feeling it, or when we don't want anyone else to know what we are feeling. Put simply, using a feelings defense is when we *feel* one way, but *act* a different way.

With the kids, name eight feelings defenses. Let the kids suggest some, or use the following list. As you name a defense, draw a face of what it looks like (or write it) on a Styrofoam cup (turn the cup upside down). Place these defense cups in the middle of your table. Some common defenses are:

***Clowning*—We make jokes of situations that make us feel uncomfortable.**

***Bullying*—We get angry and mean when we feel uncomfortable.**

***Pretending*—We pretend that something hurtful or disappointing is not happening.**

***Daydreaming*—We "tune-out" and think of other things or make up stories when we don't want to feel something.**

***Silence/Withdrawal*—We get quiet or don't say anything, even if we feel angry or disappointed.**

***Getting Sick*—We can experience headaches and stomachaches when we avoid our feelings.**

***Lying*—We tell lies or make up stories to try to make an uncomfortable situation seem better.**

***Blaming*—We make everything someone else's fault, so we don't have to feel guilt or regret.**

Defense Cups

To help the kids understand how feelings defenses work, give everyone five blank cups of their own. Now

Sometimes I feel one way but act another

hold up a stack of cups that you made earlier, which represents your personal response to a situation in your life. Place your favorite defense on the top of your stack. Tell the kids that this stack represents you, and briefly tell them about the situation in your life. Then ask:

What do you think I am feeling, based on what you see? *(They will only see the defensive behavior)*

What am I really feeling? *(They can't know, until you lower your defense and share with them what you are really feeling)*

Now look back at the skit scripts and pick one of the characters to discuss. Ask kids to name how they would feel if the events in the skit happened to them. Have them write or draw the feelings words on the cups, one word per cup. Then ask the kids to stack their cups, one on top of the other.

The stack of cups is like a person. Every day, things happen to all of us that bring about different feelings. Sometimes we like these feelings, and sometimes we don't like them at all.

Look at your stack of cups. Which of those feelings do you not like to feel? *(Probably most of them)*

What do you do to protect yourself from these feelings? Which feelings defense(s) do you use? *(Have kids identify a behavior they use to cover up feelings, choose the cup from the ones already on the table, or use their fifth cup to make a new one, and place this cup on the top of their stack)*

How does your feelings defense help you? *(Keeps you from feeling difficult feelings; keeps you from having to tell everyone you see what you are feeling)*

Do they ever hurt you? *(If we never lower our defenses, we will never understand our own feelings. People will misunderstand our actions—like Mary and Andy—and we won't get help and support when we need it)*

Defenses can help us take care of ourselves when we are facing difficult feelings. But we need to let go of them sometimes. We do that by *talking with people we trust*—safe people who can help us. This is called *lowering our defenses* and we all need places we can do this.

End your session by giving each child a copy of "Safe People in My Life" list (page 228). Help the kids fill them out. Remember, these will vary: Dad may be a safe person for one child in your group, but an unsafe person for another. Help kids see that they can find safe places to share their feelings and talk about what's real! If they need help, read some of the following examples and have kids evaluate which side of their sheets to write it on: Mom, Dad, other family members, schoolmates, a teacher, the principal, a school counselor, friends, neighbors, Sunday school teacher, and Confident Kids coaches.

Prayer Time

Use the kids' Joshua 1:9 posters as a focus for your prayer time. What issues did the kids list? Are there any that you need to explore further with them? *Emphasize the meaning of the verse, and encourage kids to take it seriously.* Pray that God will help each child in your small group feel His protecting presence when they are faced with frightening circumstances this week.

Bible Focus (20 Minutes)

Regathering

As in weeks past, have one facilitator lead a game, song, or activity.

"Fabulous Freddy, the Famous Feelings Finder Flatfoot, Learns More From David"

Present the skit as you have in weeks past. This week's script is on pages 224–226.

Memory Verse

This is the last week you will use Joshua 1:9. Review it together at this time, then offer a small prize to anyone who can say it from memory.

Closing Prayer Huddle

Close the meeting as in weeks past.

Snack (5 Minutes)

Distribute the snack the child brought. Before the kids leave, choose another child to take the snack tin home for next week.

Characters

- Mary, Jane, and Cindy

Needed

- A clown prop of some kind, such as a mask, wig, or nose

Skit 1: The Clown

Mary and Jane enter. Mary is wearing the clown prop and talking a mile a minute about nothing in particular. Jane is walking beside her, looking sad.

Jane Mary, would you be quiet long enough for me to tell you something? I've been trying to get a word in edgewise for the last hour! *(Freezes)*

Mary *(Steps away from Jane, removes clown prop, and addresses kids)* I noticed she was upset about something right away. I'm afraid of what she is going to say. It might be bad news, or worse yet, she might be mad at me! I don't want to hear anything bad, so I'm going to keep everything funny! *(Puts prop on again and returns to Jane)*

I just want to tell you one more thing! Did you hear that Mike Becker brought his frog to school yesterday and it got loose in the cafeteria? Mrs. Brooks—

Jane Mary, be quiet! Everyone knows about that stupid frog! I'm trying to tell you something important!

Mary OK, OK! What's more important than Mike Becker's frog?

Jane My dad told us last night that we have to move to Texas. He's got a different job and he starts next month. *(Freezes)*

Mary *(Steps toward kids and removes clown prop; looks anguished)* Oh, I knew it was something bad, I just knew it! Jane is my best friend in the whole world, and I don't think I can live without her! How could this happen? This hurts too much for me to face! *(Puts prop back on and returns to Jane)*

Hey, Texas! You'll look great in a cowboy hat! Are you going to have your own horse?

Jane *(Looks shocked)* How can you be so cheerful? I thought you were my best friend! Don't you understand? We aren't going to be together anymore!

Mary	I heard! But I think Mike Becker's frog was more exciting! Did you hear it even got in the soup? Everyone—
Jane	I thought you were my friend, but I guess I was wrong! You don't even care that I'm moving away, or that we won't be together, or that I feel hurt! All you ever do is make dumb jokes and laugh! I hate you! *(Runs out)*
Mary	*(Stares after her, then slowly removes clown prop)* I blew it again. I feel awful! Now my best friend is not only moving away, but she hates me, too. I feel like I want to die! What am I going to do?
Cindy	*(Enters)* Hi, Mary! What's new?
Mary	*(Puts clown prop back on and responds cheerfully)* Nothing much! Say, did you hear that Mike Becker brought his frog to school yesterday?
Cindy	Yeah! I was in the cafeteria when it got loose!

They exit, talking about the frog.

Characters

- Andy and three other kids

Needed

- Backpack or books
- A ball

Skit 2: The Bully

Andy is walking to school, slowly and sadly. He is wearing a backpack or carrying books.

Andy Another boring day at school. I hate school.

Two kids enter and walk past Andy very quickly, laughing and talking. They bump into him, ignore him, and exit.

Andy Hey! What's the big idea, bumping into me? You did that on purpose! *(Shakes his fist and yells after them)* Just you wait until recess! I'll get even with you for that! *(Sighs and looks sad again)* Look at them. They're best friends. It must be great to have a friend. I wouldn't know; I don't have any friends. I try to make friends but no one likes me for very long. *(Looks tough)* But I don't care! I'm the toughest kid in my class and everyone is afraid of me! I can have anything I want. All I have to do is take it! Watch.

Three kids enter with a ball. They are playing catch and laughing. Andy runs up to them, pushes them around, and takes the ball.

Kid #1 Hey, Andy, you bully! Give that back!

Andy *(Looks over his shoulder and growls)* Whose gonna make me? You?

Kids all look scared and exit, saying "No way, man!" Not me!" "I'm out of here!"

Andy *(Looks sad again)* See what I mean? Now I have a new ball—and three more kids who are scared of me. My mom says I'm just like my dad. He's real tough! One time he punched a neighbor and gave him a bloody nose, all because the guy said I'd beat up his kid. My dad said, "If your kid can't defend himself, that's his problem. I teach my boy to take care of himself!" Then the neighbor said, "I teach my son that violence doesn't solve anything!" That's when my dad punched him, and then said, "Oh, yeah? Well I think it just solved this problem." And he slammed the door in his face. Then he said to me, "The kid's a wimp. He's not worth your time." Then he winked at me. Cool, huh?

Two kids see Andy and call out, "Bully, bully! Bet you can't catch us!" They laugh and run offstage.

Andy *(Sighs)* I should catch them and teach them a lesson! But I don't care. Who are they, anyway? Dumb kids. All the kids in this school are dumb.

Three kids enter and sit down in a tight circle. They are whispering quietly.

Andy Look at those kids. They are always together. I don't really need any friends, but if I did, I'd like to be friends with them. They share secrets and play games and go places. But, who needs that? They're wimps and I'm tough! Tough is more important! *(Pauses and looks at the kids for a moment. They keep on talking quietly)* Well, maybe just this once I'll see if I can join them. *(He walks up to the circle and clears his throat. The kids look up at him, surprised.)*

Kid 2 Andy!

Kid 3 What do you want?

Andy I—I just wanted to join you for a while.

Kids No way! Leave us alone, OK? *(They get up and leave)*

Andy *(Talks tough)* Who needs them anyway? Just wait until recess! I'll show them! My dad is right! You gotta be tough and take care of yourself in this world! *(Exits)*

From

- Psalm 142 (*ICB*, modified) and 1 Samuel 21–24)

Characters

- Fabulous Freddy (a detective), King David, and young David

Needed

- Detective outfit and a Bible for Freddy
- A royal biblical costume for King David
- A biblical costume for young David
- A little container of mud

Suggested

- A recording of the theme from "Mission Impossible" or other appropriate music

Fabulous Freddy, the Famous Feelings Finder Flatfoot, Learns More From David

The stage is empty; the music recording starts to play. Freddy enters, sneakily, with his coat collar turned up, his hat low on his forehead, wearing his sunglasses, and carrying a Bible.

Freddy *(Sees the kids and addresses them)* Hey, good to see you all again! This caper is coming along just grand! My boss was really pleased with this "Book of Pa-salms" I showed him last week! I've been reading some of this stuff *(Flips through the pages; stops on Psalm 142)* and, you know, that David guy was right! There's every feeling you can imagine in here! Listen to this: I cry out to the Lord. I pour out my problems to him and tell him my troubles. When I am afraid, you, Lord, know the way out. Look around me and see. No one cares about me. I have no place of safety. No one cares if I live or die.

King David *(Enters)* Ah, that was one of my favorites!

Freddy Your favorites? Sounds to me like you were feeling pretty awful!

King David Well, I was running away. When I wrote that, I was hiding in a cave, fully aware that if the people chasing me ever caught me, I'd be dead!

Freddy Who was chasing you?

King David This was in the time before I was king. The first king—the man I replaced—was the one chasing me. His name was Saul.

Freddy But why did he want to kill *you*?

King David Because I had already been chosen by God to be the next king, and Saul knew it. We actually started out as friends, but Saul became jealous and afraid of me and tried to kill me several times! Finally, I had to run for my life! Talk about feelings! I can't begin to tell you how I felt! "It's not fair!" "How can this be happening to me?" "What's going to happen to me? Is Saul going to find me and kill me?" I felt all those things, and much more!

Freddy Where did you go?

King David Now that's an interesting story! I finally ended up in a place called Gath. Gath had its own king, and I went straight to him.

Young David *(Runs in, out of breath. Gets down on his knees and speaks as if talking to the King of Gath.)* Please, sir! I am a fugitive from Israel. There are men there who want to kill me, and I come to you seeking protection. May I stay here? I promise not to cause you or your people any trouble! *(Pauses)* Oh, thank you! May God be good to you for your kindness! *(Exits)*

King David Of course, I didn't tell him who I was! If he knew I was a *future* king, running for my life from the *present* king who was trying to kill me—well, he would not have wanted to be put in the middle of that!

For awhile, everything was fine, and I started to feel safe again. Until the king's servants found out who I really was. Before I knew it, they went to King Achish and told him I was David, future king of Israel! I got scared again. I had to escape, but I didn't know how. So, I thought of a plan. Now that I think about it, I guess you could say that I used a defense. Here's what I did.

Young David *(Enters, with his costume messed up, and holding his headpiece in his hand. He brings a little mud, too. He is obviously scared, and looking around for someone.)* I hope this works! *(Spreads a little mud on his face; looks up)* Uh-oh! Here comes King Achish and his guard! *(He puts his headpiece on so it covers half his face. Then he starts acting as if he is insane—drooling, laughing, staggering, falling down, yelling things like, "Where is everyone? I'm all alone!" etc. After a few moments, he falls down and looks up as if someone is talking to him.)* What? Who am I? I have no name! *(Cries)* My mother left me before I was born and gave me no name! I'm nameless! I'm nobody! *(Gets up, as if the guards were pulling him to throw him out of the city)* Hey, what are you doing? Where will I go? Is my mother out there? Mother! Where are you? *(Exits)*

Freddy Wow! You did all that?

King David Yes! I acted as if I were crazy so the king wouldn't be afraid of me, and the guards would throw me out of the city. Then I ran as quickly as I could until I found a cave. I hid in there and wrote that Psalm you were reading a few moments ago.

Freddy But you said this was one of your favorites! Sounds frightening—and lonely—to me!

King David True, but when I read those words, I remember that even in that dark, terrible time, God heard my prayer! He took care of me through all the time King Saul tried so hard to find me and kill me! As bad as I felt at times, God never stopped taking care of me! And when I read those words, *that's* what I remember!

Freddy *(Looks at the Bible, still open to Psalm 142)* You see all that in there? *(Looks confused)*

King David Yes, I do! Well, Freddy, I must be going. Hope this helps! *(Exits)*

Freddy Helps? I'm blown away! *(Theme music comes back on; Freddy pulls his collar up, pushes his hat down, and dons his sunglasses)* What can possibly happen *next* week? Let's meet back here and find out! See you then! *(Exits, as music plays)*

Joshua 1:9

Have I not commanded you?
Be strong and courageous.
Do not be terrified; do not
be discouraged, for the Lord
your God will be with you
wherever you go.

(NIV)

Safe People in My Life

Safe People	Unsafe People

Goals

- Emphasize our need to express our feelings
- Practice healthy ways of expressing feelings and help kids identify their personal preferences
- Begin assembling a Feelings Box
- Write a Psalm with the help of Freddy and David

Needed

- Group rules poster
- Props for opening skit
- A pillow, a telephone, a notebook and pen, a pair of running shoes or a tennis racket, drawing paper and markers or paints, a box of tissues, stationery with envelopes, and a large red heart (one set per facilitator)
- "Feelings Prayer Journal" (one per child)
- "My Feelings" feelings box inventory (one copy per child)
- *Optional:* Medium-size boxes and as many of the items (or pictures of the items) listed on the "My Feelings" inventory as you would like to provide
- Prayer journals
- Items for regathering, if any
- Props for Bible Story skit
- "Confident Kids Psalm 1" (one copy per every two kids)
- "Confident Kids Psalm 1" reproduced on a poster or overhead transparency
- Philippians 4:6 poster

Express Those Feelings!

Preteen Session 4 Outline

Opening (25 Minutes)

Knots

Group Rules

"The Feelings Stuffer"

Small Groups (40 Minutes)

Discussion of Session Theme

Feelings Prayer Journals and Feelings Boxes

Prayer Time

Bible Focus (20 Minutes)

Regathering

"Fabulous Freddy, the Famous Feelings Finder Flatfoot, Learns How to Write a Psalm to the Lord"

Memory Verse

Closing Prayer Huddle

Snack (5 Minutes)

The snack can be served during the Bible Focus regathering.

Express Those Feelings!

Preteen Session 4

Opening (25 Minutes)

Knots

As soon as five or more children arrive, begin this activity. Ask kids to bunch up, standing as close together as possible. Have them put their arms straight up over their heads, reach across the "bunch," and take hands. The idea is to take hands randomly, so as to form a human knot. When all hands have connected, tell the group that their task is to untangle themselves. The only rule is that they may not let go of the hands they are holding. Allow the group to accomplish the task without your help. When the kids are done, or after the rest of the kids arrive, start again with everyone participating.

Group Rules

Review the group rules again, if necessary.

"The Feelings Stuffer"

Present the skit without introduction (script is on pages 234 and 235).

Small Groups (40 Minutes)

Discussion of Session Theme

Use the following questions to discuss the session theme, "I can express my feelings in healthy ways."

> **What do you think it means to "stuff your feelings?"** *(Keeping your feelings to yourself)*
>
> **What happened to the Stuffer in the skit to make her stuff her feelings?** *(Her dad was drunk when she brought her friends home)*

What happened to her when she stuffed her feelings? *(She got sick)*

What was the result? *(Her feelings finally erupted)*

Have you ever felt like you were going to explode if you didn't tell someone when you were happy or upset? *(Share examples)*

What things cause you to want to stuff your feelings? *(Let kids respond)*

Everyone has the same feelings. When something good happens, we feel ___. *(Let the kids supply the answer: happy, excited)* When we are with someone who takes care of us or is kind to us, we feel ___. *(Love, grateful)* When we do something wrong, we feel ___. *(Guilty, sorry)* When we lose something or someone we love, we feel ___. *(Grief)* But even though we may all have the same feelings, we don't all express them in the same ways. For instance, when I feel happy, I ___. *(Finish this by telling the group what you do when you feel happy. Then ask kids to share different ways they express happiness. Repeat, using different feelings, like sad, angry, etc.)*

I can express my feelings in healthy ways

Some feelings are easy to express, and some are very hard. Some feelings we don't like to feel, so we try to hide them or pretend we aren't feeling them. ***But all our feelings need to be expressed, even the difficult ones. Ignoring our feelings does not make them go away.*** Instead, it just stuffs them down inside of us where they will struggle to get out. The harder we try to ignore them, the harder they will struggle. Eventually they will come out, but probably in very unhealthy ways. For example, holding our feelings inside can give us headaches and stomachaches. Or, they can work like a volcano. When we finally can't hold them in any more, they explode and we end up doing or saying things we don't really mean. But we can avoid all that by remembering that all our feelings need to be expressed, and by learning healthy ways to express them.

Ask kids to think of some unhealthy ways of expressing feelings. In the discussion, guide the kids to the following two rules about expressing feelings:

It is unhealthy to express our feelings by hurting another person or property. **Throwing or breaking things, and hitting or saying hurtful things to someone else are never OK!**

It is unhealthy to express our feelings by hurting ourselves. **Using alcohol or drugs, getting physically sick, and thinking about suicide are never good ways to handle feelings!**

Let's talk about *healthy ways* to express our feelings!

Pass out the following items to the kids. Distribute them equally around the circle: a pillow, a box of tissues, a telephone, a pair of running shoes (or a tennis racket), a notebook and pen, drawing supplies, stationery with envelopes, and a large red heart.

Ask the kids to look at their object(s) and decide how each one can help them express their feelings in positive ways.

***Pillow*—Hit it when you are angry; cry into it when you are sad.**

***Telephone*—Call someone you trust and talk about your feelings.**

Notebook and pen—Journal your feelings; write a poem.

Stationery with envelopes—Write a letter about your feelings and give it to someone you trust.

Drawing supplies—Drawing or scribbling helps get your feelings out.

Box of tissues—Sometimes you just need to cry!

Running shoes—Doing something physical helps get your feelings out.

Large red heart—Talk to someone you love about your feelings. Ask for a hug.

Read the following scenario:

Your parents have just told you they are getting a divorce.

Then go around the circle and ask each child to answer the following questions:

How would you feel in this situation?

How would you use the object you are holding to handle your feelings in a healthy way?

Now have the kids pass one of their items to the person on their right. Then read the following scenario and repeat the process:

Someone makes fun of you in front of the other kids at school

For the remainder of the scenarios, place all objects in the middle of the group. Have kids choose an object that they would personally use to express their feelings in that situation. Use these scenarios:

Your dad promises to take you on a camping trip (or something you really wanted to do) and then cancels.

You bring home a bad report card and your parents yell at you.

Your dog gets run over by a car.

Your best friend wants to go to the school fair with someone else from your class instead of you.

Add situations *your* kids struggle with.

Feelings Prayer Journals and Boxes

Before the session, prepare a "Feelings Prayer Journal" (pages 239 and 240) for each child. Photocopy one cover and three inside pages for each journal. Distribute the pages to the kids so they can assemble the pages into a booklet. Let kids personalize the covers as you explain how they can use the journals to express their feelings to God. Point out Philippians 4:6, 7, verses that teach us that expressing our feelings to God in prayer can bring us God's peace. *Note:* If you have used prayer journaling in the past, share with the kids what it meant to you.

Next, distribute copies of the "My Feelings" box inventory (page 241). *Optional:* Provide a box for the kids to take home and use as a feelings box. Place one or more of the items (or pictures of items) from the "Inventory Sheet" in the box.

It is important to have options when you need to express your feelings. If you keep this box (or paper) in your room, you can pull it out and use the items in it when you are having trouble expressing your feelings. This box (or paper) can remind you of all the healthy ways open to you. Remember:

Never express your feelings by hurting another person or property, or by hurting yourself!

Prayer Time

Use your group's prayer journal to review past prayer requests. How many have been answered? Use the prayer journals kids just made as the focus of today's prayer session.

Bible Focus (20 Minutes)

Regathering

As in weeks past, have one facilitator provide a game, song, or activity.

"Fabulous Freddy, the Famous Feelings Finder Flatfoot, Learns How to Write a Psalm to the Lord"

Present the skit (script is on pages 236 and 237). *Optional:* When the kids have completed their Psalms, collect them to copy and make into booklets. Distribute these to the kids next week.

Memory Verse

Review Philippians 4:6, 7 (it's also in the kids' "Feelings Prayer Journal") by displaying a poster of it and having the kids read it together:

> **Do not be anxious about anything, but in everything, present your requests to God. And the peace of God will guard your hearts and minds in Christ Jesus.**
> **Philippians 4:6, 7 (*NIV*, condensed)**

Closing Prayer Huddle

Close the meetings as in weeks past.

Snack (5 Minutes)

Distribute the snack the child brought. Before the kids leave, choose another child to take the snack tin home for next week.

Characters

- Stuffer, Joy, and Anger

The Feelings Stuffer

Stuffer enters with Anger and Joy on each side.

Stuffer	Hi! I want you to meet my friends. This is Anger *(Puts arm around Anger)* and this is Joy. *(Puts arm around Joy)* Say "hello" to the kids!
Anger	*(Growls)* Hi.
Joy	*(Brightly)* Hello! I'm so happy to be here! I've been looking forward to this all week! I feel so happy when I get to do stuff like this—
Stuffer	OK, OK! *(To kids)* Joy would bubble on forever, if I let her! Anger, on the other hand, doesn't say much at first. But when he lets go, he really blows up!
Anger	*(Looks at Stuffer)* What are you talking about? I don't blow up! *(Increasingly agitated)* Are you trying to make me look bad in front of all these kids? I could get really upset if you were trying to make me look bad—
Stuffer	See what I mean? Well, as you can see, my two friends are very different. But they are both important to me! They help me express my feelings to others. For instance, when something good happens, Joy comes out and helps me share my good feelings with my friends.
Joy	*(Bubbly)* Yeah, like the time that really cute boy *(Or girl)* sat next to you at lunch and you got all fluttery inside and you weren't going to tell anyone. But I came out and made you tell your mom and your brother and call Sally. *(To kids)* Sally is her *(Or his)* best friend. We had fun!
Stuffer	*(Glaring at Joy)* I am thoroughly embarrassed! You don't have to tell my personal stuff in public! Honestly! But you are right. It's more fun to be happy with the people I love most than to keep it all to myself. But then there are other times when things happen that make me mad and Anger comes out to help me get those feelings out.

Anger *(To kids)* If it weren't for me, she *(Or he)* would never get mad about anything! Everyone needs to get good and angry once in a while!

Stuffer That's true! But sometimes things happen and I don't want anyone else to know how I'm feeling. In fact, sometimes I don't want to feel my own feelings! *(Pushes Anger and Joy behind her [or him], and keeps pushing them down to the floor)* So, I stuff them way down inside of me so I won't have to feel them! *(Takes a few steps toward the kids to get further away from Joy and Anger)* Once they are out of sight, I figure I'll stop feeling anything at all!

Anger and Joy begin yelling from where they are: "Hey, quit squishing me!" "Why are you afraid to let me out?" "You can't do this to me!" "Are you crazy?" "Let me out!" etc. Start out softly and as Stuffer continues talking, build in intensity.

Stuffer *(Ignores the voices; speaks loudly enough to be heard over them)* Like the time my dad came home drunk when I had some friends over. I felt so scared and embarrassed. I wanted to die! But I pretended nothing was wrong and talked to my friends as if I wasn't feeling anything! *(Looks over shoulder and yells)* Be quiet! I don't want to feel anything right now so go to sleep! *(Voices quiet for a moment, and then continue with increased intensity. Stuffer is now beginning to look irritated and upset and begins to hold her [or his] head and stomach. Anger and Joy start rising and very slowly move forward. The more active they become, the more sick the Stuffer becomes.)*

Stuffer Unfortunately, stuffing my feelings out of sight doesn't get rid of them! It just makes me feel sick because my feelings are trying so hard to get out! The day my friends were over, I felt so sick one of them asked me if everything was OK. I said, "Sure," even though it was a lie! *(At that, Anger growls loudly)* Well, I finally learned that stuffing my feelings doesn't get rid of them! After a while—

Anger and Joy burst forth, and begin chastising the Stuffer: "Why do you do that?" "You know you get sick when you keep us locked up!" "We're going to get out anyway, so knock it off, OK?"

Stuffer None of you ever do anything like stuffing your feelings, do you?

They exit.

Characters

- Freddy and King David

Needed

- Detective outfit and a Bible for Freddy
- A royal biblical costume for King David
- One copy for every two kids of "Confident Kids Psalm 1" (page 238) plus one copied onto an overhead transparency or enlarged onto poster board

Suggested

- Theme music

Fabulous Freddy, the Famous Feelings Finder Flatfoot, Learns How to Write a Psalm to the Lord

The stage is empty; the music recording starts to play. Freddy is out of sight and does not enter on cue. David enters, carrying the poster (or transparency and overhead projector) and a "Feelings Prayer Journal." He looks around for Freddy.

David *(Searching for Freddy)* Now where is that young fellow? Have you seen him? *(Kids respond)* I do hope he turns up; I have something very exciting to show him.

Freddy *(Runs in, out of breath, with his coat, hat, and sunglasses all askew, as if he has been roughed up by someone)* Oh, my! Am I glad to see all of you! *(Pants; sits down to catch his breath)* Spying on bad guys can get pretty dangerous! Those guys back there were going to tear me apart, piece by— *(Notices David is carrying something; stands to look at it)* Hey, what have you got there?

David Oh, I'm so excited to show you this! Ah, but are you sure you're all right? You look sort of, well, messed up!

Freddy Occupational hazard. *(Takes poster from David)* What is this?

David *(Flips through the prayer journal)* When I saw this "Feelings Prayer Journal," I got an idea! I thought maybe you would like to write a psalm, like the ones I wrote in my book.

Freddy Wow! That would be great! How do I do it?

David *(Hangs the poster board or projects the transparency)* It's easy. All we have to do is follow the directions and fill in the blanks.

David helps Freddy write a psalm, using the poster/transparency.

David Look at what you have, Freddy. This is an expression of your feelings to the Lord. You can pray this psalm to the Lord, or you can make up a little tune and sing it to Him. Why don't you have the kids say your psalm with you?

Freddy leads the kids in reading the psalm together.

Freddy I'm enjoying this so much, I wish all the kids could do it, too.

David I'm glad you brought that up, because I just happen to be prepared for that. Here, give me some help.

Freddy and David divide the kids into pairs and give each pair a copy of the Psalm 1 sheet. Give the teams a few minutes to write a psalm, then ask for volunteers to come forward and read their psalms.

Freddy We just learned how to write a real psalm! *(Gets an idea)* I know what I'll do! I'll make a book of our Confident Kids psalms for all of us! Let me collect all our sheets and I'll bring back the finished books next week. *(He collects the sheets as David makes his final statements)*

David You know, Fred, I've enjoyed being with you these weeks, but it is time for me to move on. There are so many more people in the Bible who could help you with your mission. I wouldn't want you to think my book is the only place in the Bible where you can find feelings.

Freddy *(Looks disappointed)* But, how will I find them without you? I—

David Just be here next week as usual. I'll send someone new to help you. There are many who would love to talk with you! But for me, my time is done. I must move on. And remember to use your "Feelings Prayer Journal" to help you express your feelings to God, and you'll be fine! (*Show journal*) Good-bye, my friends! *(Exits)*

Freddy *(Sadly)* I'll miss him. *(Gets excited; theme music comes back on; he pulls his collar up, hat down, and dons his sunglasses)* But I wonder who he'll send to us next week? I'll meet you back here next week, same time, and we'll find out! I'm outta here! *(Exits)*

Confident Kids

Psalm 1

1: Address God and tell Him how you feel about Him.

Oh God, You are my

and I

2: Tell God how you are feeling today and why (what happened to make you feel that way).

Today I feel

because

3: Tell God what you wish about what you wrote in #2.

I wish

4: Ask God for what you want Him to do about it (what you wrote in #2).

Oh Lord, please

5: Tell God you trust Him to take care of you.

Thank you that no matter what happens, You will never stop taking care of me. I know You will never hurt me or let anything completely destroy me.

6: Repeat exactly what you wrote in #1.

Oh God, You are my

and I

You!

Do not be anxious about anything, but in everything, present your requests to God. And the peace of God will guard your hearts and minds in Christ Jesus.

Philippians 4:6, 7 (NIV, condensed)

Feelings Prayer Journal

Date: ____________

Today I feel: ____________

Mad
Scared
Excited
Guilty
Afraid
Proud
Lonely
Loved
Surprised
Stupid
Confused
Disappointed
Hateful
Powerful
Content
Left Out
Included
Forgiven
Smart

Draw how you feel

I feel this way because: ____________

I expressed my feeling by: ____________

Dear God,

Right now I feel ____________

I wish that ____________

Please help me to ____________

Thank You for ____________

What else do you want to say to God? ____________

Amen!

Date: ____________

Today I feel: ____________

Mad
Scared
Excited
Guilty
Afraid
Proud
Lonely
Loved
Surprised
Stupid
Confused
Disappointed
Hateful
Powerful
Content
Left Out
Included
Forgiven
Smart

Draw how you feel

I feel this way because: ____________

I expressed my feeling by: ____________

Dear God,

Right now I feel ____________

I wish that ____________

Please help me to ____________

Thank You for ____________

What else do you want to say to God? ____________

Amen!

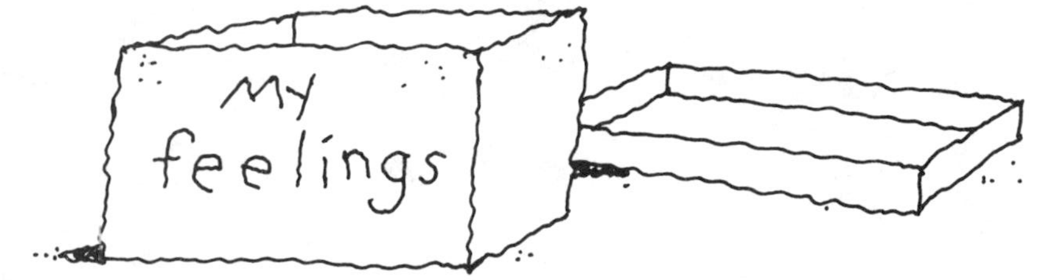

Collect as many of the following items as possible and put them into a box. Keep the box in a convenient place so you can use it whenever you are having trouble expressing your feelings. Choose an item or two that will help you get your feelings out in a healthy way!

Pillow: Hit it when you are angry; cry into it when you are sad

Telephone: Call someone you trust and talk about your feelings

Notebook and pen: Journal your feelings; write a poem

Stationery with envelopes: Write a letter about your feelings and give it to someone you trust

Drawing supplies: Drawing or scribbling helps get your feelings out

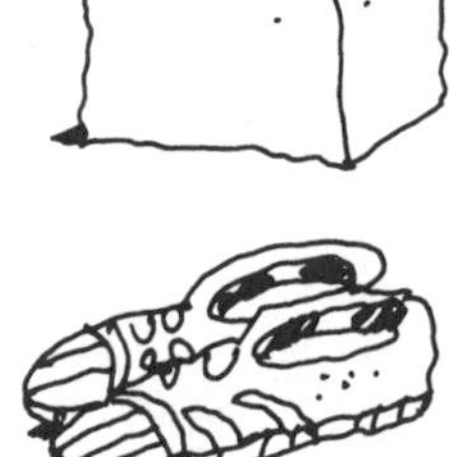

Box of tissues: Sometimes you just need to cry!

Running shoes: Doing something physical helps get your feelings out

Large red heart: Talk to someone you love about your feelings. Ask for a hug.

Goals

- Name feelings that are difficult to handle
- Identify circumstances that generate difficult feelings
- Learn and practice a three-step process to resolve difficult feelings
- Learn about difficult feelings when Freddy meets Peter

Needed

- Items for gathering activity (facilitators' choice)
- Group rules poster
- Copies of "The Losers' Club" activity
- Poster board (one prepared for each small group)
- "I Didn't Do It!" and "Instant Replay" cartoons (one copy per small group)
- "Advice Chair Situations" (one copy per small group)
- Prayer journals
- Ephesians 4:26, 27 poster
- Items for regathering, if any
- Items for Bible skit

Some Feelings Are Difficult to Handle

Preteen Session 5 Outline

Opening (25 Minutes)

Facilitators' Choice

Group Rules

"The Losers' Club"

Small Groups (40 Minutes)

Discussion of Session Theme

The Advice Chair

Prayer Time

Bible Focus (20 Minutes)

Regathering

"Fabulous Freddy, the Famous Feelings Finder Flatfoot, Meets Peter"

Memory Verse

Closing Prayer Huddle

Snack (5 Minutes)

The snack can be served during the Bible Focus regathering.

Some Feelings Are Difficult to Handle

Preteen Session 5

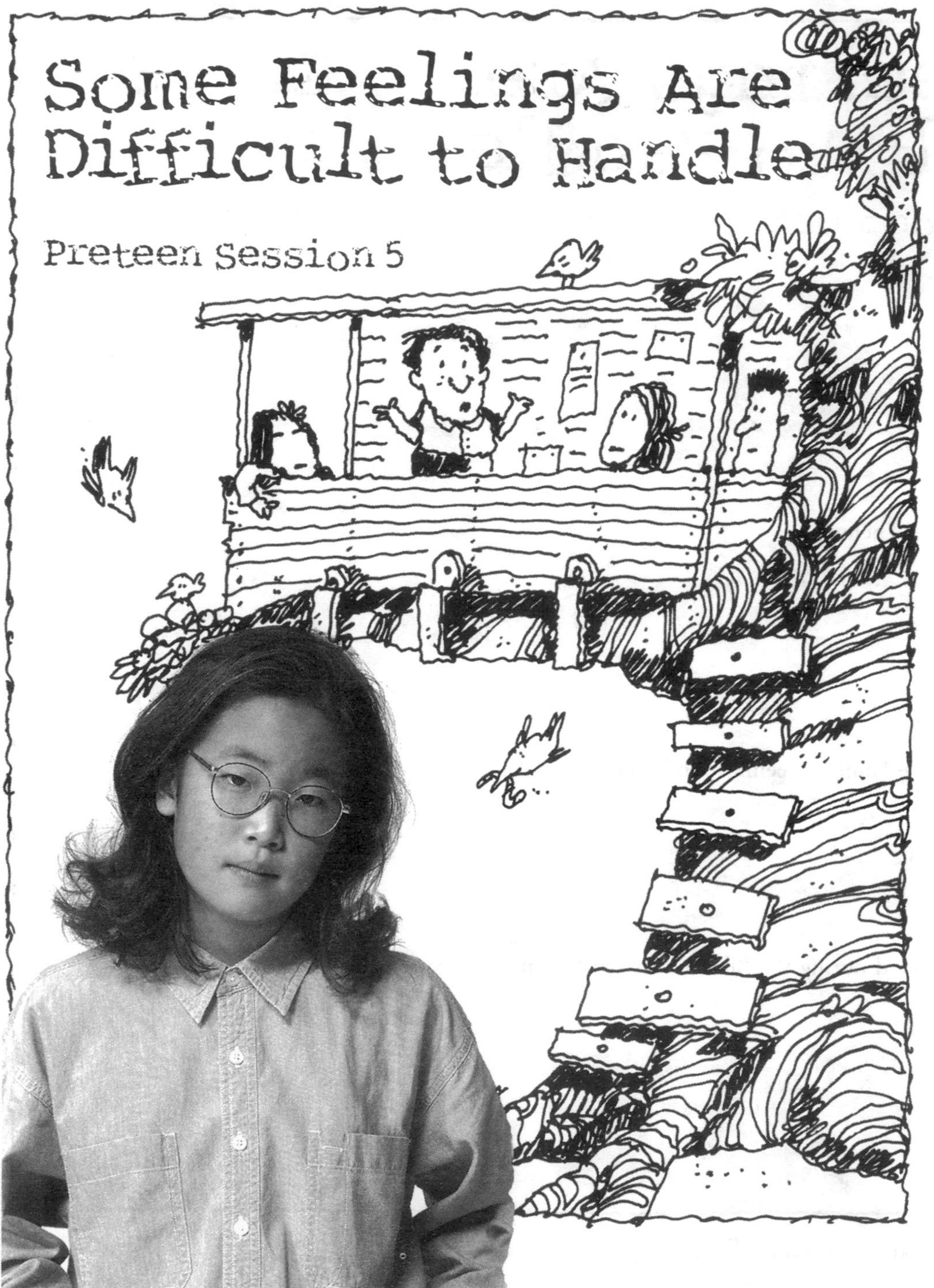

Opening (25 Minutes)

Facilitators' Choice

Choose a gathering activity that the kids have enjoyed, or involve the kids in a game or craft you know they will enjoy. *Note:* Choose kids to present the skit for this session and give them time to practice during this time (the script is on pages 248–250).

Group Rules

Using the group rules poster, remind everyone of the rules and the consequences for breaking them.

"The Losers' Club"

Have those presenting the skit do so now.

Small Groups (40 Minutes)

Discussion of Session Theme

Use the following questions to discuss the session theme, "Who's in control here—me or my feelings?"

> **What feelings did the characters in the skit experience?** *(Anger, fear, self-blame, hurt)*
>
> **What happened to bring those feelings about?** *(Review the story line)*
>
> **What did each character do, or plan to do, to handle his or her feelings?** *(Ernie gave into his anger; Jack blamed himself for being stupid and withdrew from everyone; Lucia wanted to avoid it by running away)*

Which character represents how you deal with your feelings when you are upset? *(Let kids respond)* **If none, how *do* you handle difficult feelings?** *(Let kids respond)*

Many feelings in life are not fun to feel, and we don't like to feel them. What are some of them? *(Brainstorm a list of these with the kids)* **Like most things in life that we don't like, we usually try to get rid of those feelings in whatever way we can. But when we react to difficult feelings like Ernie, Jack, and Lucia did, we only make matters worse. *We let our feelings control us; we do not control our feelings.* We need to learn to handle our difficult feelings in ways that will help us, and not hurt us, so we can be in control of our feelings!**

Display a poster board on which you have lettered *I'm in Control of My Feelings!* across the top, and *Step #1*, *Step #2*, and *Step #3* down the side.

We are in control of our feelings when we follow these three steps: *(Add each step and its corresponding question to the poster board as you talk about it)*

Step 1: Name the Feeling—Many times we react to feelings in unhealthy ways, like hiding from them or pretending we aren't feeling them, because we don't really know what we are feeling. Until we name the feeling, we can't go on to figure out what to do about it. We need to answer the question: "What am I feeling?"

Step 2: Stop and Think—When we do things like blow up when we are angry, or shut down when we are sad, or blame ourselves if we feel hurt, we are not thinking clearly. We're letting our feelings take control of us. We stop and think about our feelings when we answer this question: "What is really going on here?"

Step 3: Work It Out—When we let our feelings control us, we usually don't make very good choices. But if we know what we are feeling, and stop and think about what's really going on, then we can make a healthy choice about what to do next. Answer this question: "What is the best thing to do right now?"

You might need to do something by yourself to get your feelings out (use your feelings box to help you), or you might need to apologize to someone or make a compromise, or you might need to get to work and get something done—like study for your next math test instead of feeling stupid that you got a bad grade.

Following these steps when you have feelings you don't like will not be easy at first. But as you practice and get better at it, you will take control of your feelings. They won't take control of you!

Who's in control here—me or my feelings?

As a way to illustrate how the three steps work, show the "I Didn't Do It!" cartoon (page 255) to the kids and read it to them. Ask:

Who is in control: the boy or his feelings? *(He is letting his feelings control him)*

Then show them the "Instant Replay" (page 256) and ask the same question. Read the three steps. Be sure the kids understand how using the three steps made a big difference in the outcome of the situation.

The Advice Chair

Have the kids sit in a circle with a chair in the middle (or mark an *X* on the floor if you are not using chairs) and make sure all of them can see the three-step poster. Tell the kids that they are about to become wise counselors to some kids who are having trouble handling one of our most difficult feelings: anger.

As each child tells his story, have the rest of the group use the three steps as guidelines to help the child deal with the situation. They can do this by asking questions or giving wise advice. You function as the guidance counselor so that you can direct the interactions. Use the comments below to help direct the kids, and keep the activity on track.

Give one of the "Advice Chair Situations" (page 257) to a volunteer, who then takes a seat in the middle of the circle and reads the situation to the group. Using the three steps as a resource, give the group a few minutes to interact. Encourage all to participate, including the child in the middle who can answer questions and add information (role play) to keep the discussion going. End each scenario by having the child in the middle choose a course of action.

Here are some guidelines:

Ernie

This is the character from the skit. Ernie wants to know what to do when his dad insults his mom. Here are some possible things for Ernie to think about:

> **Step 1—Be sure Ernie understands that he is feeling hurt more than angry. He is also feeling protective of his mom.**
>
> **Step 2—Ask Ernie: "What is going on with your dad?" Ernie needs to see that his dad is feeling hurt and angry, too. Seeing his dad's side of the divorce may help him to control his anger.**
>
> **Step 3—Ask Ernie to think of several solutions to this situation such as: asking his dad not to criticize his mom, telling his dad in a conversation or in a letter how criticism of his mom makes him feel, walking away when the subject comes up, etc.**

Jackie

Jackie's problem is that her mom makes her responsible for her younger sister. Some ideas for Jackie are:

> **Step 1—Jackie is feeling angry, but she is also feeling jealous and violated.**
>
> **Step 2—Ask Jackie: "Whom are you really mad at?" If Jackie stops and thinks, she can see that the problem is with her mom, not her little sister. Also ask: "How do you think your sister feels?" Help Jackie see that her sister is unhappy and maybe even scared. None of this is her little sister's fault.**
>
> **Step 3—Offer Jackie suggestions about how to let her mom know what she is really feeling. Also, help her discover ways she could have treated her sister in the park: Was there a playground nearby where she could have played? Could she have been given a small part in the soccer game (chasing balls)?**

Kenny

Kenny's problem is that kids tease him and he has no friends. Some ideas for Kenny are:

> **Step 1—Kenny is angry, but he's also feeling rejected and hurt.**
>
> **Step 2—Kenny needs to see that his own behavior is keeping him separate from the other kids. Ask Kenny: "What would happen if you didn't respond when the kids tease you?" If Kenny can stop and think, he may see that as long as the kids get the response they want, nothing will change.**

Step 3—Help Kenny think of things he can do instead of responding to the teasing with anger and name-calling. Encourage him to keep talking to his teacher and ask her to help him find other ways to act toward the kids. He could also talk to his mom about getting involved in activities where he can find a new group of friends.

Prayer Time

Talk about dealing with anger in your prayer time, using Ephesians 4:26, 27:

> **"In your anger do not sin": Do not let the sun go down while you are still angry, and do not give the devil a foothold. (*NIV*)**

Briefly discuss what actions constitute sinning when we are angry. *(Destructive actions such as hitting, kicking, verbal attacks, breaking things, or lying about another person to get even. Also, self-destructive actions such as withdrawing, refusing to do homework, etc.)* Now ask the kids if they have any prayer requests regarding anger. Perhaps there are times they let their own anger control them or someone in their lives is taking out their anger on them (e.g., parents, older siblings, teachers who are physically or verbally hurting them).

Bible Focus (20 Minutes)

Regathering

As in weeks past, have one facilitator provide a game, song, or activity.

"Fabulous Freddy, the Famous Feelings Finder Flatfoot, Meets Peter"

Present the skit (script is on pages 251–254).

Memory Verse

Reinforce this session's teaching on anger by involving the kids in a "Popcorn Bible Verse." See Appendix B, "Resources," for directions.

Closing Prayer Huddle

Close your meeting as in weeks past.

Snack (5 Minutes)

Distribute the snack the child brought. Before the kids leave, choose another child to take the snack tin home for next week.

Characters

- Ernie, Lucia, Jack, and Kim

Needed

- Two chairs and perhaps a floor pillow, a couple of cans of soda, a few books etc., scattered around to look like a clubhouse

The Losers' Club

Ernie is pacing back and forth; he is angry and scared. Lucia is sitting with her head in her hands; she is sad and scared. Jack is reading a book, not paying attention to the others. Kim is offstage.

Kim *(Approaches the "door" and "knocks")* Knock–knock! Hello in there!

Ernie Say the secret password!

Kim Come on, Ernie, open up!

Ernie Say it!

Kim *(Rolls eyes)* OK! "Abra-cadabra is the word; if you don't know it, we'll change you into a nerd!" Now let me in!

Ernie *(Opens the "door"; Kim walks "in")* It's about time you got here.

Kim That is the *stupidest* password we've ever had!

Lucia *(Insulted)* Hey, next month *you* can write a better one, *OK*?

Ernie Oh, who cares what the dumb password is? I call this meeting of the Mighty Rocketeers to order, OK?

Lucia So why did you call this meeting, Ernie? We aren't supposed to meet until tomorrow.

Ernie *(Starts pacing again)* I—I couldn't wait that long. I'm sort of in some trouble.

Jack *(Finally puts his book down and joins the others; speaks sarcastically)* So what else is new, O fearless leader?

Kim Knock it off, Jack. Ernie looks pretty upset. What happened?

Ernie I got into another fight with my dad. This was the worst one yet. We were yelling and screaming until I was sure the neighbors were gonna call the cops. He started raggin' on my mom again, and I just couldn't take it!

Lucia	Wow! What happened?
Ernie	I finally ran out of the house—you know what my dad is like when he gets mad! I came here and called this meeting. What am I gonna do? I'm supposed to stay with my dad for two weeks, but I want to go home now. My mom will worry if I ask to go home early, and my dad will kill me if I go back there!
Jack	When are you gonna learn to control your temper, Ernie? You're always in trouble for getting mad at someone! I don't think I feel sorry for you one bit!
Kim	Lighten up, will you, Jack? What would *you* have done if your dad was raggin' on *your* mom?
Jack	Who cares? I got other stuff to worry about.
Lucia	Yeah? Like what?
Jack	Like I got another F on the math test yesterday, that's what. When my parents find out, I'm grounded for a month! *I'm so stupid*! I can't believe it!
Lucia	You're not stupid!
Jack	Oh no? What do you call it?
Lucia	You just don't understand it, that's all! When are you going to go and talk to Mr. Garcia about it?
Jack	*(Sighs, turns his back to the others, and goes back to his book)* Never. The problem here is that I'm too *stupid* to learn math. I'm dumb, dumb, dumb!
Ernie	*(Gets angry)* Hey, wait a minute! I called this meeting to talk about *my* problem! Jack's being stupid is not the issue here!
Kim	Knock it off, Mr. Hothead! Jack is not stupid! *(Pauses)* So Ernie, what do you want from us?
Lucia	*(Starts to cry)* Who cares about your dumb problem, Ernie!
Kim	*(Sighs)* You, too, Lucia? What's going on with you?

Lucia	I'm just so upset, I don't know what to do. My mom's going into the hospital tomorrow for some kind of surgery. She's going to die, I just know it! I'm so scared! I just want to run away from home!
Ernie	*(Sarcastically)* Oh that's a great response! That'll make everything better again!
Kim	Wait a minute, you guys. Will you look at us? This is supposed to be the Mighty Rocketeers Club! Looks more like the Losers' Club to me!

All exit.

Characters

- Freddy, Peter, and Jesus

Needed

- Detective outfit and a Bible for Freddy
- A biblical costume for Peter
- A white robe for Jesus

Suggested

- Theme music
- A long wig for Jesus

Fabulous Freddy, the Famous Feelings Finder Flatfoot, Meets Peter

The stage is empty; the theme music begins. Freddy enters carrying his Bible. He starts searching for someone.

Freddy Oh, hi everyone! Have you seen him yet? I don't see anyone. I sure hope King David didn't screw up and forget—

Peter *(Enters, in a hurry)* I hope this is the right place! *(Sees Freddy)* You there! Are you Freddy, the Famous Foot—uh—something or other?

Freddy Yes, sir! I'm Fabulous Freddy, the Famous Feelings Finder Flatfoot. Who are you?

Peter Oh, thank goodness! I went to the wrong place and I was afraid I'd miss you by the time I figured out what happened! My name is Peter. *(Shakes Freddy's hand)* I see you have a Bible. You'll find me in the second half of that book, the New Testament.

Freddy *(Starts looking through the Bible)* Really? Where?

Peter In the first five books: Matthew, Mark, Luke, John, and Acts. Oh, never mind. *(Takes the Bible away)* Let's just talk. So, you're looking for feelings in the Bible?

Freddy Yes, sir. Are there any in those books you just mentioned?

Peter *(Laughs)* Of course! "Those books," as you call them, are the greatest books ever written! They tell about Jesus, God's own Son, who came to earth to show us what God is like. He died on the cross so we could be God's children.

Freddy *(Looks confused)* Wait a minute, sir. You'll have to run that by me again!

Peter	Just call me Peter, OK? Those first five books of the New Testament tell about how Jesus was born, grew up, and spent three years traveling around telling the people about God and how they could know Him and healing people who were sick. Finally, He was put to death on a cross. But—and here's the best part—He didn't stay dead! In three days He came back to life, stayed with us and taught us for awhile, and then went back to Heaven to be with God again. That's when all the fun really began!
Freddy	Wow! Sounds like lots of feelings were going on during all that! But how do you fit in?
Peter	Well, I'm here because I was one of Jesus' twelve closest friends, or disciples as we were known in those days. And King David chose me to talk to you because I was the most impetuous!
Freddy	Impet—imp—what?
Peter	You know—noodle-brained, impulsive. I expressed my feelings regularly and most of the time without thinking first!
Freddy	Sounds like you're just the man I need to talk to! Give me an example of a time you were impet—imp—acted without thinking.
Peter	Oh, my. There are so many! But one of my favorite memories is the time all twelve of us were in a fishing boat out on the Sea of Galilee, but Jesus wasn't with us. He had gone off by himself for awhile and sent us on without Him. Well, in the middle of the night, a terrible, terrible wind came up! *(Peter starts acting out this story; he sways back and forth as if on a ship in a storm)* It was one of the worst I'd ever seen! We were all terrified! We thought we were going to drown for sure!
Freddy	What did you do?
Peter	We all handled our fear in different ways. Some of us started yelling, "Where are you now, Jesus? Now that we need You, You're not here! Why don't You save us?" Others were so scared they just huddled in the bottom of the boat, wanting it to be over. And then, we saw *Him*.
Freddy	*(Excited)* Whom? Whom did you see?

Peter	*(Stares off into the distance, toward the back of the room)* It was the most unbelievable thing. At first we thought we were seeing a ghost!
Freddy	A ghost? A real ghost?

Jesus enters quietly from the back and walks very slowly toward Peter. He stops behind the kids.

Peter	No, it was Jesus. But, He was *walking on top of the water*! We all started screaming different things: "It's Jesus!" "No, it's a ghost—He's dead!" "We're hallucinating, or maybe *we're* dead!" And then, over the sound of the wind and the waves, we heard—
Jesus	Don't be afraid! It's really me!
Freddy	Was it an hallucination?
Peter	Oh, no! It was Jesus all right!
Freddy	How do you know?
Peter	Because I called out, *(He yells this out and takes two small steps toward Jesus)* "Lord, if it's really You, let me walk to You on the water!"
Jesus	Come on, Peter!
Peter	*(Walks slowly toward Jesus)* So I did! I stepped out of the boat, without even thinking! I looked straight at Him and walked on top of the water! Until—
Freddy	Until what? What happened?
Peter	*(Stands halfway between Freddy and Jesus)* Until all of a sudden I realized how *stupid* this was! I had acted without thinking about what I was doing! I looked down at the waves and at my feet on top of the water and suddenly I began to sink! *(Falls to the floor)* "Lord," I cried out, "help me. I'm going to drown!" *(Reaches out toward Jesus)*
Jesus	*(Walks to Peter, takes his hand, and pulls him up)* Oh, Peter. Why do you doubt? All you have to do is trust me, and I'll take care of you! *(He turns and leaves the room. Peter goes back to the front)*
Peter	And then He climbed in the boat with us, and the storm stopped.

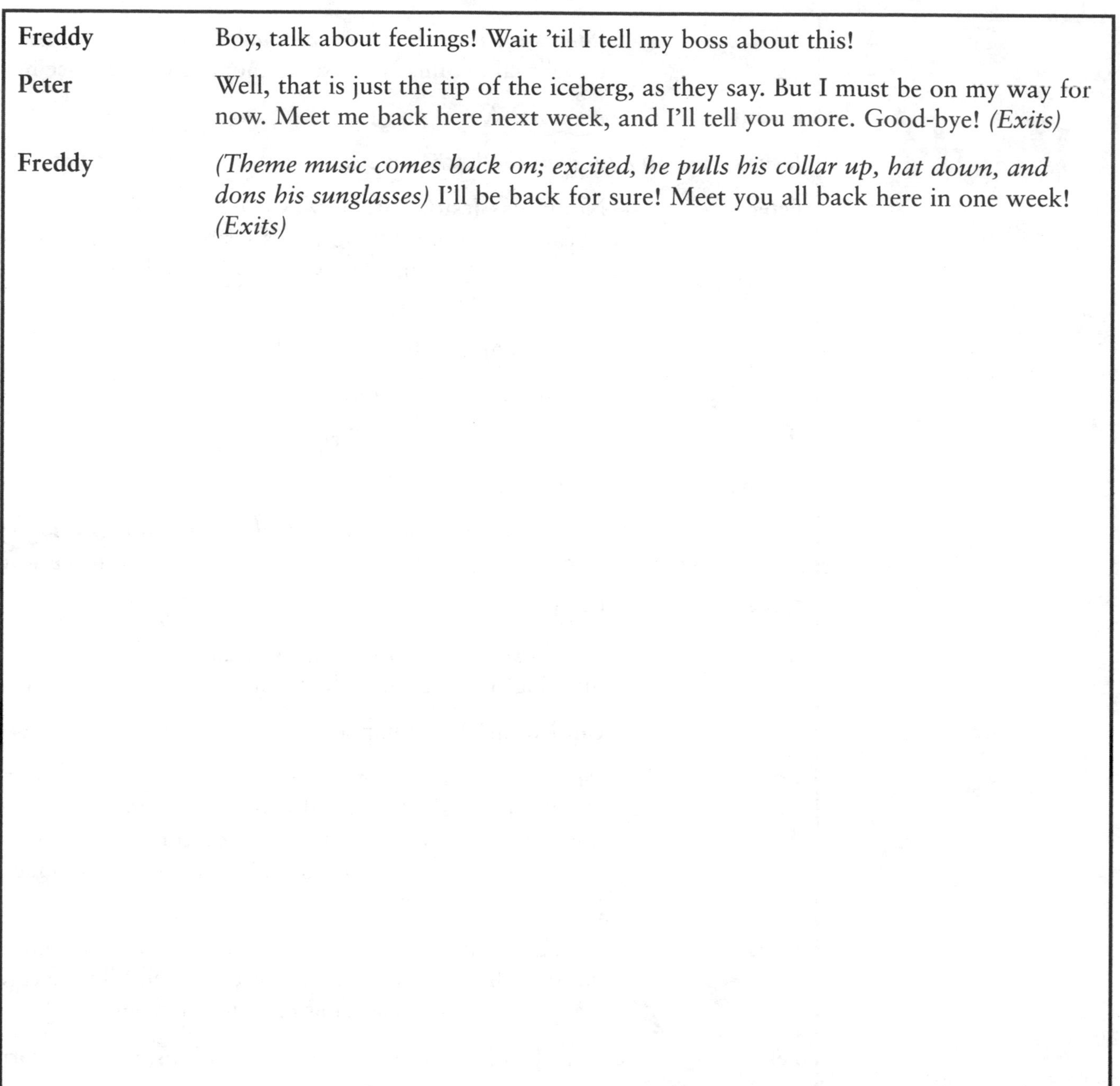

Freddy Boy, talk about feelings! Wait 'til I tell my boss about this!

Peter Well, that is just the tip of the iceberg, as they say. But I must be on my way for now. Meet me back here next week, and I'll tell you more. Good-bye! *(Exits)*

Freddy *(Theme music comes back on; excited, he pulls his collar up, hat down, and dons his sunglasses)* I'll be back for sure! Meet you all back here in one week! *(Exits)*

I Didn't Do It!

Joseph, I understand you were fighting again.
I wasn't!
One more time and I'll send you to the principal's office!
But I wasn't fighting!
It's all your fault! You told Mr. Brown on me!
I did not! Don't go blaming me if you get in trouble!
Did too! You're not my friend, idiot!
You don't need my help to get into trouble, jerk-face!

Instant Replay

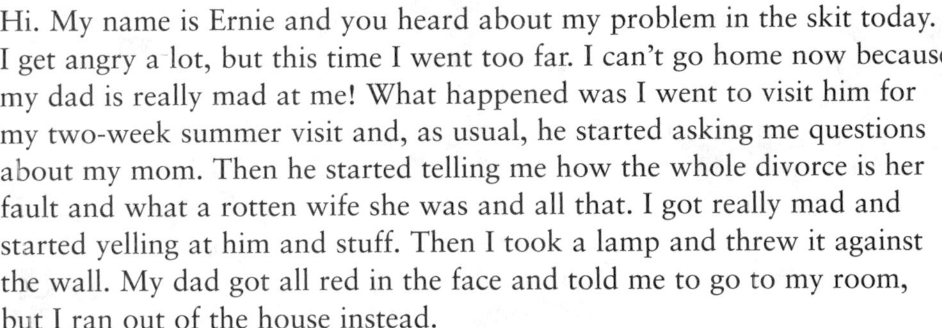

#1: Ernie

Hi. My name is Ernie and you heard about my problem in the skit today. I get angry a lot, but this time I went too far. I can't go home now because my dad is really mad at me! What happened was I went to visit him for my two-week summer visit and, as usual, he started asking me questions about my mom. Then he started telling me how the whole divorce is her fault and what a rotten wife she was and all that. I got really mad and started yelling at him and stuff. Then I took a lamp and threw it against the wall. My dad got all red in the face and told me to go to my room, but I ran out of the house instead.

So, my question to you all is: What should I do when my dad acts like that and what can I do about going home now?

#2: Jackie

Hi. My name is Jackie. My problem is about how angry I get at my six-year-old sister sometimes. Well, to be honest, almost all the time. She's not so bad really, but it seems like she gets all the attention in our house. "Isn't Jana cute?" "Let Jana watch what she wants on TV because she's younger than you." But what I hate most is that my mom is always making me take care of her. Like yesterday. I was leaving the house to go to the park with my friends and my mom called, "Just a minute, Jackie! I want you to take Jana to the park with you. I'm going out for a while!" I screamed and yelled about it; we were going to ride our bikes and meet some other kids to play soccer. Well, I got really mad that my mom would spoil our plans, so I was really mean to my sister. I yelled at her to get her stupid bike and I made sure she was in the back of the line all the time. I made her sit on the grass and watch us and "shut-up." I wanted to show my mom what a terrible thing she had done to me! Jana started to cry, and I felt kind of bad, but I didn't stop.

So, my question is: How can I handle my anger toward my sister?

#3: Kenny

Hi. My name is Kenny. My problem is the kids tease me all the time and I don't have any friends. I'm not sure why the kids tease me, but my teacher said it's because I "set myself up." That means when the kids tease me, I get mad and start a fight or call them names, which makes them want to tease me more. But it hurts when they make fun of me! I tell everyone I don't care, but the truth is, I'm lonely and I wish I had a friend to be with.

So, my question is: What should I do when the kids tease me, and how can I make friends with them?

Goals

- Identify the barriers that keep kids from asking for help
- Identify the signs that it's time to ask for help
- Learn how to ask and practice asking for help
- Make personal directories of people the kids can turn to for help

Needed

- Letter cards for gathering activity
- Group rules poster
- Copies of "The Reporter" script
- A reporter's hat, a small notebook and pen, and a fake microphone (one per facilitator)
- *Optional:* A real video camera and player
- Copies of "Asking for Help" cards, copied onto card stock, and envelopes or resealable sandwich bags
- Prayer journals
- Items for regathering, if any
- Items for Bible skit
- Philippians 4:6, 7 verse

Asking for Help

Preteen Session 6 Outline

Opening (25 Minutes)

Unit Slogan Game

Group Rules

"The Reporter"

Small Groups (40 Minutes)

Discussion of Session Theme

"Asking for Help" Cards

Prayer Time

Bible Focus (20 Minutes)

Regathering

"Fabulous Freddy, the Famous Feelings Finder Flatfoot, Learns More From Peter"

Memory Verse

Closing Prayer Huddle

Snack (5 Minutes)

The snack can be served during the Bible Focus regathering.

Asking for Help

Preteen Session 6

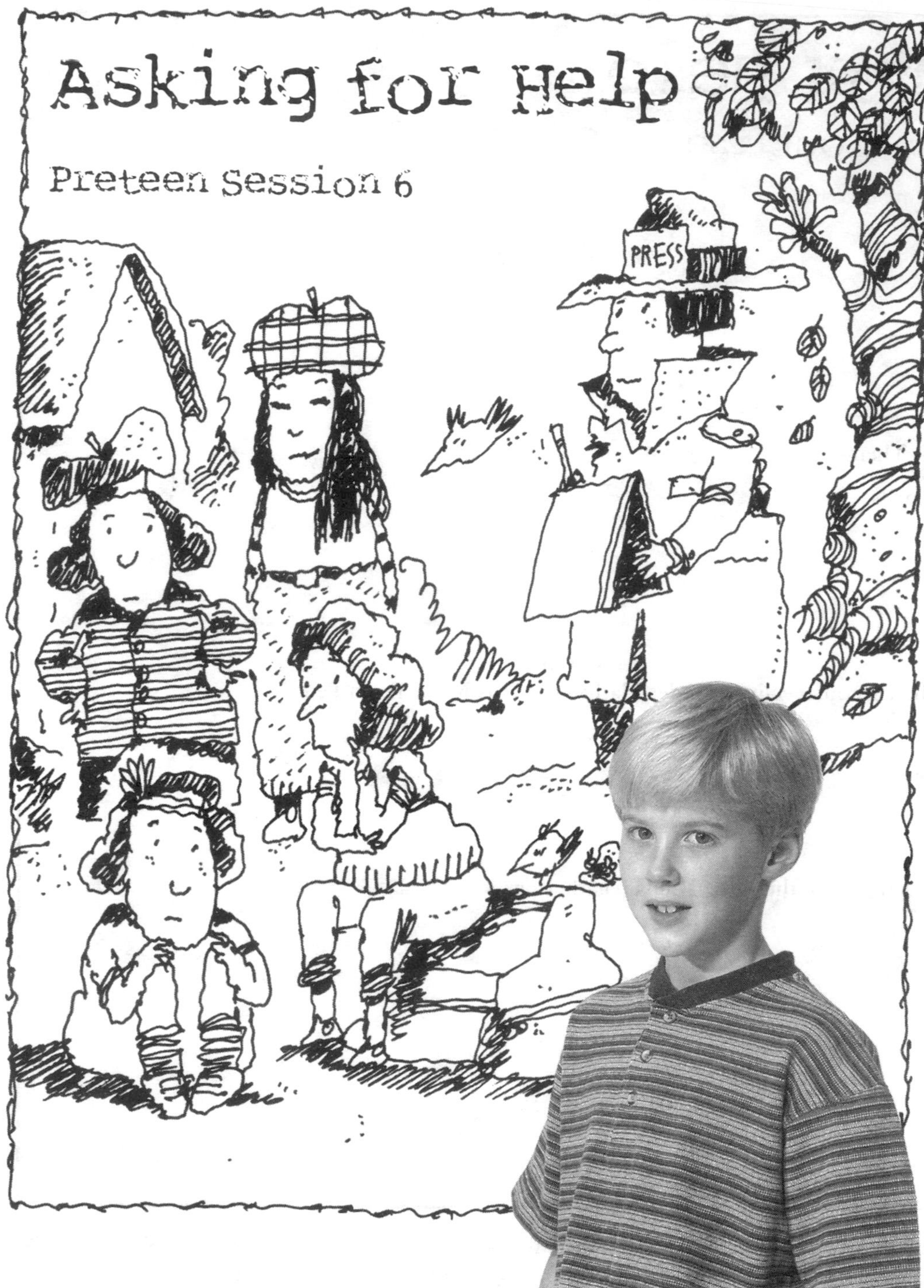

Opening (25 Minutes)

Unit Slogan Game

This game is played like "Wheel of Fortune," or hangman. In advance, prepare a set of cards (approximately 6" x 6") that will spell out the phrase, "All My Feelings Are OK." Place only one letter on each card. Pin these to a bulletin board, or tape them to the wall in order, with the letters facing the wall so that they cannot be seen. To play, divide the kids into two teams. Have the teams take turns guessing a letter. If the letter is in the phrase, turn the card(s) over so it can be read. Continue alternating between teams until one is ready to guess the phrase. If the team is correct, award points. To play additional rounds, have cards ready with other phrases, such as song titles or slogans the kids will know, and display them in the same manner. *Optional:* You can simply print dashes on a blackboard or piece of large paper instead of making cards. Play as long as time permits.

Note: Choose kids to present the skit for this session and give them time to practice during this time (script is on pages 263–265).

Group Rules

Review the group rules, if necessary.

"The Reporter"

Have those presenting the skit do so now.

Small Groups (40 Minutes)

Discussion of Session Theme

Use the following questions to discuss the session theme, "It's OK to ask for help!"

Do you think it is hard to ask for help? *(Let kids respond)* **Why or why not?** *(Let kids respond)*

What help did each of the skit characters need? *(Review story)*

What reasons did each one give for not asking for help? *(Review story)*

Put on the reporter's costume (hat and fake microphone) and assume the role of a reporter. Use the microphone as if you were recording all of the following, including your own comments. *Optional:* Record this segment on video. The kids love to see themselves on TV, and may take their answers more seriously!

Hello out there in TV land! This is _____, *(Facilitator's name)* **reporting to you live from Confident Kids here in beautiful _____.** *(Insert name of a "feelings city," such as "Lonelyville" or "Anger Park")* **Today we are trying to learn more about *how and when to ask for help*. Let's see what we can find out from this fine looking group of kids here with me today.**

Continue with the role play by interviewing each of the kids, using the following questions. To help with the flow, include your own personal comments about asking for help, and refer back to your "experience" in Lonelyville (e.g., "When I was in Lonelyville, I met a person who didn't think anyone had time for her problems. What do you think about that?") You may want to use these questions:

Tell us about a time this past week when you asked for help. *(Let kids respond)*

Tell us about a time you needed help, but didn't ask for it. Why didn't you ask? *(Let kids respond)*

How do you know when you need help? *(We need help when we are confused, scared, worried so much we can't sleep, etc.)*

Who do you know who can give you help when you need it? *(Parents, teachers, coaches, relatives, neighbors, police, etc. Get kids to give names)*

Whom would you never ask for help? *(Gang members, drug dealers, etc. in general; kids can give specific answers from their own experience)*

What do you think is the hardest part about asking for help? *(Embarrassment, knowing whom to ask, etc.)*

End the role play with appropriate "reporter" comments:

That's all the time we have for today; this is _____, *(Facilitator's name)* **live with Confident Kids. See you next time on "Roving Reporter."**

"Asking for Help" Cards

Copy the "Asking for Help" cards (pages 269 and 270) onto card stock. Distribute the copies to the kids, and have them fill out the cards. Be specific and encourage them to fill in phone numbers or other contact information when they get home. Then look at the cards together.

Sometimes the hardest part of asking for help is that we don't know exactly what we need! Looking at these cards can help you pinpoint specific things you may need at any given moment. When you know what you need, choose an appropriate person to ask for help. Let's summarize:

1. Realize that you *need* help. (You feel confused, scared, etc.)

It's OK to ask for help!

2. Use the cards to help you pinpoint *what* you need.

3. Find the right person to ask for help.

Finish by cutting the cards apart and placing them in envelopes or resealable sandwich bags to store them.

Prayer Time

Use today's verse, Philippians 4:6, 7, to emphasize that prayer is one of the best sources of help we have. Be sensitive to the fact that some of the kids may have asked God for help many times and felt that He did not answer (e.g., their parents got divorced anyway). Now is a great time to talk about that openly, and encourage kids that God never stops caring for us, even when His answers are not what we may have wanted or expected. Include a personal testimony of how God helped you in direct answer to your prayers.

Bible Focus (20 Minutes)

Regathering

As in weeks past, have one facilitator provide a game, song, or activity.

"Fabulous Freddy, the Famous Feelings Finder Flatfoot, Learns More From Peter"

Present the skit (script is on pages 266–268).

Memory Verse

This week's memory verse is Philippians 4:6, 7:

> **Do not be anxious about anything, but in everything present your requests to God. And the peace of God will guard your hearts and minds in Christ Jesus.** (*NIV*, condensed)

Write the verse on large sheets of paper, placing two or three words on each sheet. Distribute the sheets to the kids, asking them to arrange themselves so the verse can be read. Have everyone read the verse. Then choose two kids to turn their sheets over, so the words cannot be seen. Have kids read the verse again, filling in the missing words. Choose two more kids to turn their sheets over, and repeat. Continue until they can say the verse from memory.

Closing Prayer Huddle

Close your meeting as in weeks past.

Snack (5 Minutes)

Distribute the snack the child brought. Before the kids leave, choose another child to take the snack tin home for next week.

Characters:

- The Reporter and four additional kids

Needed

- A hat with a sign that says *Press* and a large notebook and pen for the reporter
- A pair of sunglasses
- A dollar bill
- A backpack

The Reporter

Reporter enters, scratching his head and looking confused.

Reporter Boy, this assignment is weird. I'm in this town called "Lonelyville," and I'm supposed to interview the residents to find out how they ask for help when they need it. Sounds boring to me. Who's going to read this? Oh, well, what the boss wants, the boss gets! Now let's see, how should I do this? Guess I'll just start with the five basic questions—uh, that's—uh—oh, yeah! Who, what, when, where, and how!

Kid 1 *(Enters, wearing sunglasses and looking tough and "cool")* Hey, man! What's with the funny hat? You new around here, or what?

Reporter I'm from the Confident Kids *Daily Press* and I'm doing a story about how the residents of Lonelyville ask for help when they need it.

Kid 1 Ask for help? You nuts or something? Nobody around here asks for help, man! That stuff's for sissies! Look, this world is tough, see? You gotta learn how to take care of yourself, 'cause ain't nobody gonna take care of you but you! I don't need no help from no one! Got it? Good. *(Exits)*

Reporter *(Looks shocked)* Yeah, I got it. Sheesh, what an attitude! I'd better find someone more helpful than him. *(Starts to write in his notebook)*

Kid 2 *(Enters, holding a dollar bill; looks confused, bumps into Reporter who is still writing)* Oh, excuse me. I didn't see you.

Reporter No problem. Since you're here, can I ask you a question? *(Pauses)* Ah, is there a problem with that dollar bill? You're staring at it like it's going to talk to you, or something.

Kid 2 No, I'm just trying to figure out if this is right. I just bought a pack of gum for a quarter. I handed the man a ten-dollar bill, and he gave me this one back. That's right, isn't it?

Reporter	*(Looks shocked)* Are you kidding? You got taken, big time!
Kid 2	Oh dear, I was afraid of that. Well, I never was much good in math. It's so confusing to me. I used to sit way in the back of the room and just try to get through it!
Reporter	Didn't you tell your teachers you needed help? I mean, lots of kids have trouble understanding math at first!
Kid 2	Oh, I could never do anything like that! I'd be too embarrassed! What would the teacher think of me? It's no big deal. Who needs math anyway? *(Exits)*
Reporter	*(Shakes his head) Who needs math?* This from a kid who just lost $8.75 from a crooked gum dealer? This is some town! *(Makes a few notes)* Let's see, who else can I find? Ah, here comes someone! *(Kid 3 enters)* Excuse me, I'm doing a story on asking for help. Can you tell me when you ask for help?
Kid 3	*(Looks worried)* Oh, I don't have time to talk now. I'm on my way to the hospital.
Reporter	I'm sorry! Are you sick, or something?
Kid 3	No, my friend is in there. He has a broken arm and a concussion.
Reporter	Wow, how did that happen?
Kid 3	*(Snaps at him; acts nervous and scared)* Why did you ask me that?
Reporter	Hey, back off! I just wondered, that's all! Are you OK?
Kid 3	I'm sorry! It's just that, well, he told me a secret and made me promise not to tell. I've been a wreck ever since. I just never thought it would end up like this.
Reporter	So the secret has something to do with why he's in the hospital?
Kid 3	*(Sad and scared)* Yes.
Reporter	Look, you are really suffering with this secret, and your friend is in the hospital with serious injuries. Isn't it time for you to get some help?

Kid 3	*(Agitated)* Don't you think I want to? But I can't! I promised! *(Exits)*
Reporter	*(Shakes his head and writes in his notebook)* What a weird town! No wonder it's called Lonelyville! I'll give it one more try. Excuse me!
Kid 4	*(Enters, wearing a backpack, looks depressed)* Me?
Reporter	You see anyone else around here? Yes, you! I'm doing a story about asking for help. Can you tell me how you ask for help when you need it?
Kid 4	Ask for help? What do you mean?
Reporter	You know, like when you have a problem or something is bothering you, how do you ask for help?
Kid 4	Oh. Well, no one cares about my problems, so I guess the answer to your question is, I don't ever ask for help.
Reporter	Not you, too! What's wrong with the people in this town? Look, there must be lots of people who care about you! What about your parents? Your teachers?
Kid 4	Well, maybe they care, but they're all so busy! My parents are tired when they come home from work. My teachers rush around everywhere. My problems aren't important enough to take up anyone's time, so I just keep them to myself. *(Sighs deeply and exits)*
Reporter	*(Throws pen up in the air)* That's it! I've had it! I can't find one person in this town who asks for help! There's no story here! *(Gets an idea)* Wait a minute! Now I know what the boss wanted me to do! I'll write a story about a town called "Lonelyville" where everyone is lonely because no one asks anyone else for help! What a great story! Everyone will want to read this one! *(Exits, excitedly)*

From

- Matthew 26; Mark 14; Luke 22; John 13, 18

Characters

- Freddy, Peter, Judas, a servant, and Jesus

Needed

- A detective outfit and a Bible for Freddy
- A biblical costume for Peter
- A rubber ear (e.g., from a Halloween costume)
- A white robe for Jesus

Suggested

- Theme music
- A long wig for Jesus

Fabulous Freddy, the Famous Feelings Finder Flatfoot, Learns More From Peter

The stage is empty; the theme music begins. Freddy enters carrying his Bible.

Peter *(Enters)* Hello again, my friends! You came back!

Freddy *(Shakes hands with Peter)* Are you kidding? I've been waiting all week for this! *(Holds up his Bible)* I've been reading in those books you told me about—Matthew, Mark, Luke, John, and Acts. You were some kind of character! You were right about being impet—impert—you know, acting without thinking. Did you really cut off a guy's ear?

Peter Ah, you got that far, did you? Sadly, that whole night was the worst night of my life! Talk about feelings!

Freddy Please tell us about it!

Peter It was the night Jesus was arrested, right before He died on the cross. Actually, it was the worst night of His life, too, but we didn't know it. He was so sad at dinner, and He kept trying to tell us that He was going to die, but we wouldn't believe Him. Even when He said, "One of you will betray me tonight," and Judas ran out of the room, we still didn't understand what was happening.

After dinner, Jesus looked almost sick with worry. He wanted to go to this beautiful little garden to pray. *(Paces back and forth, obviously upset)* While we were walking, He said to all of us, "Tonight all of you will run away because of me." That just sounded so silly to me. Run away? Why, I had given my whole life to follow Jesus! Run away? I'd fight to the death for Jesus!

Freddy I remember reading about that! *(Looks through the Bible excitedly)* It's right here! You said, "Even if everyone else runs away from You, I never will!"

Peter	Yes, and then He said something I'll never forget. It's burned in my heart for all eternity!
Freddy	What? What did Jesus say to you?
Peter	He looked straight into my eyes and said, "I tell you the truth, this very night before the rooster crows, you will disown me three times." Talk about feelings! I was devastated! I shouted back at Him—
Freddy	*(Reading from Mark 14:31, NIV)* "Even if I have to *die* with you, I will never disown you!" It's right here! So when did you cut the guy's ear off?
Peter	I'm coming to that. It was just a little later. Jesus had just returned from praying by himself. *(Jesus enters, wearing a white robe)* Suddenly, from out of nowhere, Judas showed up with a whole bunch of people, walked over to Jesus, and kissed Him on the cheek. *(Judas and the servant enter; Judas kisses Jesus on the cheek)*
Freddy	What did all that mean?
Peter	It was a sign to the Roman guards to arrest Jesus! Without thinking, I drew a sword and attacked the man next to me! *(Peter pretends to draw a sword and swings it at the servant. At the same time, the servant drops a rubber ear to the floor, and screams, holding his ear.)*
Jesus	*(Looks at Peter)* Put your sword away, Peter! Anyone who lives violently will die violently! *(He picks up the ear and "heals" the servant)* Don't you think I could ask my Father to send ten thousand angels to rescue me? But then, how could I do what needs to be done? It must happen in this way! *(Jesus, Judas, and the servant exit)*
Peter	And then—*(Pauses; looks down)* we all ran away and left Jesus alone with the guards.
Freddy	And that's when you broke down and cried!
Peter	Oh no, there's more! I was so determined to stand up for Jesus that I snuck back to the city to try to find Him. I went to the place where the crowd was gathered, hoping to hear some news. It was cold outside by then, and I went to a fire to warm myself. That was a big mistake.

Freddy	Why?
Peter	Because in the light, people recognized me. *(Squats down and rubs hands together, as if warming himself by a fire)*
Servant	*(Enters, warms himself opposite Peter for a moment, and then recognizes him. He points at Peter and says loudly)* Hey! I know you! You're one of those guys with Jesus! Hey, look everybody! This is a Jesus-follower!
Peter	Hush up! You're mistaken! I don't know this man!
Freddy	No way! You really said, "I don't know this man?"
Peter	*(Stands)* It's all there in the Bible. Read it for yourself!
Servant	*(Stands, looks intently at Peter)* It is you! You were with Jesus! Hey, everybody! Look over there— *(Runs out)*
Peter	It happened one more time that night—and then—
Freddy	The rooster crowed! Just as Jesus said it would! Wow!
Peter	And *that's* when I went out and cried my heart out! I felt as though I had been shattered into a million pieces, and would never be the same again. But Jesus understood about my feelings! If you come back next week, I'll tell you how everything turned out. But now, I must go. Good-bye, until next week! *(Exits)*
Freddy	*(Theme music comes back on; Freddy pulls his collar up, pushes his hat down, and puts his sunglasses on. He says thoughtfully)* I feel sad! Sure hope there is a happy ending to this story! Guess we'll find out next week. See you all then! *(Exits)*

Who can help me in my family?

Who can help me at school?

Who can help me in my neighborhood?

Who can help me at my church (or anywhere else)?

I'm confused —
I need help to understand.

I'm upset —
I need comforting.

I feel pressured —
I need to say NO!

I'm lonely —
I need friends.

I'm angry—I need to express it in a healthy way.

I'm tired—I need to slow down.

I'm scared because I need to do something hard.

I need:

I need to write a letter to tell someone how I feel.

I need God's help!

I was wrong—I need to apologize.

I'm upset—I need some physical exercise.

Goals

- Explore the feelings Jesus experienced during the final days of His life and discover that we feel the same feelings today
- Learn that Jesus understands everything we experience and feel and can help us
- Give the kids an opportunity to ask Jesus to come into their lives
- End the unit with an affirmation of God's love and forgiveness

Needed

- Invitations for Family Night
- Copies of "Confident Kids Psalm 1" from Elementary Session 4
- One copy of "Daddy Letters," from Elementary Session 7
- Bibles for every child (or at least every other child)
- As many visuals as possible that depict the events of the Easter story
- Paper lunch bags (one per child)
- Copies of "Inside Me" activity
- Copies of "Jesus" activity, copied onto red paper and cut apart (one per child)
- Props for Bible skit
- Joshua 1:9 and Philippians 4:6, 7 prepared as directed
- Copies of "Affirmation Balloons" and unit certificates from Appendix A, pages 377 and 379

Jesus Helps Me with My Feelings

Preteen Session 7 Outline

Opening (25 Minutes)

Family Night Invitations

Practice Confident Kids Psalm 1

Group Rules

"Daddy" Letters

Small Groups (40 Minutes)

Discussion of Session Theme

Jesus Bags

Prayer Time

Bible Focus (20 Minutes)

Regathering

"Fabulous Freddy, the Famous Feelings Finder Flatfoot, Learns About Jesus' Forgiveness"

Memory Verse Review

Closing Prayer Huddle

Snack (5 Minutes)

The snack can be served during the Bible Focus regathering.

Jesus Helps Me With My Feelings

Preteen Session 7

Opening (25 Minutes)

Family Night Invitations

Next week is the final session of this unit, which is a Family Night. Tell the kids that next week you will host a party, and they can invite their parents to come with them. Talk about the party enthusiastically to build a sense of excitement for sharing the group with their parents. Have the kids make invitations (page 279) or use purchased party invitations.

Practice Confident Kids Psalm 1

During Family Night, your kids will be asked to share with their parents the psalm they wrote in Session 4. If you still have the psalm, enlarge it onto a poster or copy it to an overhead transparency so the kids can learn it. If you no longer have it, or simply want to do so, have the kids write a new one at this time. Also, you can prepare it as a choral reading by designating who should say each line: all, boys only, girls only, or a solo. Once you have a finished psalm, practice it for next week's presentation.

Group Rules

Review the rules again, if necessary.

"Daddy" Letters

The "Daddy" letters (pages 166–173) are a collection of letters written by Amy, an eleven-year-old girl, during the months her father was being treated for cancer. She never showed these letters to anyone until after her father recovered. They were Amy's secret journal, her way of handling her feelings through a difficult period of her life. Read them with the kids with expression, highlighting places where she talks about prayer.

Small Groups (40 Minutes)

Discussion of Session Theme

Use the following questions to discuss the session theme, "Jesus understands my most difficult feelings."

Have you ever had anything happen in your life that made you feel like Amy? *(Let kids respond)* **What were some of her feelings?** *(Let kids respond)*

Amy talks about praying for her Daddy. In the first letter she says, "I've been praying that you don't (have cancer), but sometimes that doesn't matter." What do you think she meant by that? *(Let kids respond)*

Do you think Amy ever wondered if God was answering her prayers? *(Let kids respond)*

Have you ever asked God, "Why is this happening to me?" as Amy did? *(Let kids respond)* **Have you ever been angry with God for what was happening in your life?** *(Let kids respond)*

During the hardest times of our lives, it is only natural to think that God does not understand what we are feeling, or that He has stopped taking care of us. As hard as it may be, God asks us to *trust* Him when times are really tough. Let me tell you about a time when I felt God stopped taking care of me. *(Give a short personal testimony of how God has taken you through a time when you found it hard to trust Him)* **Did you know that even Jesus had a hard time getting through the last part of His life? Let's find out how many hard feelings Jesus experienced before He died on the cross.**

Jesus understands my most difficult feelings

Distribute Bibles to kids. Help them look up and read each of the following verses, one at a time. Ask the group to name Jesus' feelings in each verse before moving on to the next one. Also, use any visuals you can find to help the kids get the picture of Jesus' suffering (e.g., teaching pictures, a large nail or spike, a crown of thorns, a whip). The more objects you can gather, the better.

Hebrews 2:18—This verse sets the stage. Because Jesus suffered when He was here on earth, He can now help us when we suffer.

Luke 22:39–44—Jesus prays in the Garden of Gethsemane. His prayer is essentially, "Please God, I am very sad. Must I do this?" He was so upset, He was sweating very hard and God had to send angels to help Him get through it! *(Feelings: fear, anguish, but also trust)*

Matthew 26:47, 55, 56—Jesus is arrested. Give kids a little word picture of what that scene must have looked like. Emphasize the flight of the disciples. *(Feelings: fear, abandonment by closest friends)*

Matthew 26:59–63—Jesus is set up by the chief priests who are looking for false evidence against Him. *(Feelings: accused of things He didn't do, misunderstood)*

Matthew 27:27–31—Jesus is mocked by the soldiers. Talk about the physical suffering Jesus endured, as well as the emotional. *(Feelings: loneliness, physical pain, humiliation)*

Matthew 27:45, 46—Jesus cries out from the cross. *(Feeling: great agony and abandonment by God)*

Matthew 28:1–7—Jesus is resurrected. The story does not end with abandonment. Jesus' unending trust of God wins out. Because of Jesus' experience, we can trust God, too! During times *we* feel abandoned, we can ask Jesus to help us keep trusting and get us through.

Jesus Bags

This activity is designed to do two things. First, it will reinforce the concept that Jesus knows and cares about everything in our lives. Also, it will give you an opportunity to make a salvation presentation. Guide the kids to understand that accepting Jesus as Savior is the beginning point of having God in their lives. Pass out paper lunch bags and the "Inside Me" activity (pages 280 and 281). Proceed as follows:

***Each of us has an inside and an outside life.* Our *outside* lives are that part of us that everyone can see. What might that include?** *(What we look like, what we are good at, what we like or don't like, who our friends are, our families, etc.)* **Our *inside* lives contain all the private things no one knows unless we choose to tell them.** *(Our feelings and reactions to situations; our fears, likes and dislikes we never talk about; our hopes and dreams; etc.)*

***Pretend this lunch bag is you.* It has an outside and an inside. Decorate this bag to make it like you. On the outside, write or draw the things about you that are known to everyone.** *(Family members, activities, favorite color, etc.)* **Now use the "Inside Me" worksheet to write about some things that are part of your inside life. Put these private things inside your bag.**

***Hebrews 2:18 tells us that Jesus knows not only the outside part of your life, but He understands your private inside life as well.* And no matter what is inside your heart, He cares about those things and understands them because He has experienced them, too. That is why we can come to Jesus in prayer about anything in our lives.**

***Jesus wants to live in the inside place of our lives.* I want to give you one more piece to put inside your bags.** *(Pass out one "Jesus" heart—page 282—to everyone)* **The Bible teaches us that if we ask Him to, Jesus will come to live in our inside lives and be there with us forever. And, one day when we die, God will take us to be with Him in Heaven because Jesus is in our inside lives.** *(Place "Jesus" heart inside the bag. Staple the bag shut to symbolize that once Jesus is in our hearts, He will never leave us.)*

***You can invite Jesus into your inside lives right now.* God wants to live inside each of you, but He will only do so if you ask Him. I hope each of you has already made a decision to live for Jesus, but if you have not done so, you can do so right now.**

Optional: If you have pamphlets describing how kids can give their lives to Jesus, distribute them at this time. The children's ministry department of your church might have such a resource. If not, check with your local Christian bookstore for material consistent with your beliefs.

Lead a simple prayer of dedication. To avoid peer pressure, ask kids to pray silently and invite them to tell you what they prayed when the group is dismissed.

Prayer Time

This is your last prayer time for this unit. Review all the answers to prayer you have seen in the past few weeks and encourage kids to keep praying for those concerns not yet answered. Close with a special prayer for each child, asking God to help them know in their hearts that no matter what life is like right now, He never stops loving them.

Bible Focus (20 Minutes)

Regathering

Have one facilitator lead in music or an activity.

"Fabulous Freddy, the Famous Feelings Finder Flatfoot, Learns About Jesus' Forgiveness"

Present the skit (script is on pages 276–278).

Memory Verse Review

Your kids may also present Joshua 1:9 and Philippians 4:6, 7 to their family next week. Prepare for this by saying Joshua 1:9 as a "Memory Verse Wave," and Philippians 4:6, 7 as a "Popcorn Verse." See Appendix B, "Resources."

Closing Prayer Huddle

Close your meeting as in weeks past.

Snack (5 Minutes)

Distribute the snack. Thank all of the children who brought snacks during this unit.

Note

Facilitators will need to take home copies of the "Affirmation Balloons" and the unit certificates from Appendix A (pages 377 and 379). Have them complete one for each child in their small group, so the balloons and certificates can be presented during next week's Family Night program.

From

- Luke 21

Characters

- Freddy, Peter, and Jesus

Needed

- Detective outfit and a Bible for Freddy
- A biblical costume for Peter
- A white robe for Jesus

Suggested

- Theme music
- A long wig for Jesus

Fabulous Freddy, the Famous Feelings Finder Flatfoot, Learns About Jesus' Forgiveness

Theme music begins. Freddy enters carrying his Bible.

Freddy Hi, guys! You know, I felt so bad for Peter last week! Imagine, telling Jesus that you'll stand up for Him forever—even die for Him—and then running away and denying that you even know Him! Three times! No wonder he sobbed his heart out!

Peter *(Enters, staggering a bit)* Am I glad to be here! The trip through the time tunnel was a bit rough this week! So, how was your week?

Freddy Fine. But enough about me! Let's get back to your feelings! Last week you said that Jesus understood all about your feelings. What did you mean by that?

Peter Impatient, aren't we! Now let's see. Where did I leave off?

Freddy You denied Jesus three times and the rooster crowed and you were a sobbing, broken shell of a man. Then what happened?

Peter Ah, yes. Well, the next few days are a blur to me. None of us ever expected Jesus to die! We were so scared, we went into hiding.

Freddy But then Jesus came back from being dead! And that made everything all right, right?

Peter Well, not exactly.

Freddy	But for Jesus to come back from the dead! And you saw Him and touched Him and talked to Him! The only person who ever died and came back to life! You must have been ecstatic!
Peter	There were so many feelings in those days—powerful feelings. But me, well, I was mostly embarrassed and ashamed. I didn't think there was anything I could say or do to make things right. But, Jesus knew what I was feeling and before He went back to Heaven, He did something special to let me know everything was all right.
Freddy	I knew it! I knew Jesus would come through somehow!
Peter	It all started one night when I said to some of the others, "I'm going fishing. Want to come?" We went out and fished all night—but caught *nothing*! Not even a minnow! We were tired and hungry and started back to the shore. As we approached, we heard a voice call to us—
Jesus	*(Calls from the back of the room)* Friends, did you catch any fish?
Peter	*(Calls back)* No, sir! We've fished all night and have nothing!
Jesus	Throw your net on the right side of the boat and you will find some!
Peter	*(To Freddy)* Now, you have to understand. We didn't recognize this man. But we did it anyway and bingo! Almost two hundred of the largest fish I've ever seen!
	It was John who first realized what was happening. He said, "It is the Lord!"
Freddy	I know what you did next. You jumped into the water and swam ashore, ahead of everyone else!
Peter	Yes! *(Run to the back where Jesus is kneeling, pretending to cook fish)* And when I got there, Jesus had a fire made and was cooking fish for our breakfast. After we ate together, I realized why Jesus came to us that morning. It was just for *me*!
Jesus	*(Stands)* Come on, Peter. Let's take a walk. *(They start to walk slowly to the front of the room)* Peter, do you care about me?

Peter	Yes, Lord, You know I care about You!
Jesus	But, Peter, do you really care deeply about me?
Peter	Yes, Lord. I told You. You are more important to me than anyone!
Jesus	But Peter, do you *love* me?
Peter	Lord, why are You asking me this? You are God's Son. You know everything! You know that I love You very much!
Jesus	Then I have a job for you. I want you to care for my people all your life. It won't be easy, but it is what I have planned for you. And remember, I will always be with you through my Spirit. Nothing can ever happen to you that will separate you from me! *(Exits)*
Freddy	So, Jesus came that day, just to talk to you?
Peter	Yes! Don't you see? I had denied Him three times—
Freddy	*(Excited)* Oh, I get it! And He asked you three times if you loved Him! One time for each of the times you denied Him! Cool!
Peter	Jesus knew I needed His forgiveness for what I'd done. And by giving me a job to do, He let me know that He still trusted me. All He wanted from me—all God ever wants from any of us—is our love and trust.
Freddy	You know, Peter, when I started this case I never thought I'd find feelings in the Bible! But you and David have shown us that God knows about us and cares about every single feeling we have! There's not one feeling we need to be afraid of or stuff inside.
Peter	Just give them to God, and no matter what happens, keep trusting! I must leave you now! Good-bye, and God's very best to you! *(Exits)*
Freddy	*(Theme music comes back on; Freddy pulls his collar up, pushes his hat down, and puts his sunglasses on)* Well, I guess that wraps up this case for good. Hey, I'll miss coming here each week to see you all, but my work is done. Go with God, my friends! *(Waves good-bye and exits)*

An Invitation

To

From

Please Come!

To Family Night at Confident Kids

A Ministry of Confident Kids

Date

Time

Just like Jesus, I feel ...

Things I wish for:

Things I fear:

My greatest hope
for the future is:

Jesus
Jesus
Jesus
Jesus

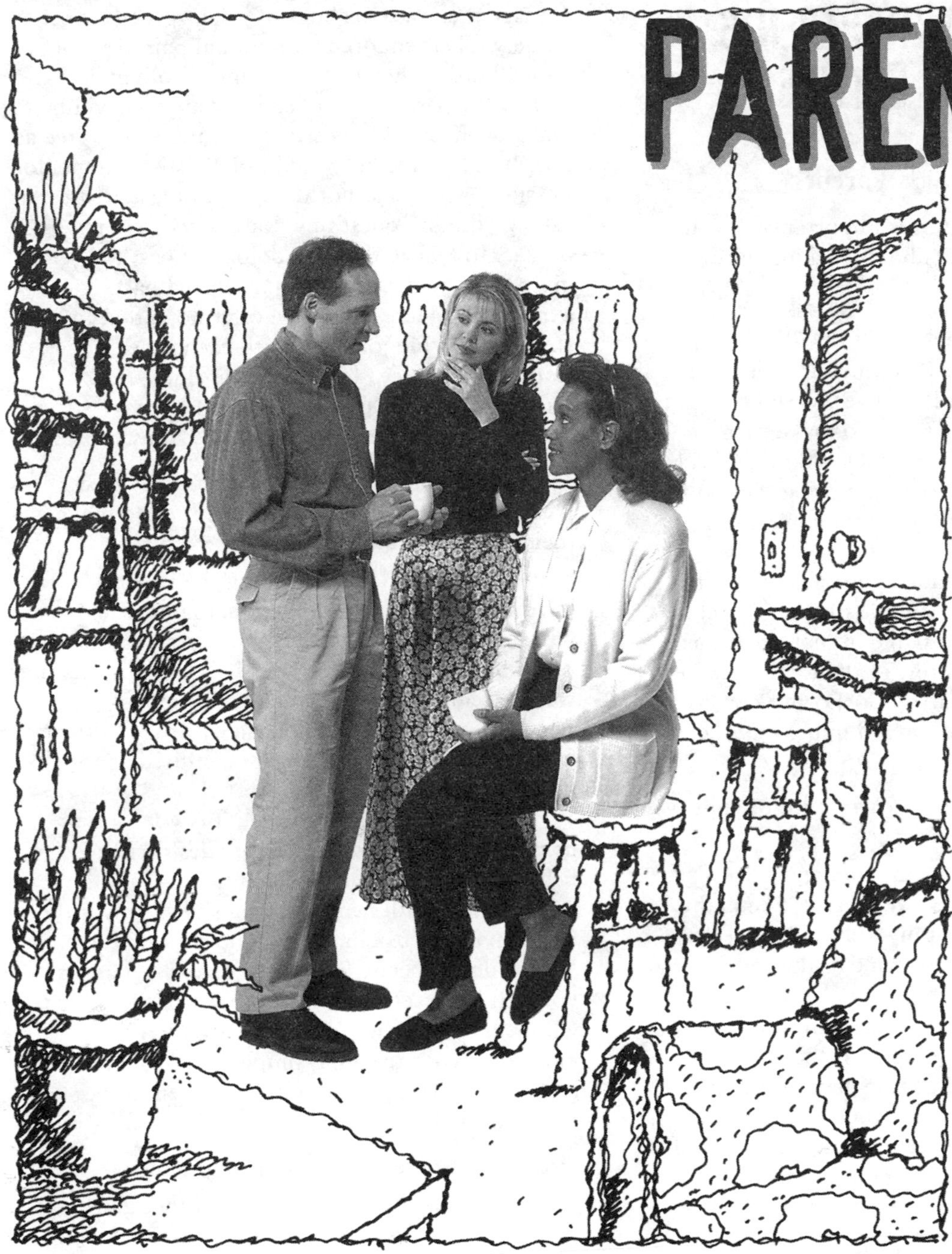

PARENT SESSIONS

TIPS FOR WORKING WITH PARENTS IN A SUPPORT-GROUP SETTING

Understanding Confident Kids Parents

As you begin the parent group, it is important for you to understand a few key points about working with parents of high-stress kids.

- **Stressed-out kids have stressed-out parents.**

  Many of the parents who come to your group will be feeling desperate about their lives, with little idea of where to turn for help or how to make their family a healthier place. They will see Confident Kids as a lifeline, a place where they can bring their kids to get some help in ways they seem unable to provide themselves.

  As the parent group leader, your job will be to reassure parents that there is hope for their families, and that you see them as capable of managing their own stress levels and the stress of their children. Let them know that being a part of Confident Kids was a great step for them to take toward improving the quality of their family life.

- **Confident Kids parents typically carry a lot of guilt and shame about their children.**

  "It's my fault my kids are having these problems," or, "If I were a better parent, we wouldn't be in this mess," or, "I'm terrified that my kids will grow up to be totally screwed up," are some of the statements we've heard in parent groups. Although guilt and shame about their kids is what brings parents to Confident Kids, an even deeper issue is the guilt, shame, and sense of failure parents have about their own lives. Parents who are struggling to manage a painful, unwanted divorce; the financial pressures of being unemployed; or the challenges of raising a child with attention-deficit hyperactivity disorder or other kind of disability have all they can do to manage their *own* feelings of grief, revenge, or anxiety. Their children's emotional pain becomes an added burden they feel ill-equipped to handle.

  As the parent group leader, your task will be to make Confident Kids as stress free and shame free as possible. This means we do not chastise parents for missing sessions, or not doing at-home activities, or asking "dumb" questions. Rather, *we do encourage parents* to realize they are doing the best they can, given their present circumstances and past experiences. Here again, we offer hope that by sharing their life journeys with each other, and learning some new, healthy living skills, their families can make progress toward effective stress management and improved relationships.

- **Most of the parents will have little or no idea of what a healthy family is, let alone how to make their family a healthy place.**

  Many parents today are reaping the results of having grown up in dysfunctional families. Many have no models of effective parenting to guide them. Since the natural response is to parent as they were parented, today's parents are simply reproducing the dysfunction they learned in their families of origin, and they are confused as to why things keep getting messed up.

  As the parent group leader, it is your job to help the parents learn to identify destructive behavior patterns learned in childhood, and how to replace them with healthy living skills. This is the function of the teaching time and the weekly "Reflection" sheets. Remember that the material you will be covering is new to most of the parents who will be coming to your group; therefore, you must keep your teaching simple, cover the basics, and have patience with those who seem to be resistant to change!

- **Stressed-out parents feel isolated and alone.**

  Many times we hear parents say, "I thought I was the only one in the whole world who was having such awful problems with their children!" As ridiculous as this may sound to those of us who work with families in today's culture, it is indicative of the nature of pain. No matter what the source of our emotional pain, it is true that we feel isolated and alone when dealing with *our* issues.

As the parent group leader, your job will be to facilitate open sharing among group members. As valuable as the teaching about healthy life skills is, many parents will receive the most benefit from hearing other parents share their experiences. This lets the parents know they are not alone and gives them the opportunity to have others who understand their feelings listen to them as they tell their stories. There is tremendous power in this support-group dynamic.

- **Parents come to the parent group expecting to hear about how to help their children, not how to work on their own issues.**

Parents who place their kids in Confident Kids groups are concerned only with the problems their children are having and how they can help them. Most of the parents will not be thinking about how their own personal growth—or lack of growth—directly affects their kids. They will be expecting to hear about what their kids are learning in the group, and how they can reinforce those concepts at home.

As the parent group leader, it is your job to respect this basic expectation the parents have in coming to the group. It is also your job to guide the parents into their own personal growth by helping them discover the following truth:

- **Parents cannot take their children any further in the journey of life than they have come themselves!**

Parents cannot expect their children to learn how to grieve, express their feelings, or make wise choices if they cannot do these things themselves. This becomes the leverage by which you can get the parents working on their own growth issues.

Once parents realize that the best thing they can do for their children is to grow themselves, they will work much harder on their own issues.

Expectations and Limitations of the Parent Group

As you begin the parent group, it is important to think through exactly what you are expecting to happen as a result of this experience. This is a two-sided coin; what can happen in the group (expectations), and what cannot happen in the group (limitations).

Expectations of what *can* happen in the group include:

- Parents receive encouragement as they realize they are not alone in their pain.
- Parents receive hope as they realize they can learn new living skills.
- The entire family system of relationships improves as parents and kids work on the same issues at the same time.
- Families that need additional help can be guided to appropriate places for professional help.

Limitations, or what *cannot* happen in the group, are:

- Confident Kids is a support group, not a therapy group. We do not offer therapy in any way, nor do we want to!
- We cannot fix anyone's problems for them, or "save" them from difficult life circumstances. We can offer a supportive, caring environment; teaching; and insights aimed at the goal of personal growth, but we cannot do the parents' work for them!
- We will not be able to help all the families that come to us. Some families are simply not able to benefit from the support-group experience.
- It is not our goal to encourage parents to stay in the support-group setting forever. Parents need to know up front that Confident Kids is a limited

program. Parents will need to set new goals on how to care for their families' continued growth.

Referring to Other Sources for Help

In a program such as Confident Kids, you will be working with many families who may need more help than the support-group setting can provide. Before you begin your first group, be sure you know what to do when parents say or do things that concern you. If you are not the Confident Kids program administrator, your first step is to go to the person who is responsible for the Confident Kids program at your location, who will have a clearly defined procedure for dealing with such cases. This procedure should have been discussed during your training time. If not, be sure to ask about the procedure you are to follow for making referrals and/or reporting abuse (page 10).

OVERVIEW

This session focuses on the fact that there are no good or bad feelings, but that all feelings have a purpose. Our feelings give us valuable information that will help us live healthy lives.

NEEDED

- Letters of welcome from page (??) for new parents (if you did not use the "Welcome to Confident Kids" session last week)
- SKILL handout (page 349)
- Topic overview (page 351)
- Session Summary for Parents (page 355)
- "Reflections" worksheet
- "Building on God's Word" worksheet
- Prayer journal

FEELINGS ARE AN IMPORTANT PART OF LIFE

PARENT SESSION 1 OUTLINE

Getting Started (20 Minutes)

Check-In

Group Rules

Review Session Summary for Parents

Teaching Time (20 Minutes)

"All My Feelings Are Important to Me"

Making It Personal (35 Minutes)

Reflections: "Feelings Word Inventory"

Group Sharing

Building on God's Word (15 Minutes)

Bible Focus

Prayer Time

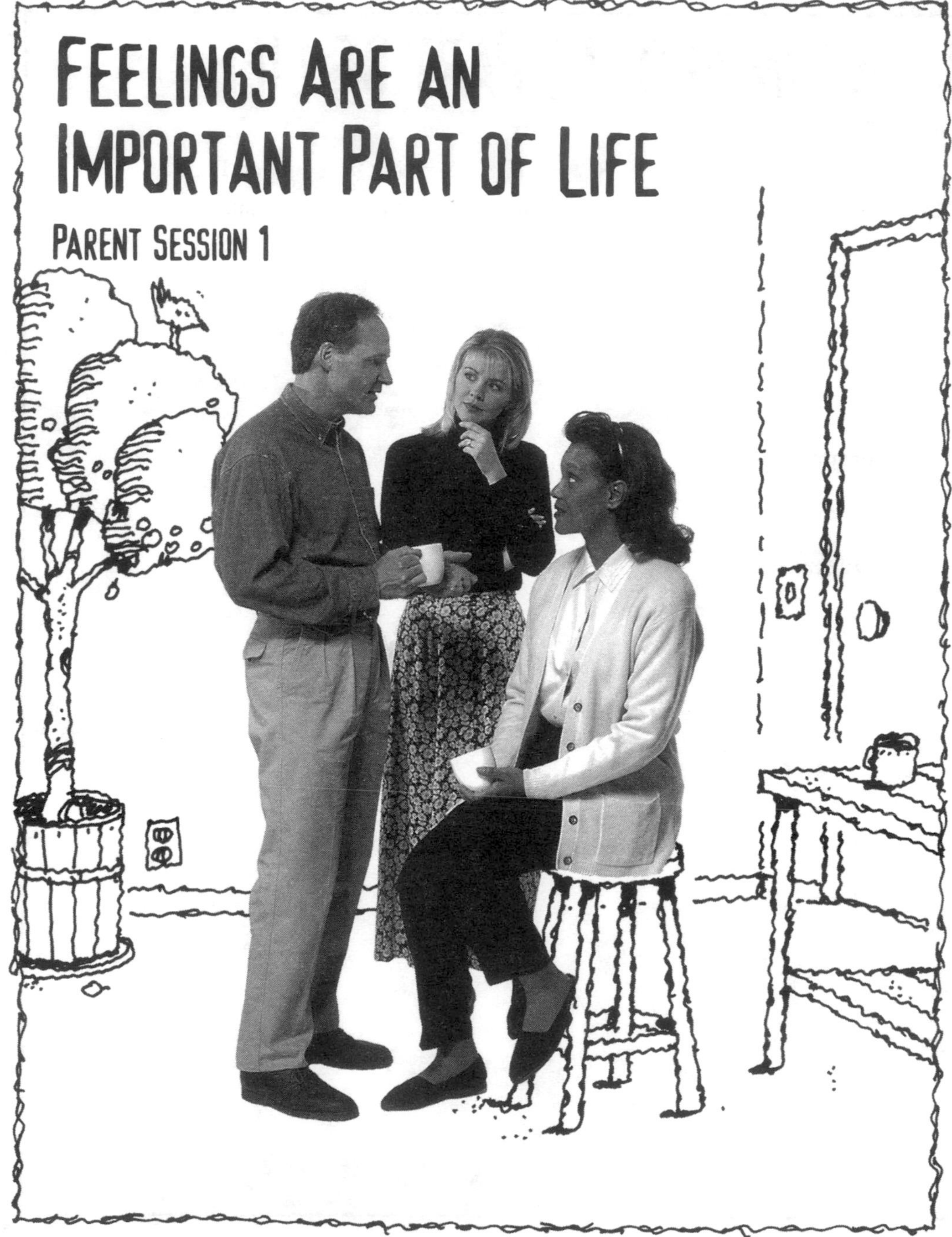

FEELINGS ARE AN IMPORTANT PART OF LIFE
PARENT SESSION 1

GETTING STARTED (20 MINUTES)

CHECK-IN

Form a circle of chairs and have group members introduce themselves. Distribute and review the welcome letter and the SKILL handout, if you did not use the "Welcome to Confident Kids" session last week. Then distribute the topic overview to everyone and use it to introduce the unit theme.

GROUP RULES

Review the three basic rules of Confident Kids' parent sessions. Be sure everyone understands them. (See "Getting Started" on page 24 for information about group rules.)

1. Confidentiality
2. No advice giving
3. The right to pass

REVIEW SESSION SUMMARY FOR PARENTS

Read through the "Session Summary for Parents" (page 355). Be sure parents understand that this handout summarizes what their children will learn in their session today.

TEACHING TIME (20 MINUTES)

ALL MY FEELINGS ARE IMPORTANT TO ME

Introduce the session theme, "All my feelings are important to me."

> **It was the first morning of a new Confident Kids unit. Joey walked into the room, stood in front of his leader with his**

ALL MY FEELINGS ARE IMPORTANT TO ME

hands on his hips, and announced, "I shouldn't be here, 'cause I don't have any feelings. So, I got nothin' to talk about!" For the entire eight weeks of the unit, Joey held tenaciously to his position that he had no feelings—except for one incident that captured his attention.

During Session 5, the kids were using puppets to role-play various hypothetical situations. When they got to the one that said, "Your parents just told you they are getting a divorce," Joey's hand shot up. "I want to do that one," he said. Using a puppet, he continued, "If I had feelings—which, of course, I don't, but if I did—I'd feel angry." He paused for a moment, then added, "Because parents don't tell you when they're gonna get a divorce—they just leave!"

Joey was in second grade, and he had already discovered that life is full of feelings that are not fun to feel. In response he simply decided not to feel them. What he was too young to understand, however, is that it is not possible to shut out only certain emotions. When we choose not to feel some feelings, we cut ourselves off from the ability to feel at all. The result? As Joey said, "I don't have any feelings. So I got nothin' to talk about!"

Many of us grew up just like Joey. Somewhere along the way, we discovered that some feelings are not fun to feel, and we responded by finding ways not to feel them. In the process we cut ourselves off from one of the most important aspects of living a healthy life—the ability to feel all our feelings. Our first task, therefore, is to give ourselves and our children permission to feel all our feelings. Here are three simple steps to help us get started:

Realize There Are No Good or Bad Feelings

Most people instinctively believe that if a feeling feels good, it is good; if it feels bad, it is bad. If we are to feel all our feelings, we must realize that feelings are neither good nor bad. They are simply an expression of what is happening inside of us. Changing the way we refer to feelings from "good" and "bad" to "comfortable" and "uncomfortable" (or "difficult") is a simple way to begin opening up to the whole range of feelings God has placed within us. When we label certain feelings as "bad," we are really sending a message that tells us to get rid of them, for we were taught, and we teach our children, to stay away from or cleanse ourselves of bad things. Saying that a feeling is "uncomfortable" or "difficult" invites us to find a way to deal with it. Uncomfortable experiences may not be fun, but handling them appropriately is a normal part of healthy living.

Discover the Purpose of Each Feeling

Every feeling provides us with valuable information we must have to stay safe, meet our personal needs, and develop sound relationships. For instance:

Fear warns us of danger and tells us to seek protection and comfort.

Anger signals that our own or someone else's rights are being violated. It is a safety valve that helps us release strong

emotional pressure and generate strength to handle whatever situation is before us.

Loneliness tells us that our basic need for relationships and intimacy is not being met and motivates us to reach out to others.

Pain lets us know that something significant has hurt us. It says we are in need of healing.

Joy indicates that our needs are being met.

Pride tells us that we are doing something well, thereby affirming our sense of self-worth.

And so on. Each feeling we experience plays a part in letting us know whether our needs are being met. When we cut ourselves off from even one feeling, we shut down a significant source of information.

Learn to Name Feelings Accurately

To effectively gather the information our feelings provide, we must be able to name our feelings. For example, it is not helpful to say, "I feel awful." "Awful" is too vague. However, saying "I feel lonely" is helpful. I now know that my relational needs are not being met. In response, I can find a way to reach out. In the same way, "I feel happy" is not very informative. It is also vague. But "I felt welcomed and included at the neighborhood picnic today" helps me see that I have found a place to get the important need of "belonging" met.

Feelings are a tremendous gift from God. Knowing that "all my feelings are OK" is the first step to living the emotionally healthy lives God intends.

MAKING IT PERSONAL (35 MINUTES)

FEELINGS WORD INVENTORY

Distribute copies of the "Reflections" worksheet (page 291) to all participants and give them a few minutes to fill them out. They will also need the "Alphabetical List of Feelings Words" (page 353) that accompanied the topic overview they received earlier.

GROUP SHARING

After everyone is finished, share responses around the circle. Remind everyone of the "Right to Pass" rule before starting. *Optional:* If you have more than eight parents in your group, you may want to divide them into groups of four or five.

BUILDING ON GOD'S WORD (15 MINUTES)

BIBLE FOCUS

Distribute copies of the "Building on God's Word" worksheet (page 293) and discuss it together. Encourage parents to use this sheet at home during the coming week as a means of spiritual encouragement and connecting to God.

PRAYER TIME

Ask parents to fill in the prayer request line on their "Building on God's Word" activity sheet. Give opportunity for parents to share these requests with the rest of the group. As the leader, you can keep a journal of these requests for your own prayer time during the week, and help the group track the requests shared each week. End the session with a time of open prayer.

FEELINGS WORD INVENTORY

1. **Read your "Alphabetical List of Feelings Words." Paying attention to your emotional reaction to each one, identify the following:**

   Feelings you are comfortable feeling and expressing:

   Feelings that frighten you:

   Feelings you are unable to feel at all:

   Patterns or insights you see:

2. **In your family of origin:**

   Which feelings were acceptable?

   Which ones were unacceptable?

Feelings Word Inventory

3. **What experiences can you remember that might have caused you to block out certain feelings?**

    __ Parents' divorce
    __ Chemically dependent family member
    __ Emotional, physical, or sexual abuse
    __ Teasing in school for being too fat, tall, dumb, etc.
    __ Other:

4. **What experiences helped you open up to your feelings?**

    __ Parents allowed me to talk through all my feelings
    __ Schoolteachers, youth sponsors, scout leaders, coaches, or other mentors took a special interest in me
    __ Recovery groups, counseling, and other support systems helped me as an adult
    __ Other:

JOSHUA 1:9

Learning to feel all our feelings can be frightening and painful. If you are struggling with this part of your life, remember that you do not have to face this journey alone. You can have the presence and power of God to guide you through it. Let this promise from God's Word give you hope and strength:

> **"Have I not commanded you? Be strong and courageous. Do not be terrified, do not be discouraged, for the Lord your God will be with you wherever you go." Joshua 1:9 (*NIV*)**

List below any feelings or circumstances you are facing this week that are frightening or discouraging:

Write a prayer to God, asking Him to make Joshua 1:9 real to you in the midst of these feelings or circumstances.

Dear God,

Your #1 prayer request for this week:

Overview

This session focuses on the dangers of labeling feelings as either "good" or "bad." Although we may not like to feel certain feelings, it is important that we stay in touch with the whole range of emotions God has placed within us.

Needed

- Session Summary for Parents (page 356)
- "Reflections" worksheet
- "Building on God's Word" worksheet
- Prayer journal

All My Feelings Are OK!

Parent Session 2 Outline

Getting Started (20 Minutes)

Check-In

Group Rules

Review Session Summary for Parents

Teaching Time (20 Minutes)

"All My Feelings—And That Means All—Are OK!"

Making It Personal (35 Minutes)

Reflections: "Good Versus Bad"

Group Sharing

Building on God's Word (15 Minutes)

Bible Focus

Prayer Time

All My Feelings Are OK!

Parent Session 2

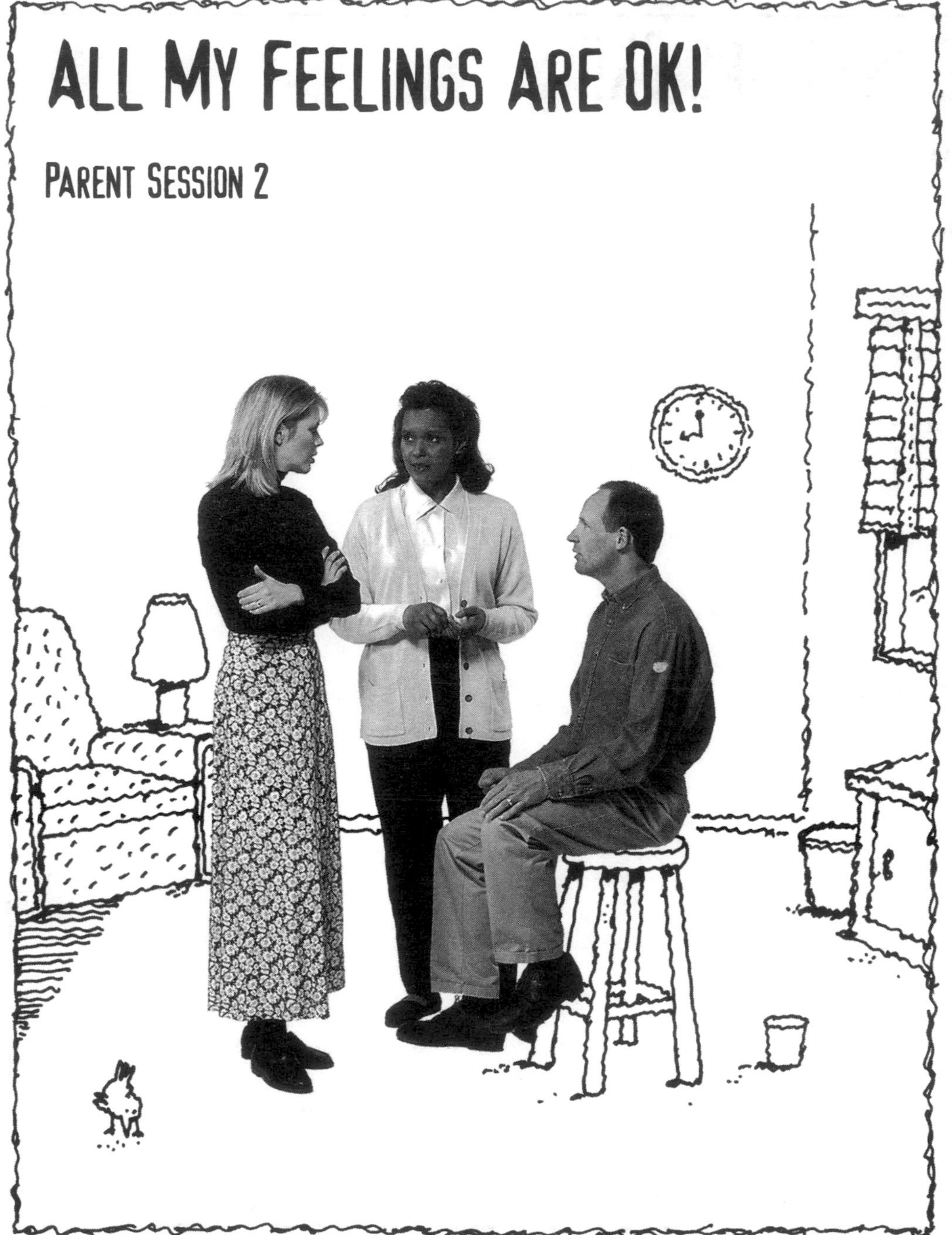

Getting Started (20 Minutes)

Check-In

Ask parents to share one feelings word that describes how they are feeling as they come to group today. Then ask if anyone has a question or follow up to last week's session.

Group Rules

Review the three basic rules of Confident Kids' parent sessions.

1. Confidentiality
2. No advice giving
3. The right to pass

Review Session Summary for Parents

Read through the "Session Summary for Parents" (page 356). Be sure parents understand that this handout summarizes what their children will learn in their session today.

Teaching Time (20 Minutes)

All My Feelings—and That Means All—Are OK

Today's emphasis is, "All my feelings—and that means all—are OK!" Begin this session by asking parents how many of them believe there are good feelings and bad feelings. Make a two-column chart listing feelings we usually label as *good* in one column and *bad* in the other column. Then discuss why we make these distinctions.

> **Many of us learned which feelings are "bad" in our childhood. We grew up with messages that denied us our feelings:**

ALL MY FEELINGS—AND THAT MEANS ALL—ARE OK!

"You shouldn't feel that way!"

"What are you crying about? We'll get you another dog."

"Big boys don't cry" or, "Nice girls don't scream."

"Stop making such a fuss."

"The Bible says 'don't be angry,' so you can't act that way in this house!"

"Dad does not have a drinking problem. Don't you ever say that again!"

The problem with labeling certain feelings as "bad" has to do with what we do with things in our lives that we consider to be bad. We get rid of them. We cleanse ourselves of them. When we label certain feelings as bad, we will do the same thing with them—get rid of them! We learn lots of ways to do this, such as: behaving in certain ways, *(Don't cry, don't be angry, don't grieve, always smile and be happy)* not talking about what's real, *(Don't mention Dad's drinking, don't tell anyone about the way Uncle George touches you, keep quiet about your fears)* or pretending you don't feel pain *("There's nothing to deal with, thank you very much!")*

What other ways did you use to get rid of your feelings? *(Let parents respond)*

But we must remember that it is not possible to get rid of only the "bad" feelings. To cut ourselves off from a certain range of feelings means we must cut ourselves off from the ability to feel at all. An example of this truth is *(At this point, share a personal example from your own life. If you don't have one, read the following example from the author's life)*

My friends in college used to say, "Linda, you are the most emotionally stable person we know. We'd give anything to be like you!" At the time I remember responding, "Thank you," but silently thinking that something about that comment didn't feel right. I didn't know what—I just knew that what they were saying wasn't right. It wasn't until many years later at a particularly difficult time of my life that I finally began to understand why. What my friends had seen in me and interpreted as stability was in reality a state of being emotionally frozen. I was your basic "flat-line feeler"!

God has created us to feel a wide range of emotions, which often seems like both a blessing and a curse. Along with the ability to feel deep love, pleasure, and excitement, He has also given us the capacity to feel great pain, anger, and loneliness. The unmistakable truth is this: We cannot have one without the other! Cutting ourselves off from emotions that make us uncomfortable seriously hampers our ability to feel anything at all.

In the weeks ahead, we will look at how to open ourselves up to the whole range of emotions. For now, let's just remember that to deal honestly with the feelings we don't want to feel we must do three things:

1. **Recognize that the feeling exists.**
2. **Talk to someone about it. Laying it out immediately takes out its destructive power.**
3. **Ask the Lord to heal us.**

Making It Personal (35 minutes)

Good Versus Bad

Distribute copies of the "Reflections" worksheet (page 299) to all participants and give them a few minutes to fill them out.

Group Sharing

After everyone is finished, share responses around the circle or divide into smaller groups of four or five. Remind everyone of the "Right to Pass" rule before starting.

Building on God's Word (15 minutes)

Bible Focus

Distribute copies of the "Building on God's Word" worksheet (page 301) and discuss it together. Encourage parents to use this sheet at home during the coming week as a means of spiritual encouragement and connecting to God.

Prayer Time

Ask parents to fill in the prayer request line on their "Building on God's Word" worksheet. Give opportunity for parents to share these requests with the rest of the group. Use your prayer journal to refer back to requests mentioned last week and ask for updates. End the session with prayer.

GOOD VERSUS BAD

1. **Which feelings do you label as "bad"?**

   Why?

2. **What behaviors do you use to "cleanse" yourself of these negative feelings?**

   __ Stuff them inside (ignore them)
   __ Get drunk or use medications
   __ Take them out on my kids, spouse, or friends
   __ Blame myself for being dumb, stupid, etc.
   __ Other:

3. **Describe any steps you've taken to deal with the feelings you listed in question 1 in healthier, more positive ways:**

Good Versus Bad

4. What unhealthy tendencies do you see in your children when they must deal with difficult feelings?

5. What steps can you take as a family to deal with all your feelings openly and in a healthy manner?

    1.

    2.

    3.

JOSHUA 1:9

> **"Have I not commanded you? Be strong and courageous. Do not be terrified; do not be discouraged, for the Lord your God will be with you wherever you go." Joshua 1:9** (*NIV*)

Think of this verse as God's promise to help you face all your feelings openly and honestly. Remember, since God created all your feelings, He is not threatened by any feelings you have. You can bring all your feelings to God in prayer and ask Him to help you face them and the circumstances behind them. As you pray this week, choose two feelings you would like God to help you face honestly:

__ Anger: About?

__ Loneliness: Why?

__ Fear: Of what?

__ Guilt/shame: From what?

__ Confusion: Where?

__ Failure: In what?

__ Other:

Your #1 prayer request for this week:

Overview

Feelings defenses are actions or behaviors we use to cover up (defend against) deeper feelings that are perceived as threatening, scary, or painful. Everyone uses defensive behaviors to some extent. This session focuses on the unhealthy use of defensive behaviors, and how to lower these defenses to look honestly at our deepest feelings.

Needed

- Session Summary for Parents (page 357)
- Five Styrofoam cups and one marker for each participant
- "Reflections" worksheet
- "Building on God's Word" worksheet
- Prayer journal

Feelings Defenses

Parent Session 3 Outline

Getting Started (20 Minutes)

Check-In

Group Rules

Review Session Summary for Parents

Teaching Time (20 Minutes)

"Everyone Uses Feelings Defenses"

Making It Personal (35 Minutes)

Reflections: "Lowering My Defenses"

Group Sharing

Building on God's Word (15 Minutes)

Bible Focus

Prayer Time

FEELINGS DEFENSES

PARENT SESSION 3

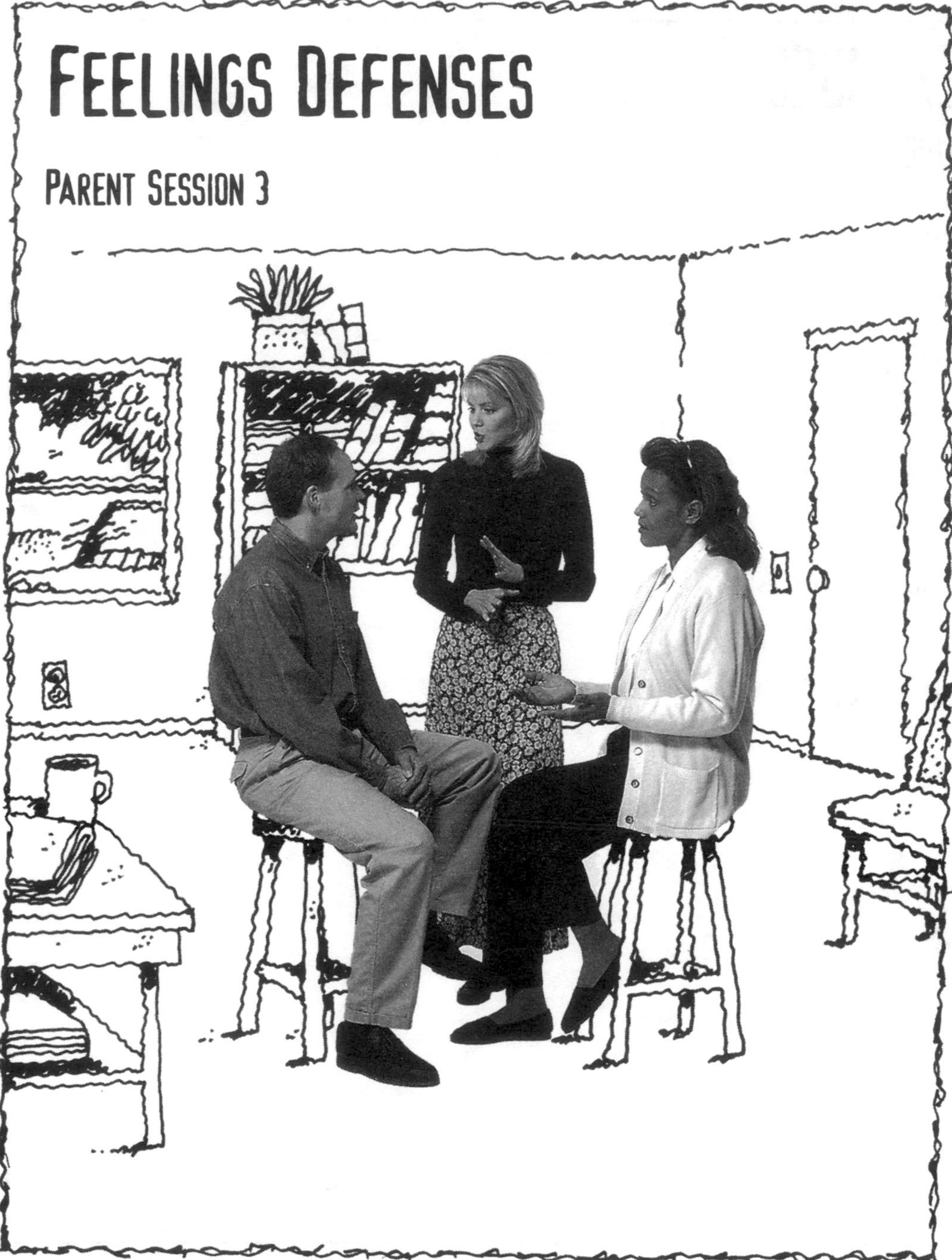

GETTING STARTED (20 MINUTES)

CHECK-IN

Ask parents to share one feelings word that describes how they are feeling as they come to group today. Then ask if anyone has a question or follow up to last week's session.

GROUP RULES

Review the three basic rules of Confident Kids parent sessions:

1. Confidentiality
2. No advice giving
3. The right to pass

REVIEW SESSION SUMMARY FOR PARENTS

Read through the "Session Summary for Parents" (page 357). Be sure parents understand that this handout summarizes what their children will learn in their session today.

TEACHING TIME (20 MINUTES)

EVERYONE USES FEELINGS DEFENSES

Today's emphasis is, "Everyone uses feelings defenses."

Do you know anyone who uses a feelings defense? Perhaps you know someone who:

—Cracks jokes constantly, especially in the midst of a conflict.

—Has problems that always seem to be someone else's fault.

—Never gets angry or seems to be bothered by anything.

—Talks a mile a minute and never lets anyone respond.

These are examples of people who use what is known as feelings defenses. We call certain behaviors "defensive" because that is exactly what they are—a way to defend or protect us from life's most painful and threatening experiences. Feelings defenses work as decoys or distractions, keeping the focus away from whatever feels threatening or painful. When a person is using defensive behavior, what we see in terms of outward behavior may be very different from what the person is actually feeling inside. For instance, in the examples above, what we see is:

—A comedian or clown

—A poor soul who is always caught in everyone else's ineptitude

—A likable person with an easygoing personality

—A chatterbox

What is real for these people, however, may be something very different. They may be struggling with some of life's most difficult and painful experiences—and we may never know it!

People use many defensive behaviors. Common ones are: clowning, lying, blaming, silence or withdrawal, pretending or daydreaming, constant talking, people-pleasing, acting like a "know it all," or aggression. In effect, a feelings defense is any behavior that keeps us from focusing on what is real. Here are the main points to keep in mind about them:

Feelings defenses serve an important purpose. They can help us cope with the painful or dark side of life by giving us time to gather courage and strength to face whatever life has brought our way. Or they may give us a needed break from the intensity of dealing with certain situations. But feelings defenses become unhealthy when we use them to keep out painful feelings we need to face, keep out the real problem so that we never resolve the core issue, or keep out other people who could help us.

We all use defensive behaviors to some extent, having formed them when we were very young. When we were young and life felt threatening or painful, we would sometimes defend ourselves by acting in ways that took the focus off the circumstances causing them. We believed that as long as we didn't face these feelings, they weren't really there. Of course, as we learned last week, choosing not to face frightening or threatening feelings does not make them go away. They continue to live inside of us, struggling to get out.

Lowering our feelings defenses is a choice we must make for ourselves. It is the only way we can allow ourselves to face the frightening feelings and hurtful circumstances behind them and resolve the core issues in our lives.

EVERYONE USES FEELINGS DEFENSES

Use a stack of Styrofoam cups to illustrate how this works. Write typical feelings that people may try to avoid on several cups (one per cup). Then write a feelings defense on another cup. Stack the cups, putting the one with the feelings defense on the top of the stack. The stack represents a person who has many feelings and unresolved issues going on inside (the bottom cups), but is choosing to cover them up with a feelings defense (the top cup).

The illustration below (Gail's personal stack) will help you get the idea. Present Gail's story to the group or use examples from your own life.

To present the illustration, hold up the stack with the defensive behavior written on the top cup. Labels for Gail's cup stack:

—Calm control
—Fear
—Despair
—Self-hatred
—Self-destruction
—Confusion
—Loneliness/abandonment

Say:

All we know about this "person" is what we see on the outside—the feelings defense. What is really going on inside is hidden from us, and often from the person as well. We can only find out what is beneath the defense when the person chooses to look carefully at each underlying feeling and reveal it.

At this point, share your own stack of cups with the group, removing one cup at a time as you talk about the feelings/issues behind your defensive behavior, or use Gail's story below:

I was an overachiever growing up. A confident, controlled exterior was my feelings defense. *(Top cup)* **As long as I could convince people that in all situations I was never angry, sad, or confused, then I thought people would like me. My defense became an automatic reaction, and I had no idea whatsoever that I was doing it. I desperately needed everyone's approval. And I worked very hard for it. Every move I made was deliberate. I made certain that I handled myself perfectly in any given situation.**

I remember one incident that happened after I got married. My husband said something very cruel to me. I stayed very controlled and calm on the outside, although I had pain in my chest and stomach that was unbelievable. I made an effort to smile, to make things OK. My husband looked at me and told me, "Wipe that smirk off of your face." The desperation of not knowing what to do next helped me lower my defense and begin to look inside at what was really going on. What I discovered, however, was that I could not identify one feeling from another. Everything showed up as pain. Emotional pain that felt so bad that my skin crawled and hurt! Hard to describe!

I made the choice to dare to look at the inside of Gail only after many marriages, failed parenting, two emotional breakdowns, self-hatred, and continuous suicidal thoughts. Here's what I found:

(Top cup) FEELINGS DEFENSE: Calm, controlled perfectionism. **I made that decision to look at Gail's insides. I choose to live.** *(Remove cup from stack)*

(Next cup) FEELING #1: Fear. **Quiet, tormenting desperation. My parents' way of punishing me when I did not perform well was to deny my existence. I was terrified of doing anything that would cause the people in my life whom I loved to turn their backs on me and quit loving me.** *(Remove cup)*

(Next cup) FEELING #2: Despair. "Nothing will ever be OK again." I always believed I had somehow committed the unpardonable sin, but most of the time I didn't know what I had done. My parents just shunned me. No matter what I did, I couldn't find the key to making it better. I had no hope. *(Remove cup)*

(Next cup) FEELING #3: Self-hatred. I hated myself for failing—again. I took the blame in every situation. Although outwardly I would calmly point out where another person was completely wrong, inwardly I believed I had failed. *(Remove cup)*

(Next cup) FEELING #4: Self-destruction. My "way out" was ridding the world of me. Only then would I be free of the pain, and *they* would be sorry for the way they had treated me! *(Remove cup)*

(Next cup) FEELING #5: Confusion. What can I do to fix this? I never could fix it. *(Remove cup)*

(Bottom cup) FEELING #6: Loneliness/abandonment. I felt absolutely abandoned by life. No one loves me.

Learning about feelings defenses is important for two reasons. First, it helps us see the need to lower our own defenses so we can face what is real and resolve the core issues in our lives. Second, it also helps us see defensive behavior in our children so we can help them recognize and lower their defenses now, while they are still forming them. Then we can help them learn to get their needs met in healthier ways.

Making It Personal (35 Minutes)

Lowering My Defenses

Distribute copies of the "Reflections" worksheet (page 308) to all participants. Also give each one five Styrofoam cups and a marker. Allow plenty of time to work through the sheet.

Group Sharing

After all are finished, ask for volunteers to share their stack of cups with the group. Then share responses to the written questions around the circle or divide into smaller groups. Remind everyone of the "Right to Pass" rule before starting.

Building on God's Word (15 Minutes)

Bible Focus

Distribute copies of the "Building on God's Word" worksheet (page 309) and discuss it together. Encourage parents to use this sheet at home during the coming week as a means of spiritual encouragement and connecting to God.

Prayer Time

Ask parents to fill in the prayer request line on their "Building on God's Word" worksheet. Give opportunity for parents to share these requests with the rest of the group. If time allows, use your prayer journal to check back on last week's requests before ending the session with a time of open prayer.

LOWERING MY DEFENSES

1. What feelings defense do you use most often?

2. Describe your earliest memory of using it.

3. Identify the feelings and painful or threatening experiences you were defending against.

4. Describe a time in adulthood when you used a feelings defense. Include the circumstances that triggered your defensive behavior and how it kept you from getting your needs met.

5. Use the Styrofoam cups and marker to build your own stack of cups to illustrate how you use feelings defenses.

   Cup #1:
   Cup #2:
   Cup #3:
   Cup #4:
   Cup #5:

PSALM 23

We build our feelings defenses out of fear that certain emotions will destroy us or our relationships if we allow ourselves to feel them. David was well acquainted with such fears and expressed them often in the book of Psalms. Although familiar to most of us, Psalm 23 takes on new meaning when we apply it to lowering our feelings defenses. Read it now paying particular attention to verse 4:

> **Even though I walk through the valley of the shadow of death, I will fear no evil, for you are with me; your rod and your staff, they comfort me. Psalm 23:4** (*NIV*)

We can make David's prayer our own as we walk through the valley of lowering our defenses and facing the painful feelings and frightening circumstances that are behind them. Write out your prayer to God, describing to Him your defenses and the painful feelings behind them.

Dear God,

Your #1 prayer request for this week:

Overview

Central to handling our feelings in healthy ways is the ability to express all our feelings openly. That is *not* to say that all ways of expressing our feelings are healthy, nor that all people will express their feelings in the same ways. This session explores the negative consequences of holding feelings inside or expressing them in destructive ways, and offers healthy ways of expressing our feelings.

Needed

- Session Summary for Parents (page 358)
- "Reflections" worksheet
- "Building on God's Word" worksheet
- A pillow, a box of tissues, a pair of running shoes, stationery and pen, drawing paper and markers, a telephone, and a big red heart
- *Optional:* A "Family Feelings Box"
- Prayer journal

Expressing Our Feelings

Parent Session 4 Outline

Getting Started (20 Minutes)

Check-In

Group Rules

Review Session Summary for Parents

Teaching Time (20 Minutes)

"To Each His Own"

Making It Personal (35 Minutes)

Reflections: "Our Family Feelings Box"

Group Sharing

Building on God's Word (15 Minutes)

Bible Focus

Prayer Time

EXPRESSING OUR FEELINGS

PARENT SESSION 4

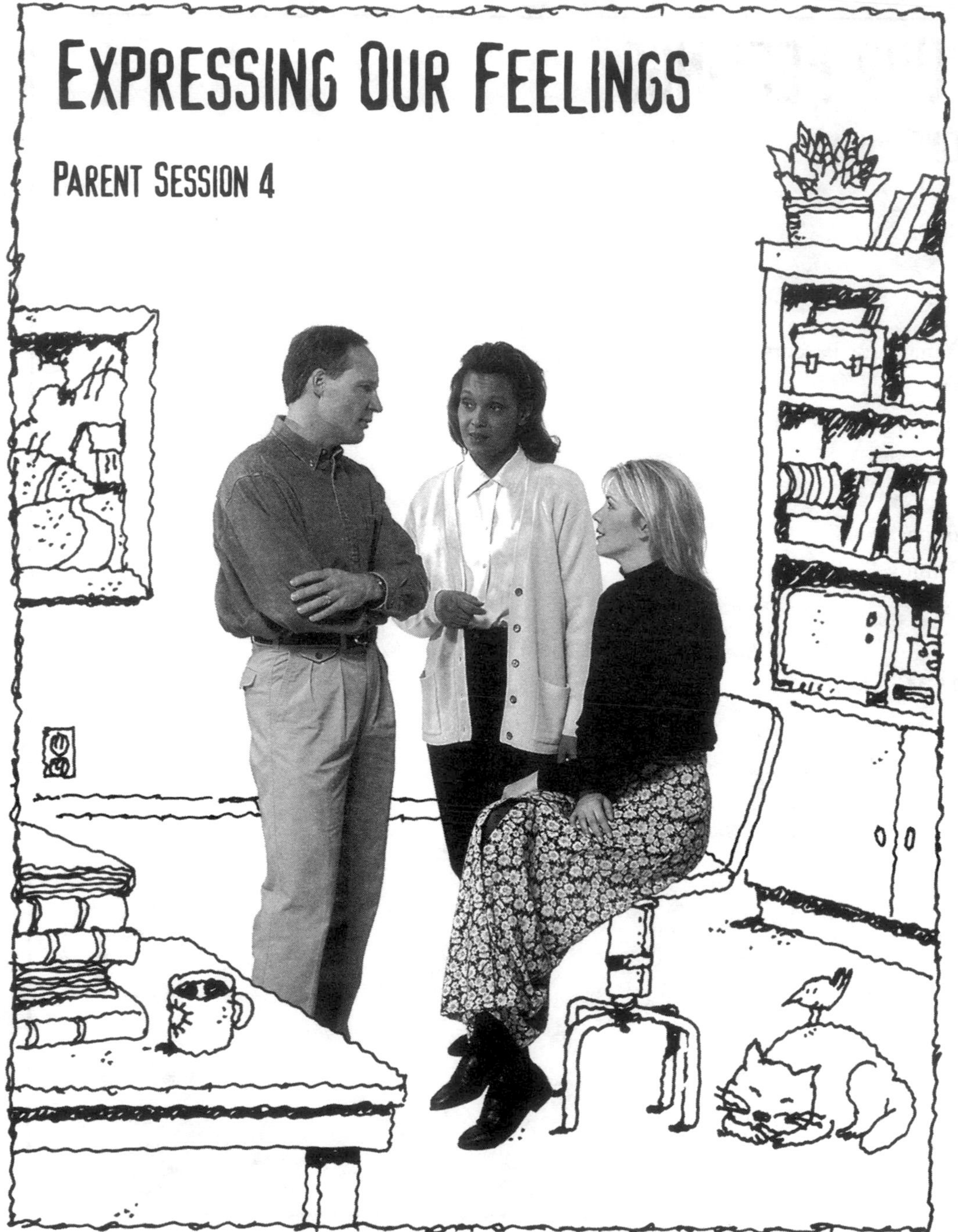

GETTING STARTED (20 MINUTES)

CHECK-IN

Ask if anyone has any feedback or questions from last week's session. Then ask parents to share one time during the past week they noticed that they used or lowered a feelings defense.

GROUP RULES

Review the three basic rules of Confident Kids parent sessions:

1. Confidentiality
2. No advice giving
3. The right to pass

REVIEW SESSION SUMMARY FOR PARENTS

Read through the "Session Summary for Parents" (page 358). Be sure parents understand that this handout summarizes what their children will learn in their session today.

TEACHING TIME (20 MINUTES)

TO EACH HIS OWN

Today's emphasis is, "I can choose a healthy way to express my feelings."

> **Have you ever heard (or made) comments like these:**
>
> **"Poor Josephine! Imagine having your husband walk out on you after twenty-five years of marriage! But she's taking it very well. She told me 'he's not worth crying over,' and 'life goes on.' I wish I**

I CAN CHOOSE A HEALTHY WAY TO EXPRESS MY FEELINGS

could be more like her. Nothing ever seems to bother her, especially crises."

"I'm so sorry about your father, Billy. But remember, you have to be strong for your mother. You're the man of the house now!"

Statements such as these reflect a denial of one of our most basic needs—to feel and openly express our emotional responses to life situations. As much as we may wish it to be true, it is not possible to handle our feelings by ignoring them or pretending they don't exist. Here are three important points to remember about expressing our feelings:

Feelings will be expressed eventually. A fundamental truth of emotional health is this: Unexpressed feelings do not go away. They simply get stuffed deep inside until they find their own way out, and that way will almost always be destructive.

Today your kids are learning about healthy ways to express their feelings. We need to do this, too. Keeping feelings stuffed inside is exhausting and will result in one or more of the following: stress-related illnesses, *(Headaches and ulcers)* excessive irritability, *(Overreacting to people and circumstances)* depression, *(Anger turned inward)* escapism/withdrawal, *(Hiding from the world)* misplaced anger *(Striking out at everyone around us, especially those we love most)*

Feelings can be expressed in many different ways. Although we all experience the same feelings, we express them in unique ways. *(Bring with you a pillow, a box of tissues, a pair of running shoes, stationery and pen, drawing paper and markers, a telephone, and a big red heart. Place all of these items in the center of your group at this time)* These items represent a wide variety of healthy ways of expressing our feelings. Our task as parents is twofold: Find the ways that work best for us, and help our children find the ways that work best for them.

Ask:

How can each of these items be used to express feelings in a healthy way? *(Most items are self-evident. The heart represents being with someone we love, asking for a hug, etc.)*

What specific ways do you express your feelings? *(Let parents respond)*

What specific ways do each of your children express their feelings? *(Let parents respond)*

We need to observe realistic limits to expressing our feelings. Finding our own way to express our feelings does not give us or our children permission to indulge in a feelings "free-for-all." Today your kids are learning a very important rule about expressing feelings: You can express your feelings any way you choose, ***except*** you may not be destructive to yourself, others, or property. For example:

It's OK to go to your room and be alone for awhile; it's not OK to cut yourself off entirely from the people who care about you (that's destructive to yourself).

It's OK to tell a friend she hurt you by telling your secret to someone else; it's not OK to spread gossip about her to get even (that's destructive to others).

It's OK to punch a pillow when you're angry; it's not OK to throw lamps or dishes through your TV screen (that's destructive to property).

Making It Personal (35 Minutes)

Our Family Feelings Box

Distribute copies of the "Reflections" worksheet (page 315) to all participants and give them a few minutes to fill them out.

Optional: Prepare a "Family Feelings Box" for your family as a visual illustration of this idea. Bring an empty box that has been decorated as a feelings box. Then following the directions in the "Reflections" worksheet, describe how each member of your family likes to express his feelings and add the appropriate items to your box.

Encourage parents to follow your example and make a "Family Feelings Box."

Group Sharing

After all are finished, point out the importance of the relationship between the answers to their "family of origin" questions, and the way feelings are handled in their own families now. Also, give volunteers time to share what items they would place in their "Family Feelings Boxes" and why. Remind everyone of the "Right to Pass" rule before starting.

Building on God's Word (15 Minutes)

Bible Focus

Distribute copies of the "Building on God's Word" worksheet (page 316) and discuss it together. Encourage parents to use this sheet at home during the coming week as a means of spiritual encouragement and connecting to God.

Prayer Time

Ask parents to fill in the prayer request line on their "Building on God's Word" worksheet. Give opportunity for parents to share these requests with the rest of the group. End the session with a time of open prayer.

OUR FAMILY FEELINGS BOX

1. **In your family of origin, how did family members express "pleasant" emotions, such as happiness, excitement, pride, and silliness?**

   __ Everyone joined in; we had a family celebration.

   __ The kids could act happy and silly, but my parents did not participate.

   __ These feelings were considered self-indulgent and we were not allowed to express them openly.

   __ Other:

2. **What happened when someone was angry, sad, or scared?**

   __ We were told, "There's nothing to be angry, sad, or scared about.

   __ We were sent to our rooms until we could calm down and act "appropriately."

   __ We were allowed to express these feelings openly, and we received validation.

   __ Other:

3. **In your present family, how do your children express their feelings?**

   __ They share them openly and the family responds appropriately.

   __ Their feelings are denied (We tell them, "Don't feel that way"; no one responds to their joy or sorrow, etc.).

   __ I don't know; I feel uncomfortable with my children's feelings so I just ignore them.

   __ Other:

4. **On a separate sheet of paper, identify how the members of your family express their feelings. Then design a "Family Feelings Box" by thinking of all the items you could gather together in a box for family members to use when they need to express their feelings. For example: "Mary likes to write letters to her dad when she is angry with him, so I'll put letter writing items in our feelings box." Do the same for each family member.**

SELECTIONS FROM THE PSALMS

The book of Psalms is actually a collection of poems, hymns, and prayers written to God. Within them can be found honest expressions of every feeling that exists. Read the Psalms listed below and identify feelings being poured out to God:

Psalm 22

Psalm 61

Psalm 66

Psalm 121

What are you feeling today? In the space below, write a psalm or prayer to God that honestly pours out your feeling(s) to Him:

Dear God,

Your #1 prayer request for this week:

Overview

Throughout this unit we have been discussing the necessity to recognize and respond to our feelings in healthy ways. This session introduces a way to explore our feelings when they seem confusing or overwhelming.

Needed

- Session Summary for Parents (page 360)
- "Reflections" worksheet
- "Building on God's Word" worksheet
- Chalkboard or flip chart
- Prayer journal

Some Feelings Are Difficult to Handle

Parent Session 5 Outline

Getting Started (20 Minutes)

Check-In

Group Rules

Review Session Summary for Parents

Teaching Time (20 Minutes)

"I'm All Shook Up!"

Making It Personal (35 Minutes)

Reflections: "Let's Sort It Out"

Group Sharing

Building on God's Word (15 Minutes)

Bible Focus

Prayer Time

Some Feelings Are Difficult to Handle

Parent Session 5

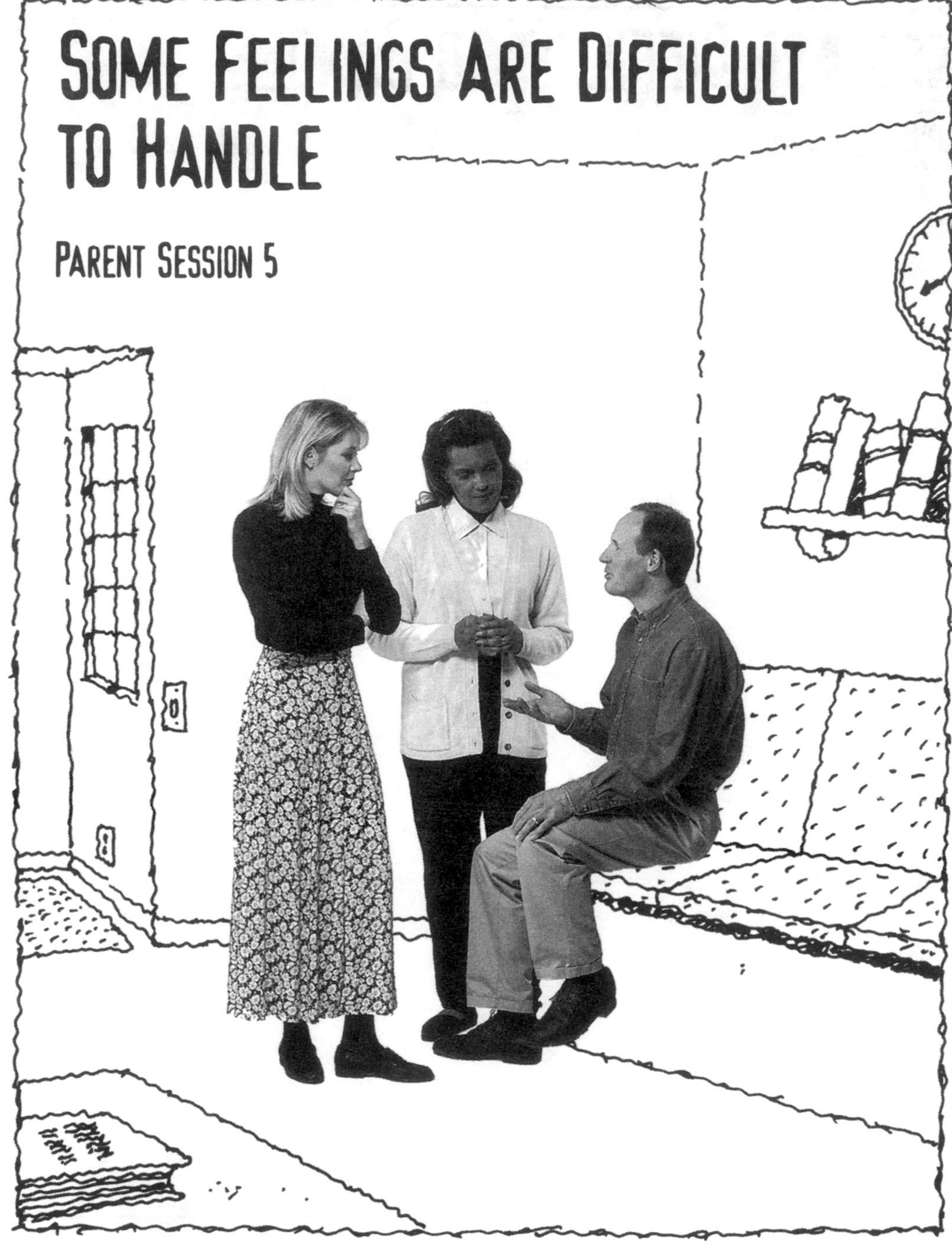

Getting Started (20 Minutes)

Check-In

Ask if anyone has any feedback or questions from last week's session. Then ask parents to share one time during the past week they noticed that they used or lowered a feelings defense.

Group Rules

Review the three basic rules of Confident Kids parent sessions:

1. Confidentiality
2. No advice giving
3. The right to pass

Review Session Summary for Parents

Read through the "Session Summary for Parents" (page 360). Be sure parents understand that this handout summarizes what their children will learn in their session today.

Teaching Time (20 Minutes)

I'm All Shook Up

Use the following story to introduce today's theme, "I'm all shook up":

> **Five-year-old Timmy had been warned about throwing things in the house time and time again. Finally, when he threw something that came dangerously close to breaking a lamp, Timmy's mom lost her cool. A loud scolding of, "How many times do I have to tell you?" and, "You**

never listen to me!" ended when Tim was sent to his room. As he stomped up the stairs mumbling such things as, "It's not fair!" and, "It just slipped out of my hand," he turned suddenly, put his hands on his head, and said, "Oww! My brain feels funny. It gets all scrambled up when you yell at me!"

Timmy's experience is not unique. In fact, it's an experience we all share, although we may have different names for it. "My stomach is in knots," "I'm losing my mind," or "I'm all shook up!" are all ways of saying the same thing—we are having an emotional reaction that short-circuits our ability to be clear about what we are feeling or thinking at that moment. Those times are scary and difficult to get through. When these times come, we must make a choice: We can choose to remain in our state of feeling "all shook up" and use a feelings defense to deal with it, or we can choose to listen to our feelings and take time to sort through them to discover what is really going on.

But how do we listen to our feelings and sort through them, especially when they are so confusing? Let's find out by tracing the experiences of three people as they work through a four-step process to sort out their feelings. The journey begins for each one as they find themselves looking in the mirror one morning, feeling down, and telling themselves the following messages: *(Write these on chalkboard or flip chart, leaving room under each statement for additional information)*

Sheila "I'm fat and ugly and that's the way I'm always going to be!"

Thomas "I'm never going to amount to anything. Nothing I ever do is right."

Jana "Poor Jason will never amount to anything as long as he has me for a parent!"

These "global" (notice the words *always* and *never*) and self-destructive messages sent a signal to all three of these people that they needed to sort out their feelings. Sheila, Thomas, and Jana took the time to sort out their feelings by using four simple steps. Let's look at these four steps.

Step One: Identify the Source of the Feeling(s)

When we feel a barrage of "scrambled" feelings, we can feel so overwhelmed that we may not know where to begin to sort them out. The place to begin is with questions such as "*When* did I start feeling this way?" and "*What happened* that started this feeling?"

The answers to these questions will give us the information we need. Identifying a particular time and event *keeps us focused on what is real* and avoids wasting time and energy on global and self-destructive messages. Notice the change in focus for each of our three friends: *(Write on chalkboard under first statements)*

Sheila "I've felt awful ever since I ate that hot fudge sundae at lunch."

Thomas "I started losing it as soon as my parents arrived for dinner last night."

Jana "It all started when the principal from Jason's school called on Monday."

I'M ALL SHOOK UP!

Step Two: Accurately Name the Feeling(s) Involved

Saying that we feel "awful" or are "losing it" is too vague to be helpful. Our task is to pinpoint the precise feelings that have been aroused by the circumstances and events identified in Step One. A list of feelings words can help. As we read through the list, certain words will grab our attention. We can keep working at it until there is a feeling of assurance that says, "Yes! That is exactly what I am feeling!" In our three examples, the feelings that each person named were *(Write on chalkboard)*

Sheila	Guilt, shamed, and dominated
Thomas	Stupid, bad, and threatened
Jana	Failure, confused, and shamed

Step Three: Decide What to Do About the Feeling(s)

Once we know exactly what feelings we are dealing with, we must make some choices. Examples of choices you might make to deal with your feelings follow:

Find a healthy way to express it. *(Have a good cry, call someone, physical exercise, notebook/pen, etc.)*

Make amends when you are wrong.

Choose to reject inappropriate and self-destructive messages. *(I do not accept that I am irresponsible; I made an honest mistake)*

Find a trusted friend or support group to help you understand the source of your feelings. *(How about Confident Kids!)*

Make an action plan. *(Call a friend if you feel lonely)*

Let's see what our three friends decided in this step:

Sheila was surprised that the feeling "dominated" surfaced in Step Two. Thinking about that helped her see that she had ordered the hot fudge sundae at lunch as a reaction to a fight she had with her husband the night before, in which she had felt completely dominated by him. For the first time in her life, she began to wonder if she was using food as an inappropriate way to deal with her feelings—a cycle that increased her feelings of shame and guilt, since she had struggled with being overweight all her life. *(Add this next line to the chalkboard)* ***Sheila's Action Plan***: She sought out counseling in a support group focused on eating issues.

Thomas had already been working on recognizing the self-destructive messages that were often triggered by his encounters with his over-demanding parents. *(Add the highlights to the chalkboard)* ***Thomas's Action Plan***: He first chose to reject the negative messages, and then he decided to list in a journal his feelings and specific ways to celebrate the relationships in his life that remind him of how worthwhile and valuable he really is.

Jana decided to take a risk by making an appointment to see the principal and telling him how confused she was about being a parent. (Jason had been born when Jana was only seventeen.) Although sharing her true feelings was not easy for her, she was able to state clearly how ashamed she felt that Jason was constantly in trouble at school. *(Add the highlights to the chalkboard)* ***Jana's Action Plan***: The principal reminded her that becoming a teenage parent presented special problems and referred her to a parenting group that met at a nearby community center. At the first meeting, Jana discovered that sharing with others who were struggling with the same issues greatly reduced her feelings of confusion and failure.

Step Four: Follow Through With the Choice Made in Step Three

There is, of course, a big difference between knowing what to do and doing it. Taking action is a big part of getting through our difficult feelings. It may involve taking risks that feel frightening or difficult. Just remember—if your plan of action feels too threatening, it's always OK to ask for help!

Learning the skills for sorting out our feelings may take some practice and patience at first, but it is well worth the effort. As parents, there is a double reason to do so. Not only is it healthy for us, but we will only be able to help our children work through their feelings when we have first learned the skills to work through our own.

Making It Personal (35 Minutes)

Let's Sort It Out

Distribute copies of the "Reflections" worksheet (page 322) to all participants and give them a few minutes to fill them out.

Group Sharing

After all are finished, share responses around the circle, or divide into smaller groups. Remind everyone of the "Right to Pass" rule before starting.

Building on God's Word (15 Minutes)

Bible Focus

Distribute copies of the "Building on God's Word" worksheet (page 324) and discuss it together. Encourage parents to use this sheet at home during the coming week as a means of spiritual encouragement and connecting to God.

Prayer Time

Ask parents to fill in the prayer request line on their "Building on God's Word" worksheet. Give opportunity for parents to share these requests with the rest of the group. End the session with a time of open prayer.

LET'S SORT IT OUT

1. Describe a time in your childhood or adolescence when you felt you had "a scrambled brain" or "knots in your stomach" or you were "losing it" and you didn't know why.

2. Describe a recent time when you had the same experience.

   What, if any, connection do you see between the two experiences?

LET'S SORT IT OUT

3. Now use the four steps to work through the experience you described above:

Step One: Identify the source of the feeling(s). When did I start feeling this way? What happened that started this feeling?

Step Two: Accurately name the feelings involved.

Step Three: Decide what you can do (or could have done) about the feeling(s).

Step Four: If it is still possible, do it!

PSALM 51:6; JOHN 8:31, 32

Honestly facing our feelings is a powerful form of truth-telling. Let's read these Bible verses, applying them to the experience of letting go of our feelings defenses and telling the truth about what is behind them.

> **Surely you desire truth in the inner parts; you teach me wisdom in the inmost place.** Psalm 51:6 (*NIV*)
>
> **Jesus said, "If you hold to my teaching, you are really my disciples. Then you will know the truth, and the truth will set you free."** John 8:31, 32 (*NIV*)

Record your immediate reactions to these verses.

God promises to guide us through our journey. Bring your struggles to Him in prayer now, asking for His wisdom to lead you to the truth that will set you free.

Your #1 prayer request for this week:

Overview

One of the consistent themes of the Confident Kids program is that it is always OK to ask for help. Many high-stress families feel isolated, without resources to provide help when they need it. This session focuses on giving parents permission to ask for help, and guides them to appropriate resources.

Needed

- Session Summary for Parents (page 361)
- "Reflections" worksheet
- "Building on God's Word" worksheet
- Prayer journal

Asking for Help

Parent Session 6 Outline

Getting Started (20 Minutes)

Check-In

Group Rules

Review Session Summary for Parents

Teaching Time (20 Minutes)

"It's My Job to Ask for Help to Get My Needs Met"

Making It Personal (35 Minutes)

Reflections: "Building a Support System"

Group Sharing

Building on God's Word (15 Minutes)

Bible Focus

Prayer Time

ASKING FOR HELP

PARENT SESSION 6

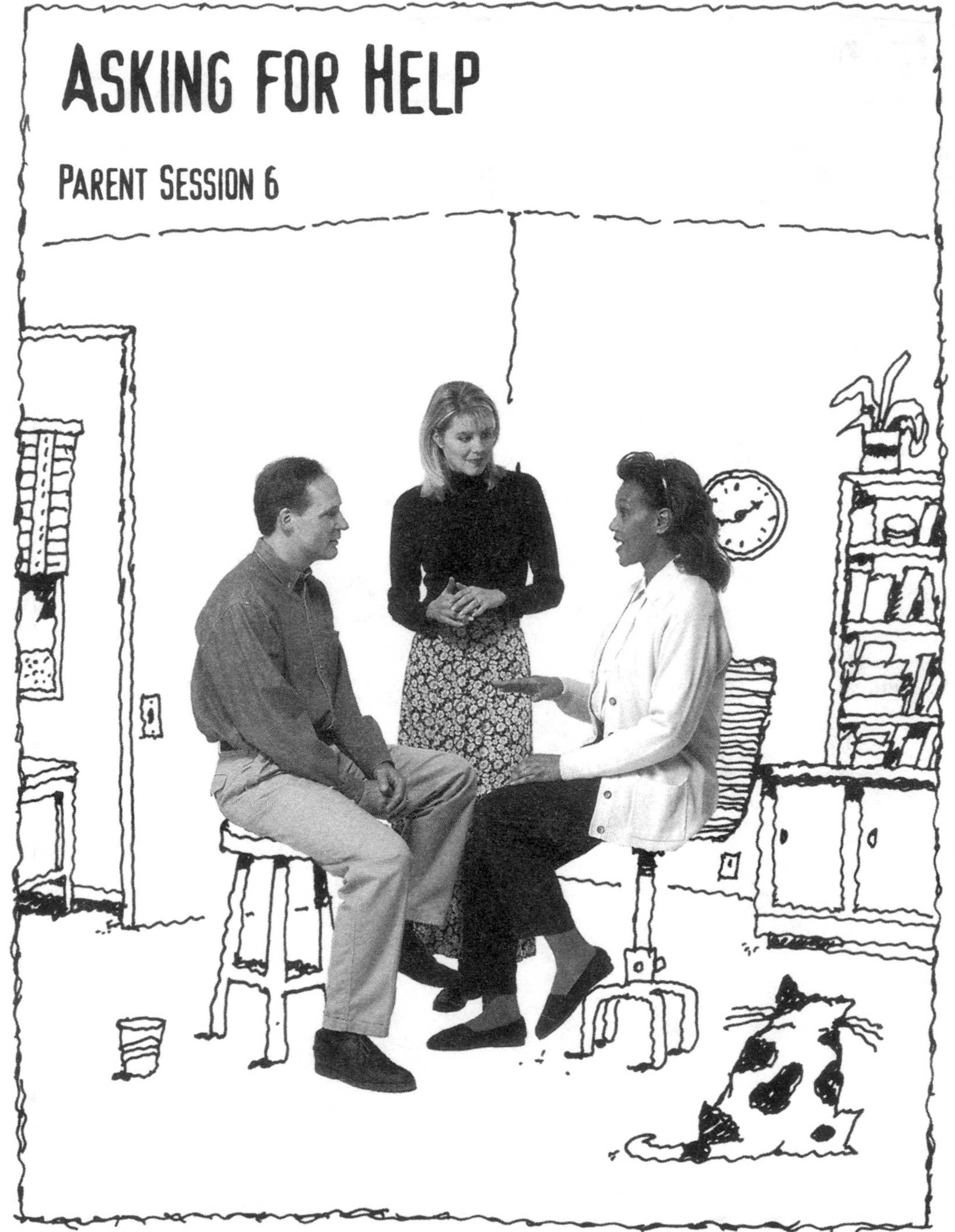

GETTING STARTED (20 MINUTES)

CHECK-IN

Ask if anyone has any feedback or questions from last week's session. Then ask parents to share one time this past week when they asked someone for help with something. Any deliberate effort to ask for help should be praised.

GROUP RULES

Review the three basic rules of Confident Kids parent sessions:

1. Confidentiality
2. No advice giving
3. The right to pass

REVIEW SESSION SUMMARY FOR PARENTS

Read through the "Session Summary for Parents" (page 361) together. Be sure parents understand that this handout summarizes what their children will learn in their session today.

TEACHING TIME (20 MINUTES)

IT'S MY JOB TO ASK FOR HELP TO GET MY NEEDS MET

Today's emphasis is, "It's my job to ask for help to get my needs met."

> **We live in a society that values privacy more than community and teaches us that life is "normal" when we are happy and living the "good life." Even some churches have propagated the belief that we won't have problems if we are truly spiritual and connected to God. As a result, most of us**

feel we should be making it on our own, and know of very few places within society (including the church) where we feel comfortable sharing our greatest areas of pain and asking for help. All of this, however, is a major distortion of what it means to be human and live in our world. Life is hard and, more often than not, the problems we face are big ones! It is also a fact of being human that we need each other to get through life. The truth is, living a healthy life is possible only when we learn how to ask for help when we need it. Here are a few points that can help us develop this skill.

It's OK to Ask for Help

Many of us grew up with a lot of misconceptions about getting our needs met. We may have lived in families in which our needs were not important. We were told to be quiet, stop crying, get our own meals, etc. Or, we might have been taught that it is someone else's job to meet our needs—without us ever telling them what those needs are. This is an "If you really loved me, you'd take care of me" mentality. A third possibility is that we may have been raised in church settings in which we were told that it is selfish and against God's will for us to center on our own needs. We should just serve God and others and not think about ourselves at all. All of these attitudes are damaging to us.

IT'S MY JOB TO ASK FOR HELP TO GET MY NEEDS MET

The truth is, no one knows what we need but us. Many people in our lives would like to help, but they don't "magically" know what we need. It is up to us to tell them by asking for help when we need it. This does not mean that we spend all our time focused on ourselves and our concerns; we must also give attention to our relationship to God and to caring for others. But sometimes the right thing to do is to take care of ourselves by giving ourselves permission to ask for help.

Everyone Needs a Support System That Includes a Variety of Helpers

The best way to ask for help is to surround ourselves with a network of people who will be available to us when we need help. Every human being needs such a support system, made up of a variety of people who will meet different kinds of needs. We need people we can turn to when we need:

Someone to listen to us when we need to "dump." Sometimes we just need to vent our feelings with a friend who will listen attentively but not try to "fix" the situation for us. They can tell when we just need to talk, but don't need advice.

Someone to be honest with us about our blind spots. There are times when we need to talk to friends who we know will tell us when they see us do something unhealthy. These friends can discern the difference between when we need to "dump" so we can move forward on our own, and when we are stuck and need an honest "kick in the pants" to move on. These are trusted friends who can speak a word of truth in *love*—not *shame*!

Someone we can "let down our hair" and "kick up our heels" with! An important part of managing stress in our lives is knowing when we need to take a break from the intensity of the situation and do something fun. These friends are the ones we want to call at those times. They always know how to make us laugh and forget our problems, even if it is for a short "breather." Everyone needs some of these friends in their lives!

Someone who can help us take care of the practical concerns of life. This may be a friend we can call when our car breaks down or the plumbing backs up, or someone who will take the kids for a day to give us a needed break. These are the people who will bring a meal when we're sick, or always seem to know whom to call when we don't know where to turn to get something done.

People who will take an interest in and be role models for our children. All parents need help to raise healthy kids. The best thing you can do for your kids is build a family support system, made up of people who share your value system and will take an active interest in your children. As kids grow older, it becomes increasingly important that they have adults other than their parents whom they can confide in and feel *they* can turn to for all the points listed above. Parents need not feel threatened if their child goes through a time when they seem to want to confide in an adult other than themselves. This is normal and healthy for our children!

Professional helpers. Many of the most stressful situations in our lives need a professional helper to get us through (e.g., a counselor, a doctor who specializes in attention deficit disorders, a lawyer, a social worker). People who live healthy lives know where to find professional helpers, and are not ashamed to ask for their services, when needed.

Building a Support System Takes Time and Hard Work; Stay With It!

Finding people who can provide the support outlined above is not easy in our isolationist society. But it is essential for coping with life in our stressful times. You can build this support system from family members, neighbors, church families, support groups, civic groups, etc. The point is that you must reach out to others; you cannot simply sit back and wish that others would come alongside and help you. As you invite people to share in your life and are willing to offer them the same kind of support in their lives, you will find others whom you—and your children—can call on when you need help.

Making It Personal (35 Minutes)

Building a Support System

Distribute copies of the "Reflections" worksheet (page 330) and give participants a few minutes to fill them out.

Group Sharing

After all are finished, share responses around the circle. Give particular attention to question 2. Ask parents to talk about whether it was difficult, or even possible, for them to come up with twenty names. Help them think of sources they might not ordinarily consider available to them (e.g., your church, if they do not attend).

Also, if time permits, have parents pair up and practice asking for the help they need, as identified in question 3. Tell them:

> **This is a role play. Pretend your partner is the person you want to ask for help. Practice what you would say to get the help you need.**

Remind everyone of the "Right to Pass" rule before starting.

Building on God's Word (15 Minutes)

Bible Focus

Distribute copies of the "Building on God's Word" worksheet (page 332) and discuss it together. Encourage parents to use this sheet at home during the coming week as a means of spiritual encouragement and connecting to God.

Prayer Time

Ask parents to share their prayer request from their "Building on God's Word" worksheet. Ask for updates on requests shared in past weeks. End the session with a time of open prayer.

BUILDING A SUPPORT SYSTEM

1. How would you rate yourself and your family's present ability to ask for help when you need it? (Make two marks on the line below; one for you and one for your family as a whole.)

Have all the support we need	So-so	We are totally isolated

2. In the space below, identify twenty people you consider to part of your support system in some way. (Family, neighbors, church group, professionals, trusted friends, etc.)

1. ______	11. ______
2. ______	12. ______
3. ______	13. ______
4. ______	14. ______
5. ______	15. ______
6. ______	16. ______
7. ______	17. ______
8. ______	18. ______
9. ______	19. ______
10. ______	20. ______

3. Identify one area that is especially difficult for you to ask for help. Fill in the blanks on the next page to make a plan to ask for help in that area.

Building a Support System

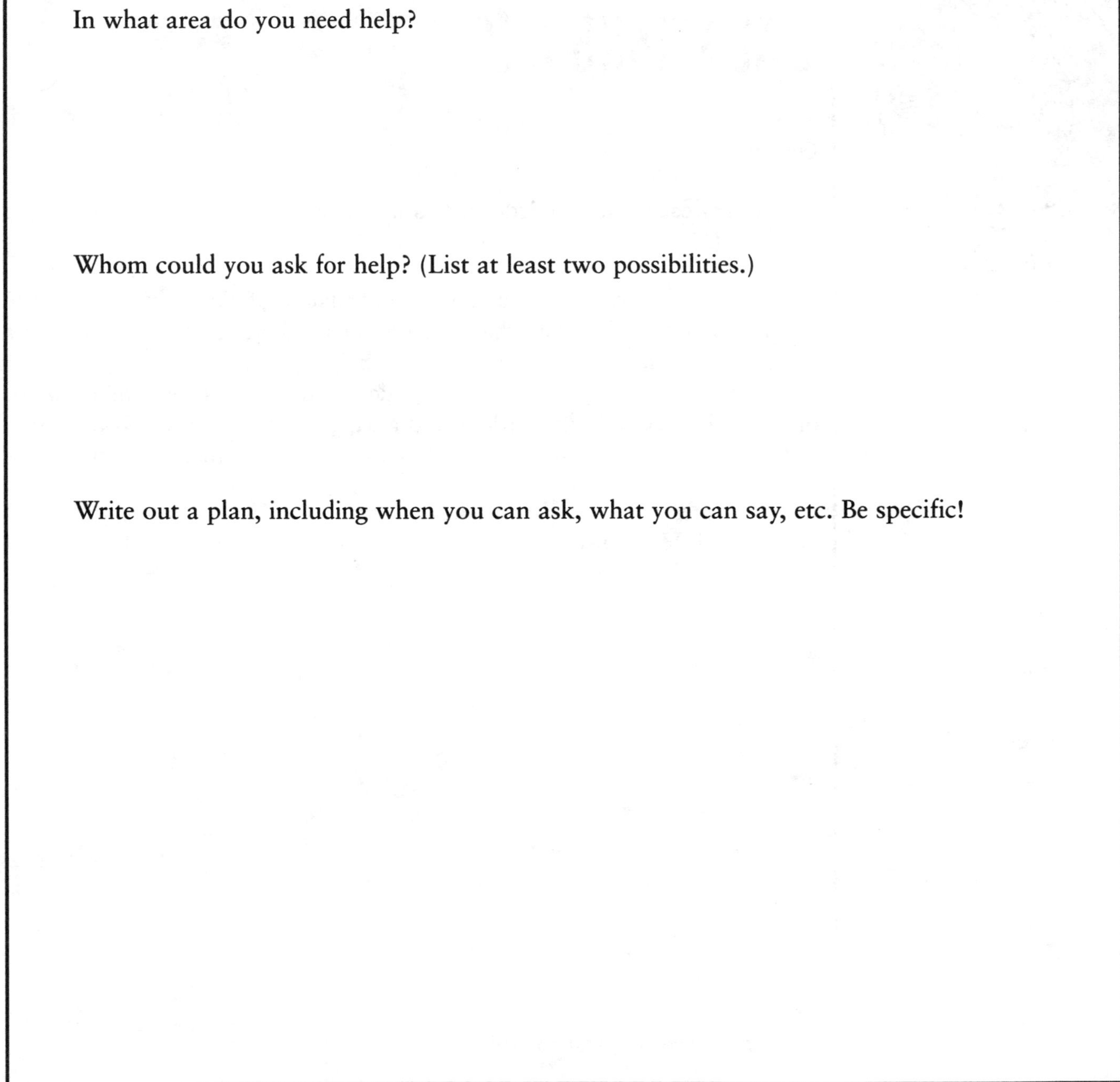
In what area do you need help?
Whom could you ask for help? (List at least two possibilities.)
Write out a plan, including when you can ask, what you can say, etc. Be specific!

GALATIANS 6:2

The Bible shows us how to care for one another's needs and pray for each other. One favorite verse is:

> **Carry each other's burdens, and in this way you will fulfill the law of Christ. Galatians 6:2 (*NIV*)**

Although at first reading this verse sounds like it is reinforcing the need for us to be centered on other people's needs rather than our own, consider this: If everyone believed they were supposed to be helpers and never the one needing help, would there be anyone for helpers to help? The words are clear: carry *each other's* burdens. That means sometimes you must let yourself be the one who is sharing your burdens and asking others to carry you for a time. This is God's plan, and we cannot live healthy lives unless we learn to balance being the "carry-er" and the "carry-ee."

In your times of prayer this week, remember that God often meets our needs through other people. Ask Him to show you how you can build a support network of other human beings He can use to answer your prayers for help! As you listen for His answer, record any insights below:

Your #1 prayer request for this week:

Overview

During the hardest of times, it is only natural to ask, "Where are You, God?" This lesson explores the spiritual questions we have when life is painful and difficult. It also involves parents in an activity that illustrates how Jesus' presence within our lives makes Him the best helper possible—for them *and* their children!

Needed

- Session Summary for Parents (page 362)
- One copy of "Daddy" from Elementary Session 7
- Copies of "Inside Me" and "Jesus" from Elementary Session 7
- Paper lunch bags (one per parent) and markers
- *Optional:* Magazine pictures and glue
- "Building on God's Word" worksheet
- Prayer journal

Jesus Helps Me with My Feelings

Parent Session 7 Outline

Getting Started (20 Minutes)

Check-In

Group Rules

Review Session Summary for Parents

Teaching Time (20 Minutes)

"Where Are You, God?"

Making It Personal (35 Minutes)

"Jesus Is My Helper" Paper Bag Activity

Building on God's Word (15 Minutes)

Prayer Time

Bible Focus

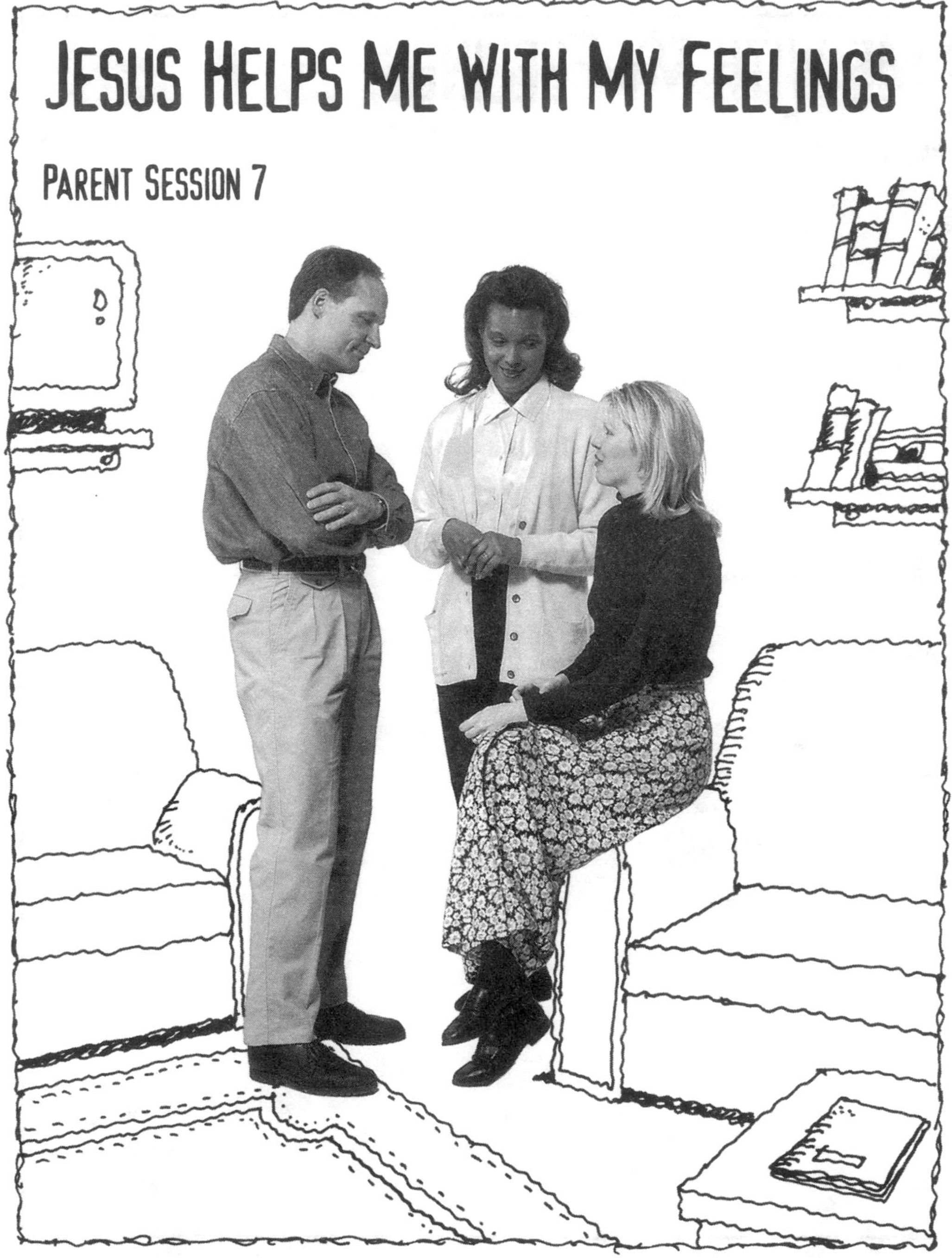
JESUS HELPS ME WITH MY FEELINGS
PARENT SESSION 7

GETTING STARTED (20 MINUTES)

CHECK-IN

Remind parents that next week is the last week of the unit, and give them any special instructions for that session, such as where to meet and whether or not to bring snacks. If you are planning to continue beyond this unit, give them a preview of the next topic, and tell them how to sign up for it.

GROUP RULES

Review the three basic rules of Confident Kids parent sessions:

1. Confidentiality
2. No advice giving
3. The right to pass

REVIEW SESSION SUMMARY FOR PARENTS

Read through the "Session Summary for Parents" (page 362). Be sure parents understand that this handout summarizes what their children will learn in their session today.

TEACHING TIME (20 MINUTES)

WHERE ARE YOU, GOD?

Today we ask the question, "Where are You, God?" You will need a copy of "Daddy" from Elementary Session 7 (begins on page 166). This is a collection of letters written by eleven-year-old Amy during her father's cancer treatment. They were Amy's way of handling her feelings through a difficult period of her life. Read them to the parents at this time, especially highlighting the places where she talks about prayer. Discuss the following:

Have you ever had anything happen in your life that made you feel like Amy? *(Let parents respond)*

Amy talks about praying for her daddy. In the first letter she says, "I've been praying that you don't (have cancer), but sometimes that doesn't matter." What do you think she meant by that? *(Let parents respond)*

Have you ever asked God, "Why is this happening to me?" as Amy did? *(Let parents respond)* **Have you ever been angry with God for what was happening in your life?** *(Let parents respond)*

During the hardest times of our lives, it is only natural to ask, "Where are You, God?" Sometimes it is hard to remember that God can be a great help to us when life gets difficult, especially when it seems as though the hard times drag on and on. During those times, it is only natural for us to question whether God loves us, or feel as if He has abandoned us. It's OK to feel that way for a time.

Ask if anyone is feeling that way today. Give anyone who wants to talk the opportunity to express her feelings to the group.

During times when we feel overwhelmed by our circumstances, we can help ourselves get through by doing two things: Talking to trusted friends about how we're feeling and relying on promises from God's Word.

Ask parents to share any promises from God's Word that have sustained them through difficult times. Share those verses with each other as a way of affirming that God is, indeed, faithful to us during the difficult moments of our lives.

MAKING IT PERSONAL (35 MINUTES)

JESUS IS MY HELPER PAPER BAG ACTIVITY

Instead of completing a "Reflections" sheet today, the parents will do the same activity their kids are doing. You will need paper lunch bags, markers, and copies of "Inside Me" and "Jesus" from Elementary Session 7 (pages 179 and 181). If you like, you can also provide a variety of old magazine pictures and glue.

Begin by reading Psalm 139 to affirm God's presence with us through every situation we face in life. Emphasize that there is no place we can go, or anything that can happen to us that is apart from God's knowledge and care. Then distribute the paper lunch bags, markers, pencils, and the "Inside Me" sheet. Proceed as follows:

Each of us has an inside and an outside life. **Our *outside* lives are that part of us that everyone can see. What might that include?** *(What we look like, what we are good at, what we like or don't like, who our friends are, our families, etc.)* **Our *inside* lives contain all the private things no one knows unless we choose to tell them.** *(Our feelings and reactions to situations; our fears, likes, and dislikes we never talk about; our hopes and dreams, etc.)*

Pretend this lunch bag is you. **It has an outside and an inside. Decorate this bag to make it like you. On the outside, write or draw (or use magazine pictures) to depict the things about you that are known to everyone.** *(Family members, activities, favorite color, etc.)* **Now use the "Inside Me" worksheet to privately write about some things that are part of your inside life. Put these private things inside your bag.**

Psalm 139 tells us that God knows not only the outside part of our lives, but He understands our private lives as well. **And no matter what is inside your heart, He cares about those things and loves you very much. In fact, there is no living person who knows us as well as God, or loves us as much. That is why we can come to God in prayer about anything in our lives.**

Now give one "Jesus" heart to each person.

Here's one more piece to put inside your bags. The Bible teaches us that if we ask Him to, Jesus will come to live in our inside lives and be there with us forever. And, one day when we die, God will take us to His home in Heaven because Jesus is in our lives. *(Place "Jesus" heart inside the bag. Staple the bag shut to symbolize that no one can get into our inside lives unless we choose to let them. This can also symbolize that once Jesus comes into our lives, He never leaves!)*

Be sure everyone understands that God wants to live in our inside lives, but will only do so when asked. Tell them that you hope each of them has made a decision to give their lives to Jesus, but if they have not they can! *Note:* Offer to help those who want to follow through with a decision to let Jesus direct their life.

Building on God's Word (15 Minutes)

Prayer Time

Due to the nature of this session, you may want to have the prayer time now, to give parents who may have never done so an opportunity to ask Jesus to direct their lives. Give all parents an opportunity to pray quietly about the "inside feelings" they placed inside their bags. Close with a prayer for all the parents, asking God to be particularly close to those having a hard time feeling His presence in their lives at this time. Welcome into God's family anyone who might have asked Jesus into their lives for the first time today.

Bible Focus

Distribute copies of the "Building on God's Word" worksheet (page 337) and review it briefly together. Encourage parents to use this sheet at home during the coming week as a means of spiritual encouragement and connecting to God.

PSALM 139

Psalm 139 teaches us how special we are to God. No matter where we are, or what is happening to us, God is always with us! He knows us inside and out, and cares deeply about everything that happens to us! Even though God may not answer our prayers in just the way we ask Him, that doesn't mean God is not there or that He does not care!

In her last letter, Amy said: "I should have listened to Mom when she told me that God does listen but He does things His way, not ours."

The fact that God is always with us makes Him the best helper we can have. Sometimes people will not be able to help us when we need it most, but God promises to be with us all the time! And we can count on that! Each day this week, read Psalm 139, asking God to sink its incredible truths deep within your heart. Write out a response to each day's reading. Notice any differences as the week goes on.

Monday:

Tuesday:

Wednesday:

Thursday:

Friday:

Saturday:

Sunday:

GOALS

- Have kids and parents share the Confident Kids group experience
- Have kids and parents play together
- Give opportunity for kids and parents to evaluate the group and reenroll for the next unit (if you are having one)
- Bring closure to this unit

NEEDED

- Name tags for parents, kids, and facilitators
- Word cards for "Feelings Charades"
- Praise tape or other means of facilitating group singing
- Items for kids' presentations
- Unit verse cards copied onto card stock and cut apart
- Evaluation sheets for parents and kids (pages 371 and 373)
- Affirmation balloons, filled out in advance (page 377)
- Completion certificates, filled out in advance (page 379)
- Snacks

FAMILY NIGHT

FAMILY SESSION 8 OUTLINE

Gathering Activity (25 Minutes)

Name Tags

Feelings Charades

Welcome and Introduction of Parents by the Kids

Split Session (20 Minutes)

Parents Review Basic Concepts From Unit

Kids Prepare for Their Presentations

Closing Program (30 Minutes)

Songs

Presentations:

Preschool: Joshua 1:9, With Motions

First Through Fourth Graders: David and Goliath Story or Confident Kids Psalm 1

Fifth and Sixth Graders: Confident Kids Psalm 1 or Memory Verses

Awarding of Certificates and Affirmation Balloon Sheets

Closing Prayer Huddle

Snacks and Evaluations (15 Minutes)

Snack Table

Evaluations and Enrollment Time

FAMILY NIGHT

FAMILY SESSION 8

GATHERING TIME (25 MINUTES)

NAME TAGS

As participants arrive, be sure everyone, including facilitators, puts on a name tag. If you like, you can make an activity out of it by letting each person design his own tag using rubber stamps, stickers, and markers.

FEELINGS CHARADES

Repeat this gathering activity from Elementary Session 2. Before the session begins, make up a set of "Feelings Charades" cards by writing feelings words on 3" x 5" cards. Make about ten cards. To play, divide families into two teams and choose one to start. Choose a child to draw a card and act the feelings word out for the rest of their team. The rest of the team calls out guesses. After three incorrect guesses, the actor gives a hint by saying: I feel this way when ________.

After the feeling has been guessed, choose a child from the other team and repeat. For Round 2, let the parents act out the words. Continue until all words have been used or you are out of time.

INTRODUCTION OF THE PARENTS BY THE KIDS

Seat everyone in a circle and ask the kids to introduce their parents to the rest of the group by giving their parent's name and one special thing about them. This could be a character quality, a favorite food, something they like to do, etc.

SPLIT SESSION (20 MINUTES)

Send the parents to their room with their facilitator to do the following:

- Review the main concepts of this topic and answer any remaining questions.
- Have parents share what they found most helpful from the unit.
- Give an overview of the next topic, if you are planning to do one, including starting date, unit theme, and any special instructions.

Meanwhile, have the kids meet in their room(s) to review their presentations.

CLOSING PROGRAM (25 MINUTES)

SONGS

Choose an energetic song leader to lead families in singing a few praise songs and Psalms set to music, or any songs the kids have been singing throughout the unit.

CHILDREN'S PRESENTATIONS

Invite the kids to make the presentations they worked on during the last session (see Session 7 for details):

- Preschoolers: Invite the kids and leaders to come forward and present Joshua 1:9, with motions.
- First Through Fourth Graders: Depending on the choices made last week, present the David and Goliath story (led by King David) or Confident Kids Psalm 1.
- Fifth Through Sixth Graders: Depending on the choices made last week, have the kids recite their version of Confident Kids Psalm 1 or review the memory verses by doing a memory verse wave. The older kids can also pass out a copy of the "Scripture Cards" (page 342) for each child to take home.

AWARDING OF CERTIFICATES AND AFFIRMATION BALLOONS

Before the meeting, have facilitators who did not already do so fill out a certificate and affirmation balloons sheet (page 377) for each child in their group. (Rolling them up together and tying with a ribbon is a nice way to present them. Real balloons would be fun, too!) Have each facilitator award these to their kids. Allow time for the facilitators to give a verbal affirmation to each child as well. Affirming kids in front of their parents is a powerful experience for the kids.

CLOSING PRAYER HUDDLE

Have the kids do their closing prayer huddle, while parents watch. Include a prayer for the unit, thanking God for each family and asking His blessing.

SNACKS AND EVALUATIONS (15 MINUTES)

SNACK TABLE

For this special event, create a special party table for families to enjoy. The facilitators can bring the treats, or you can have a potluck snack table. Be sure to include this information on the party invitations, or have facilitators write a special note to each of their kids this week inviting them to bring snacks. *Note:* Before dismissing to the snack table, set a rule that kids must go through the line with their parents! This will prevent a stampede, and will keep the families together so they can fill out the evaluations.

EVALUATIONS AND ENROLLINGMENT TIME

Place the unit evaluation forms for both parents and kids (pages 371 and 373) on the snack table. Be sure all participants take one to complete before leaving. Notice that kids and parents have different forms. Also, if you are planning to host another Confident Kids unit, invite parents to reenroll by signing the statement on the bottom of their evaluation sheet. Allow families to "hang around" and visit as long as they like!

Joshua 1:9

Be strong and courageous. Do not be terrified; do not be discouraged, for the Lord your God will be with you wherever you go.

NIV

Philippians 4:6, 7

Do not be anxious about anything, but in everything present your requests to God. And the peace of God will guard your hearts and minds in Christ Jesus.

NIV

Joshua 1:9

Be strong and courageous. Do not be terrified; do not be discouraged, for the Lord your God will be with you wherever you go.

NIV

Philippians 4:6, 7

Do not be anxious about anything, but in everything present your requests to God. And the peace of God will guard your hearts and minds in Christ Jesus.

NIV

Joshua 1:9

Be strong and courageous. Do not be terrified; do not be discouraged, for the Lord your God will be with you wherever you go.

NIV

Philippians 4:6, 7

Do not be anxious about anything, but in everything present your requests to God. And the peace of God will guard your hearts and minds in Christ Jesus.

NIV

Parent Information Handouts

Confident Kids

GETTING INFORMATION TO THE PARENTS

Parent Information Handouts are helpful for many reasons, but particularly because of the Confident Kids confidentiality rule. Elementary kids will have difficulty sorting out what is okay to talk about and what should be kept confidential. Therefore, they will typically tell their parents that their leaders told them *not* to talk about what they are doing in the group. These handouts will allay parents' fears and answer many of their questions about the program.

Parent Information Handouts will keep parents well informed about the Confident Kids program by including the following handouts:

- **Welcome to Confident Kids! Information for Parents**

  This letter gives an overview of the program and should include the name and telephone number of the person parents can contact if they have any questions about their kids' experience during the sessions.

- **Let's Learn Healthy Living Skills**

  Much of the Confident Kids material is designed to teach families healthy living skills. For many families, this material will be new, and the skill being taught will feel awkward and uncomfortable. Review this handout periodically to encourage parents to work hard at replacing old, unhealthy behavior patterns with new, healthy living skills.

- **Topic Overview**

  This piece summarizes the theme for the entire set of sessions.

- **Weekly Session Summaries**

  Each week a session summary details each week's theme and key verse, plus gives a suggested follow-up activity parents can do throughout the week.

Distribute the Session Summaries in one of these ways:

- **During the Parent Sessions**

  The best way to keep parents informed, of course, is to involve them in the parents sessions. Parents who participate will receive and review the Session Summaries as part of their meeting.

- **In the Kids' Rooms or a Central Location**

  Place the handouts where parents can pick them up when they drop off or pick up their kids each week.

- **Through the Mail**

  By mailing them each week, you will ensure every parent receives one.

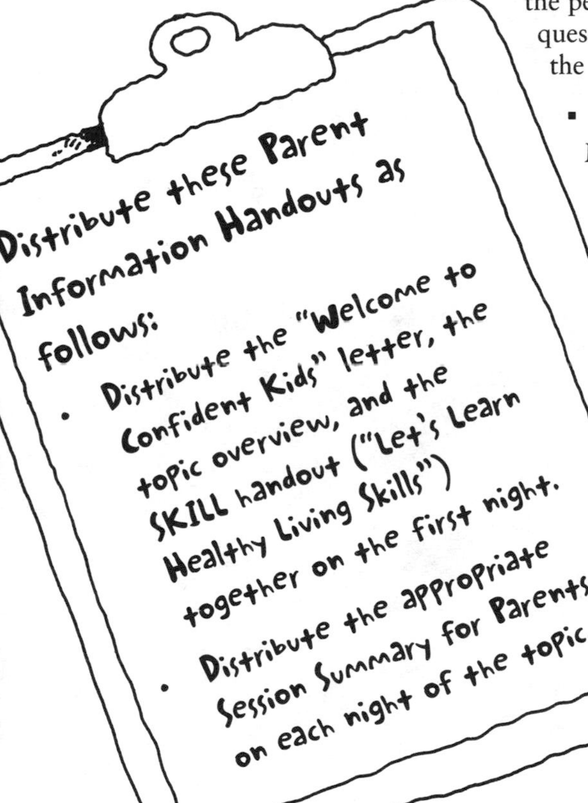

Distribute these Parent Information Handouts as follows:
• Distribute the "Welcome to Confident Kids" letter, the topic overview, and the SKILL handout ("Let's Learn Healthy Living Skills") together on the first night.
• Distribute the appropriate Session Summary for Parents on each night of the topic.

Welcome to Confident Kids!

Dear Parent or Sponsor,

Welcome to Confident Kids Support Groups. I am delighted you have chosen to involve your child in this experience. Please take a moment to read the information with this letter about the group, and be sure to keep my name and phone number close by in the coming weeks. I will be glad to talk with you about your child's experience at any time.

Deal with high-stress situations

Our Goals

In our changing society, children are having a harder and harder time growing up. There are so many stressful things for all of us to manage, and our kids are approaching overload! Confident Kids is designed to help both you and your children learn to deal with these high-stress situations in healthy and growing ways. We hope to:

- Teach children how to talk about their experiences and provide a loving and safe environment in which to do so
- Teach children skills to cope with their life experiences in healthy and positive ways
- Build self-esteem and a sense of trust through relationships with caring adults (facilitators)
- Guide children into a relationship with God and show them how prayer and the Bible are resources for dealing with their life circumstances

The Curriculum

Confident Kids is taught through a series of topics, each of which is eight weeks long and designed to teach a specific life skill. An outline of the topic you and your children are about to begin is enclosed. Each session plan uses stories, games, learning activities, and discussion questions to communicate with the children. In addition, each child is assigned to a small group, led by a carefully trained facilitator. These small groups will give your children an opportunity to build a relationship with a caring adult who will be their guide through the program.

Your Role

We ask you to take an active interest in what the children are learning. You will receive a summary of each session's theme, including an activity you can do at home to reinforce what kids are learning. If you are attending a parent group, the summaries will be distributed there. If not, they will be sent home with each child each week. Be sure to look for them.

Tested curriculum and trained facilitators

Snacks are an important part of the Confident Kids meetings. Children will take turns bringing the snack for the group each week. When the "snack tin" comes home with your child, instructions concerning what to send will be listed on the lid. Also, if there are restrictions on the snacks your child can have, be sure to call me immediately.

The last night of each unit is Family Night. You will be invited to come and share the group experience with the children. This is an important time; it brings closure to the unit, and provides an opportunity for you to meet your child's facilitator(s). Please plan to come to the party!

The Parent Group helps you, too!

The *Confident Kids* experience is most effective when you experience the program, too. To make this possible, we have a Parent Group that meets while the kids are meeting. The time is spent discussing the same topic the kids are learning, with emphasis on how to incorporate the skills at home, and time for personal sharing and prayer support. We would love for you to come.

Finally, please be aware that the information any child shares in the group will be respected as confidential. Children will be told not to share at home what others have said in the group setting; only information about themselves, if they wish to do so. Also, each facilitator has been instructed to treat every child's personal sharing as confidential, so please do not ask facilitators for detailed information. We don't want our program facilitators to be caught in the middle between you and your child. However, be assured that as the program administrator, I will monitor your child's participation carefully. If issues arise concerning your child that you need to know about, I will be sure to get you that information.

Once again, I am thrilled to have your family join us in the *Confident Kids* program. If I can help you in the weeks ahead, please do not hesitate to call me.

Sincerely,

Program Administrator

____

Phone Number

P.S. Much of the material in *Confident Kids* is designed to teach you and your family healthy living skills. If the material is new to you, you may feel awkward and uncomfortable using it at first. Let me encourage you that working at learning new life skills is worth the effort it takes to do it! I've included a copy of the SKILL Handout, "Let's Learn Healthy Living Skills," to encourage you along these lines.

Let's Learn Healthy Living Skills!

Learning new skills takes time and feels uncomfortable at first!

Remember when you were first learning to ride a bicycle or play a musical instrument or hit a baseball? It took time to perfect the skills you needed to accomplish those tasks, and much of that time was spent in boring practice sessions. You probably went through periods of discouragement and thought you would never improve. But persistence and practice eventually paid off, especially if the learning process was a group experience that took place in a friendly environment where everyone's efforts were treated with respect. It helped even more if you were guided by someone who had already mastered the skill and encouraged your every sign of progress.

Developing healthy life skills in a family setting is like that. Learning to live together in new ways will take time and commitment and patience on the part of every family member. Both you and your children will sometimes feel awkward and uncomfortable, as if things will never change for the better. There are no shortcuts to making healthy life skills a reality in your home, but knowing what to expect can keep you going. New skills normally develop in five stages, as the following acrostic illustrates:

S = **Stage 1: Seeing the Need.** All change begins here. It is only when we are motivated by the need for change that we will go through the hard work of learning a new skill.

K = **Stage 2: Keeping On.** As you start practicing a new skill, it is natural to feel awkward, so you may want to revert to behavior patterns that are familiar and comfortable. At this point, you will need lots of encouragement and the determination to keep going. This is the stage of greatest discouragement and the point at which many people give up.

I = **Stage 3: Increasing Confidence.** Over time, you will begin to see changes, and the ability to use the new skill will take root. Learning to recognize and celebrate small steps of growth will build your confidence and keep you going.

L = **Stage 4: Letting Go.** As your skill level improves, more and more you will find yourself letting go of past behavior patterns and replacing them with the new and healthier ones.

L = **Stage 5: Living It!** In this last stage, the new skill has become so integrated into your life that it becomes almost automatic. When you find yourself using it easily, you realize that the hard work of the earlier stages has paid off!

Facing My Feelings Topic Overview

Unit Slogan

All My Feelings Are OK!

Bible Lessons

Stories from the life of David in 1 Samuel 16–26, and selected Psalms

Key Verses Joshua 1:9 and Philippians 4:6, 7

Be strong and courageous. Do not be terrified; do not be discouraged, for the Lord your God will be with you wherever you go. (*NIV*)

Do not be anxious about anything, but in everything present your requests to God. And the peace of God will guard your hearts and your minds in Christ Jesus. (*NIV*, condensed)

Key Concepts

- There are no "good" or "bad" feelings; all are necessary to living a healthy life.
- It is dangerous to stuff (avoid) our feelings by using feelings defenses.
- There are healthy ways to express our feelings; we can avoid expressing our feelings in inappropriate ways.
- Our feelings tell us when it's time to ask for help.
- Jesus understands all our feelings and His presence within our hearts is the greatest resource we have to deal with them.

Session Titles

Preschool

1 I Have Lots of Feelings
2 All My Feelings Are OK!
3 Some Feelings Are Not Fun to Feel
4 I Can Talk About My Feelings
5 I Can Name My Feelings
6 Asking for Help
7 Jesus Helps Me With My Feelings
8 Family Night

Elementary/Preteen/Parents

1 Feelings Are an Important Part of Life
2 All My Feelings Are OK!
3 What Are My Feelings Defenses?
4 Express Those Feelings!
5 Some Feelings Are Difficult to Handle
6 Asking for Help
7 Jesus Helps Me With My Feelings
8 Family Night

Facing My Feelings

This unit addresses one of the most fundamental, and yet difficult parts of living a healthy life—the ability to feel the whole range of feelings God has placed within us. When properly understood, the capacity to experience feelings is an incredible gift from God. Feelings enrich our lives, help us connect with others and God, and warn us when we are in danger or need help.

Yet most of us are not always sure whether our emotional life is a blessing from God, or a curse! On one hand, we have the ability to feel love, pleasure, excitement, and pride. But on the other hand, we also feel great pain, anger, and loneliness. And here's the problem—we cannot have one without the other! We cannot pick and choose which emotions we want to feel. The only way we can avoid "bad" feelings is to shut down our ability to feel anything at all, or use unhealthy behaviors (feelings defenses) to keep them under control.

Children learn early in life that some feelings are not very much fun to feel. Unfortunately, *they also come to believe that if they feel bad, they are bad*, and therefore they must avoid or get rid of bad feelings at all costs! That one basic misconception is at the heart of much unhealthy behavior, learned in childhood and carried into adulthood. As you and your children work through the sessions in this unit, your primary goal will be to replace this misconception with the truth that there are no "bad" feelings, recognize the importance of opening up to all your feelings, and develop the skills necessary to handle them in helpful and appropriate ways.

Build a Feelings Vocabulary

An important part of this unit is teaching children (and yourself) how to *name what they are feeling, when they are feeling it*. Throughout the weeks of this unit, be aware of times you can help your children learn new feelings words and apply them to their life experiences. An alphabetical list of feelings words follows, and can help you expand your own feelings words vocabulary.

Alphabetical List of Feelings Words

accepted
afraid
angry
anxious
anxious to please others
apathetic
appreciated
attractive
awkward

beaten
beautiful
bewildered
brave

calm
cheated
closed
comfortable
compassionate
competent
concerned
confident
confused
contented
cowardly
cruel
curious
cut off

defeated
depressed
deprived
deserving punishment
desperate
disappointed in myself
disappointed in others
dominated

eager
embarrassed
envious
excited

failure, like a
fearful
friendly
friendless
frustrated

grateful
grudge-bearing
guilty
gutless

happy
hateful
hopeful
hopeless
hostile
humorous
hurt

ignored
immobilized
impatient
inadequate
incompetent
in control
indecisive
inferior
inhibited
insecure
insincere
isolated

jealous
judgmental

kind

lonely
loser, like a
loved
loyal

manipulated
manipulative
melancholy
misunderstood

needy

old beyond years
optimistic
out of control
overcontrolled
overlooked

paranoid
peaceful
persecuted
pessimistic
phony
pleased with self
possessive
pouty
pressured
proud

quiet

real
rejected
repulsive
restrained

sad
secure
shy
sick
silly
sincere
sinful
sluggish
soft
sorry
stubborn
stupid
sunshiny
superior
supported
suspicious
sympathetic

terrified
threatened
torn
touchy

ugly
unable to communicate
unappreciated
uncertain
understanding
uptight
useless

victimized
vindictive
violent

weary
weepy
winner, like a
wishy-washy

zealous

Session 1 Summary for Parents

Feelings Are an Important Part of Life

Main Points Your Child Learned Today

For the next few weeks, we will be talking with your child about managing our feelings. We began today by emphasizing that God created us with many different kinds of feelings. Some of them are pleasant and fun to feel; these feelings help us enjoy life. Others are much more difficult to feel, but they, too, serve a valuable purpose in our lives. They protect us by letting us know when we are in danger or in need of asking for help.

Your kids were also introduced to the idea that although all of us have the same feelings, we don't all express them in the same way. In the next few weeks, the kids will learn how to express their feelings in healthy and appropriate ways.

Bible Emphasis

Kids were introduced to King David today. His life will be the focus for this unit. David will talk with the kids about the many feelings he experienced throughout his lifetime, and how he learned to use poetry and music to express those feelings to God.

Joshua 1:9 (*NIV*), this unit's memory verse, was introduced today:

> **Be strong and courageous. Do not be terrified; do not be discouraged, for the Lord your God will be with you wherever you go.**

You can reinforce today's Bible teaching this week by memorizing Joshua 1:9 as a family. You can also pray together at bedtime about situations that may be causing fear in you or your children, and offer thanks for God's promise to be present and help in your lives.

Do-at-Home Activity

Make feelings vocabulary cards. Write a feelings word on one side of a 3"x 5" card. On the other side, draw a picture of that feeling or write the definition. Make a new card every day. Review the cards at mealtimes or bedtime.

Session 2 Summary for Parents

All My Feelings Are OK!

Main Points Your Child Learned Today

Last week we talked about how many different kinds of feelings there are and that feelings are a very important part of our lives. Today we talked about how some feelings feel better than others. We like to feel happy, excited, or loved—feelings we may label as "good." We don't like to feel sad, embarrassed, or hurt—feelings we may label as "bad." We must remember, however, that feelings are not good or bad. They are signals that tell us what is going on in our lives and what we need to do to stay healthy. For instance, feeling sad may not be fun, but when we have experienced a significant loss, it is good and healthy for us to feel that way for awhile.

Your children may naturally think there is something wrong with them when they have unpleasant feelings. But sometimes things happen that make us feel sad, angry, or disappointed. At those times, remind your children that *all* their feelings are important and there is nothing wrong with them because they are experiencing an unpleasant feeling. Remember, all our feelings are OK!

Bible Emphasis

Review Joshua 1:9. Remind your children and yourself that we do not have to be afraid of, or run away from, things in our lives that evoke powerful feelings. God's promise to be with us always can get us through anything life brings our way.

Do-at-Home Activity

Validate your children's feelings. Your reaction to your children's feelings will teach them if their feelings are appropriate or inappropriate. Find a quiet time this week to spend with each of your children. Let each child talk about anything that is on her mind, but listen for feelings more than content. Do not be judgmental. Set aside your parental role for this time, and by your reactions, let your child know it is OK for her to express all of her feelings to you.

Session 3 Summary for Parents

Feelings Defenses

Main Points Your Child Learned Today

Today we discussed with your child the subject of feelings defenses. To put it simply, a feelings defense is when we feel one way, but act in a different way. Feelings defenses protect (defend) us from feelings we consider to be too painful or powerful to face openly. We use them to avoid feeling uncomfortable, or if we want to hide our feelings from others.

Although any behavior can be considered a defense when it is used to avoid feelings, certain feelings defenses are particularly common. You may see a number of these at work in you or your children when your family is under stress.

Clowning—Making jokes in every situation in which we feel uncomfortable, or acting silly in emotional settings.

Pretending—Pretending that we don't feel hurt or disappointment or acting as if the situation had never happened.

Daydreaming—"Tuning out" of a conversation, thinking of other things, or making up stories when we don't want to feel something.

Acting Like a Know-It-All—Trying to gain control by always having the last word or never admitting we are wrong or at fault

Silence—Responding to pain by withdrawing and not saying anything, even if we feel angry or disappointed.

Getting Sick—Focusing on headaches and stomachaches—real or imagined—when something upsetting happens.

Lying—Covering up by exaggerating or making up excuses, or distracting others through irrelevant stories.

Being a People Pleaser—Doing everything possible to keep everyone happy to avoid conflicts that generate unwanted feelings.

Blaming—Putting down and accusing others to keep from facing internal pain.

It's important to note that everyone uses defensive behaviors sometimes, and that using them correctly is part of emotional health. The danger point is *always* using feelings defenses so that we *never* have to face our painful feelings openly. You can help your children lower their defenses by encouraging them to share their true feelings with trusted people who can offer them support.

Bible Emphasis

Review Joshua 1:9 again. Remind your children and yourself that you do not have to be afraid of, or run away from things in your lives that evoke powerful feelings. Let God's promise to be with you give you strength to lower your defenses and get the help you need!

Do-at-Home Activity

Use the Psalms to Express Your Feelings to God

As a family, read one Psalm each day and talk about what its author was feeling when he wrote it. Do you have similar feelings you can express to God in a family prayer?

Feelings Defense Cards

Make a set of cards listing the nine feelings defenses (listed here) to review with your feelings vocabulary cards (see Session 1 Summary for Parents, page 355).

Session 4 Summary for Parents

Express Those Feelings!

Main Points Your Child Learned Today

This week your children learned about expressing their feelings in healthy and positive ways. We discussed the fact that all feelings need to be expressed and that ignoring them does not make them go away. Rather, it just stuffs them deep inside where they will struggle to get out. We learned that the results of trying to keep our feelings locked inside (headaches, stomachaches, and misplaced anger) can be avoided by paying attention to our feelings and expressing them in appropriate and healthy ways.

We also discussed the fact that although all of us have the same feelings, we don't express them in the same ways. We encouraged them to find the ways that work the best for them. Possibilities for expressing feelings were presented using the following objects:

> ***Pillow***—Hit it when you are angry; cry into it when you are sad.
>
> ***Telephone***—Call someone you trust and talk about your feelings.
>
> ***Notebook***—Journal your feelings; write a poem.
>
> ***Stationery with envelopes***—Write a letter about your feelings and give it to someone you trust.
>
> ***Drawing supplies***—Drawing or scribbling helps get your feelings out.
>
> ***Box of tissues***—Sometimes you just need to cry!
>
> ***Running shoes***—Doing something physical helps get your feelings out.
>
> ***Large red heart***—Talk to someone you love about your feelings. Ask for a hug.

Finally, we also made it clear to the kids that the need to express their feelings does not give them freedom to engage in a "feelings free-for-all." There are inappropriate and unhealthy ways to express feelings that must never be used:

- **It is unhealthy to express feelings by hurting another person or property.** Throwing or breaking things, or hitting or saying hurtful things to someone else is never OK!
- **It is unhealthy to express feelings by hurting ourselves.** Using alcohol or drugs, getting physically sick, or thinking about suicide is never a good way to handle feelings!

You can reinforce this concept at home by making this rule part of your family life:

> **I must *never* express my feelings by hurting another person, hurting myself, or breaking things. I can *find a better way* to handle my feelings!**

Bible Emphasis

Today we introduced a new Bible verse:

> **Do not be anxious about anything, but in everything present your requests to God. And the peace of God will guard your hearts and your minds in Christ Jesus. Philippians 4:6, 7 (*NIV*, condensed)**

This verse teaches us that it is natural to feel worried and anxious about many things in our lives; all of us do. God knows that, and teaches us to come to Him with those feelings. Knowing that God will be with us and asking Him to help brings peace.

Do-at-Home Activity

Make a Family Feelings Box. Gather as many of the items listed above (or pictures of the items) as possible and place them into a box. Whenever any family member expresses their feelings in inappropriate ways, direct them to the Family Feelings Box to choose a healthier way to get their feelings out!

In addition, be aware of *preventive* measures you can take to keep feelings from erupting in unhealthy ways. Plan times alone with your children to talk about anything they want to talk about. Remember to accept what they share; don't use this time to reprimand. You could also go for walks, play active games more often, help them build relationships with other caring adults, etc.

SESSION 5 SUMMARY FOR PARENTS

SOME FEELINGS ARE DIFFICULT TO HANDLE

MAIN POINTS YOUR CHILD LEARNED TODAY

Today's session presented to your kids a three-step process they can use to help them handle feelings that are particularly difficult to face. Our goal was to make the kids aware that even unpleasant feelings are important and OK to feel, but that they are the feelings we will do our best to avoid, or impulsively react to in unhealthy ways. The following steps can help them get through difficult times in healthy ways:

- **Step 1: Name the Feeling**—Many times we react to feelings in unhealthy ways because we don't really know what we are feeling. When we name the feeling, we can go on to figure out what to do about it. But first, we must answer the question: "What am I feeling?"
- **Step 2: Stop and Think**—When we erupt when we are angry, shut down when we are sad, or blame ourselves when we feel hurt, we may not be thinking clearly. Before reacting impulsively, we can stop and think about what happened to start this feeling. Did something happen? Did someone say something? We answer this question: "What is really going on here?"
- **Step 3: Work It Out**—When we know what we are feeling, and stop and think about what's really going on, then we can make a healthy choice about what to do next. We might need to do something by ourselves to get our feelings out (use our feelings box), apologize to someone, or get to work to get something done (like study for the next math test instead of pouting over a bad grade). Answer this question: "What is the *best* thing to do right now?"

You can reinforce this teaching at home by guiding your children through this process whenever you see them reacting in unhealthy ways to the difficult feelings they have.

BIBLE EMPHASIS

The Bible story today came from 1 Samuel 26, which tells about some of King David's powerful feelings. Also, we reviewed Philippians 4:6, 7, emphasizing how prayer and trusting God to care for us are effective means of handling difficult feelings, especially anxiety (worry).

DO-AT-HOME ACTIVITY

Continue to build your feelings skills. Review past Session Summaries for Parents, particularly the "Do-at-Home" suggestions. Remember, these are skill-building activities. They need to be practiced regularly. Choose several that are particularly relevant to your own family situation. Make an intentional effort to work on these skills this week.

Session 6 Summary for Parents

Asking for Help

Main Points Your Child Learned Today

Today's session explored the need to ask for help when we need it. As simple as that may sound, many children and adults feel isolated and are afraid to ask for help. We must learn how to ask for help. We presented the following points to your children:

- **It's always OK to ask for help when you need it.** Children must learn early that others will not always know what they need until they speak up and ask for help.
- **You should ask for help whenever you feel uncomfortable inside.** If the kids don't understand something (are confused), feel afraid, want a hug (feel sad or lonely), they should ask for help.
- **Everyone needs a support system.** To help the children identify their own support systems, we had each child make a directory of "safe people" they felt they could turn to for help.

You can reinforce today's lesson by reviewing your child's directory and adding phone numbers to those people they could reach by phone. Plan to update the directory often, as your family's support system changes.

Bible Emphasis

The most important thing we did today was to emphasize during the prayer time that, when it comes to asking for help, God is the most important helper we can turn to!

Do-at-Home Activity

Make your own directory of helpers. Many parents in today's society feel isolated, without the resources they need. Take the time to write down those people who comprise your support system. These can be family, friends, work associates, mentors, church leaders, and professionals. Try to name at least twenty helpers among the following categories:

- People who will listen to you when you need to "dump."
- People who will be honest with you about your blind spots.
- Friends you can "let down your hair" and "kick up your heels" with!
- People who will help you take care of the practical concerns of life.
- People who will take an interest in and be role models for your children.
- Professional helpers.

If you cannot identify twenty people, take steps to build a stronger support system for you and your family. Here are some ideas: make an appointment for counseling, set up a lunch date with a friend, invite a church family over for dinner, etc. Be creative, and stay with it! Building a support system is hard work and takes time.

Session 7 Summary for Parents

Jesus Helps Me With My Feelings

Main Points Your Child Learned Today

This session is the last one for this unit, and we wanted to leave your children with the most powerful message we could. During the hardest times of our lives, it is only natural to ask, "Where are You, God?" God can be a great help to us, but sometimes it is hard to remember that when we can't see Him or touch Him. Therefore, we spent the entire session talking about God's presence in our lives. Specifically, we made the point that when we ask Jesus to live in our hearts, He comes to dwell in the deepest places of our lives and knows better than we do what we are feeling and why. This makes Jesus the perfect helper, particularly when we are going through difficult circumstances and pain. We encouraged the kids that sometimes people will not be able to help when they need it most, but God promises to be with them all the time.

It is our hope and prayer that no matter what else your children may gain from this unit, they will remember that no matter what life brings their way, God is the best helper we can have.

Bible Emphasis

Preschoolers through fourth graders focused on Psalm 139. This Psalm teaches us how special we are to God, and that no matter where we are or what is happening to us, God is always with us! He knows us inside and out, and cares deeply about everything that happens in our lives. We also reassured your kids that even though God may not answer their prayers in just the way they asked Him to (e.g., their parents got divorced, their grandparent died), that God is with us and He does care.

Fifth through sixth graders focused on the death and resurrection of Jesus. The events surrounding the last days of Jesus' life show clearly that Jesus is the perfect helper for us because He experienced many of the same things we do. (See Hebrews 2:18.) Your kids explored verses showing them how Jesus was abandoned by His friends; accused of something He didn't do; pleaded with God ("Please not make me do this!"); was betrayed by a friend; arrested; beat up; and cried out on the cross, "Father, where are You?" But He also experienced the resurrection, and today wants to give us *His power* to face the difficult events of our lives.

Do-at-Home Activity

Give attention to your own relationship to God. The message we shared with your children today of God's love, presence, and care through the circumstances of life is for you, too! Wherever you are on your faith journey, we encourage you to do whatever is necessary to build your own relationship to God. Whether that is finding someone you trust to honestly discuss questions you have or barriers that are interfering with your relationship to God, do it! God is waiting to be *your* helper, too!

APPENDIX A

FORMS

You will need the following forms as you conduct your Confident Kids unit:

Confident Kids Facilitator Application Form

Sponsoring Church/Organization: ______________________

Name: ______________________

Address: ______________________

City: ______________ State: ________ Zip: _____

Home phone: (_____)______________________

Work phone: (_____)______________________

Are you a church member?__________ Regular attender?__________

For how long?______________________

What other ministries have you been involved with, for how long, and what was your role?

Please write a brief statement describing your Christian experience, including your understanding of what it means to be a Christian and significant personal experiences that have shaped your faith:

Please tell us why you are interested in working in the Confident Kids program:

Briefly describe your childhood, including any significant issues directly relating to your work in the Confident Kids program (e.g., parental divorce, relationship to parents). Include any personal counseling or recovery process relating to your past that you have worked through as an adult:

Which areas of Confident Kids are you most interested in? Please rank in order, with 1 indicating the area of greatest interest:

_____ Facilitating a small group of children
_____ Preschool _____ Grades 1–4 _____ Grades 5, 6

_____ Facilitating a parent group

_____ Drama team

_____ Leading music

_____ Organizing and preparing materials and supplies

_____ Other:

(continued)

Background Information

Have you at any time been accused, rightly or wrongly, of child abuse, sexual molestation or neglect? _____

If yes, please explain fully:

Have you ever been arrested/convicted for anything more serious than a traffic violation? _____

If yes, please explain fully:

Have you ever been treated for any nervous or mental illness? _____

If yes, please explain fully:

I, the undersigned, authorize the Confident Kids program administrators or its representatives to verify the information on this form. Confident Kids administrators may contact my references and appropriate government agencies as deemed necessary in order to verify my suitability as a Confident Kids facilitator. I verify that the above information is completely true.

Signature: ________________________________ Date:__________

Personal References

Please attach the names, addresses, and phone numbers of three persons who are not related to you, and have known you for more than five years.

Confident Kids Family Enrollment Form

Sponsoring Church/Organization: ______________________

Unit Title: ______________________

Unit Dates: ______________________

Name: ______________________

Address: ______________________

City: ______________ State: ________ Zip: _____

Home phone: (_____) ______________________

Work phone: (_____) ______________________

Your relationship to the child(ren) listed below: ______________

List all children you would like to enroll (age four years through sixth grade), *and* younger children for child care:

______________ Age/Grade: ________ Birthdate: ________

______________ Age/Grade: ________ Birthdate: ________

______________ Age/Grade: ________ Birthdate: ________

Child(ren)'s mailing address/phone if different from yours:

Address: ______________________

Phone: (____) ______________________

If this is your first unit, please tell us why you want to place your child(ren) in the Confident Kids program:

If you are continuing in the program, please tell us any new information about your child(ren) or family that we should know:

Will you attend the Confident Kids parents group (meets at the same timc as the kids' meeting)?

(continued)

Release Statement

Please be advised that the Confident Kids program is a support group program only. It is not therapy, nor a substitute for therapy in any way. Our leaders are volunteers, not trained counselors. (If at any time you feel your child is in need of professional counseling services, we will be happy to talk with you about a referral.) All information given by both parents and children will be held in strict confidence. Information shared by children in confidence will not be passed on to adults outside the leadership of the Confident Kids program, except as deemed necessary by the Confident Kids program administrators to ensure the health and safety of the child.

Having read the above and understanding it fully, I hereby authorize my child(ren) to be enrolled in the Confident Kids program.

Signature: ______________________________ Date: ______________

Confident Kids Parent Phone Interview

Interviewed By: ______________________________

Parent's Name: ______________________________

Address: ______________________________

City: ____________________ State: ________ Zip: _____

Home phone: (_____)______________________________

Work phone: (_____)______________________________

Relationship to the child(ren) listed below: ____________________

Children in the family (list *all,* including children for child care and teen siblings):

____________________Age/Grade: ________ Birthdate: ________

____________________Age/Grade: ________ Birthdate: ________

____________________Age/Grade: ________ Birthdate: ________

Child(ren)'s mailing address/phone if different from yours:

Address: ______________________________

Phone: (____) ______________________________

Why do you want to place your child(ren) in the Confident Kids program?

What, if any, behaviors are you seeing in your child(ren) that are of concern to you? (e.g., unexpressed feelings, aggressive behavior, withdrawal):

(continued)

When did these behaviors start? If recently, were they *un*characteristic of your child(ren) before that time?

What help, if any, are you getting (or have gotten in the past) for you and/or your child(ren)? (Include counseling, divorce recovery or other support groups, school counselors/teachers, professional diagnosis of ADHD or other learning disability, medications, etc.)

Are you currently married? _____

If yes, tell your spouse's name and briefly describe your relationship, particularly as it affects your kids (e.g., loving and close, strained, dad's never around, mom's an alcoholic):

If no, describe your ex-spouse's relationship to you and your children (e.g., friendly/hostile, sees or does not see the kids regularly):

Do you understand the participation expected of you (i.e., participation in a Confident Kids parents group or other requirements)? _____

Are you willing to participate in this way? _____

Other information:

Do you (the parent) have any questions you would like to ask of me (the interviewer)?

If you are enrolling the family into Confident Kids, give the parent all necessary details. If you believe they should be referred to other sources of help rather than or in addition to enrolling them (e.g., counseling for past sexual abuse, ADHD evaluation), do so at this time. In either case, be sure to end your conversation with words of encouragement and hope.

Confident Kids Children's Evaluation Form

Unit Title:____________________

Unit Dates:____________________

Your Name:____________________

In what ways has Confident Kids helped you in this unit?

What things did you like best during this unit?

What didn't you like about this unit?

What things would you like to do that we didn't do?

How could we make Confident Kids better?

Confident Kids Parent's Evaluation Form

Unit Title:________________________________

Unit Dates:________________________________

Your Child(ren)'s Name(s): ____________________

Your Name: ____________________________

In what ways has Confident Kids been helpful to your child(ren)?

To you?

What, if any, changes have you seen in your child?

In you?

How could Confident Kids be more helpful to you and/or your children?

Re-enrollment Request

_____ Yes, please enroll us in the next eight-week session

_____ No, we will not be returning for the next session.

_____ Please keep our name on file for a future eight-week unit.

Copy these **CONFIDENT KIDS POSTCARDS** onto 8.5" x 11" card stock.

To:
From:
I like the way you
You are
You are good at
How you have grown in Confident Kids
A special quality about you is

This is to certify that

has completed

Facing My Feelings

on this, the day of

Congratulations!

Confident Kids

Signed

APPENDIX B

RESOURCES

Use resources listed here to supplement the *Confident Kids* curriculum.

Games and Activities

Memory Verse Games

The Wave

This activity simulates "The Wave," which is popular at sporting events. Have the kids sit in a straight line or in a circle. Have one child quickly stand, raise his arms over his head, say the first word of the verse, and then sit down. Ask the next child to immediately stand and do the same thing. Continue around the group. After the kids have practiced with the memory verse poster, take the poster away and repeat the wave until the whole verse, reference included, has been said. Begin again if a mistake is made.

Popcorn Verse

In advance, write out the verse, including the reference, on slips of paper. Place one word on each slip and number the slips consecutively. Have the kids sit in a long line or in a circle, and randomly pass out the slips of paper. Keep going until all the slips are distributed, even if some kids get more than one. Then have the kids read the verse by standing, saying their word, and then sitting down again. They will know their turn by the number on their slip of paper. Keep this moving as quickly as possible, like popcorn popping!

Memory Verse Puzzles

Cut 3" x 5" cards in half and print one word of the verse on each card, including the reference. Scramble the cards and then work together to put them in the right order. Increase the fun by making two or more sets, dividing the kids into teams, and having the team race to see who can assemble the verse first.

For younger children, print the verse on a larger piece of paper and cut it into pieces, like a jigsaw puzzle. Let kids assemble the verse and then read it together.

One Word at a Time

Review the verse using the verse poster, then put the poster aside. Have the kids sit in a circle and ask one of them to say the first word of the verse. Ask the next person to say the second word, and so on around the circle. If someone makes a mistake, begin again. See how quickly the group can say the entire verse without a mistake.

Memory Verse Scramble

Print the verse on half sheets of paper, placing one or two words on each sheet. Scramble the sheets and distribute them randomly to the kids. Have the kids place themselves in order so the verse can be read. Add interest for the older kids by timing them the first time, and then seeing if they can improve their speed.

Regathering Activities

The purpose of the regathering time is to engage kids who have completed their small group work in a short activity until the other small groups finish. The Bible story follows the regathering activity, so decide if your kids need to settle down with quiet activities, or burn some energy with active activities. Choose activities that a few kids can begin and the other kids can easily participate in as they arrive. Ask the kids for suggestions, or try some of the ideas below.

Songs

This is a great time for music! You can teach the kids new songs or stick to their favorites from Sunday school. If one of your leaders plays guitar or another musical instrument, have that person play and sing quietly as the kids come together. Music can be very calming to high-stress kids.

Memory Verse Games

Use the regathering time to work on memorizing unit verses.

Games and Activities for Younger Children

Younger children like these games and activities:

- Simon Says
- Duck, Duck Goose
- Follow the Leader
- Simple bending and stretching exercises
- Telling Bible stories, using a flannel board

Games and Activities for Older Children

Older children enjoy these games and activities:

- Charades, using one word or a simple phrase
- Guessing a word or phrase one letter at a time (similar to Wheel or Fortune™)
- Artist, in which one child begins drawing a simple object and continues until someone guesses what it is

Past Gathering Activities

Some of the gathering activities suggested for the opening time of the meetings are simple enough to also be used for regathering (e.g., feelings charades, graffiti board, simple crafts). Choose ones your kids particularly enjoyed and repeat them.

Games for Family Night

Some of the favorite Family Night events are the games that all family members can play together. Any game that involves entire families will work. Below are a few that have been particularly enjoyable.

Wink 'Em

You will need an odd number of players for this game. Have half of the players sit in chairs arranged in a circle. Leave one chair empty. Have the rest of the players stand behind each chair, including the empty one. The person behind the empty chair is "it." The object is for the player standing behind the empty chair to call one of the others sitting around the circle to her chair by winking at that person. The player who was winked at must then get up and move to the empty chair; however, the player standing behind him should try to stop him from moving to the empty chair by placing her hands on his shoulders. If the standing player can accomplish her goal before the seated person gets away, the seated person must remain in the chair and the person who is "it" must wink at someone else. If the person winked at gets away, his partner—whose chair is now empty—becomes the new "it."

Family Scavenger Hunt

This is a family cooperative game. Have the families sit together and be sure they have everything they brought with them, such as purses, wallets, or backpacks. Then call out a series of objects family members are likely to have brought and give each family who can produce that item a point. Be creative! Anticipate items you believe your participants will be carrying, but may be rare, such as:

- Red shoelaces
- A key ring with twelve or more keys
- A homework assignment
- Purple socks
- Hand lotion
- A watch with a cartoon character on it

You can also call out characteristics that only one family will win, such as the oldest person in the group, or the person with the longest hair, the most freckles, or widest smile.

Relay Races

Families enjoy all kinds of races. Examples include:

- Three-legged race
- Crab race
- Wheelbarrow race
- Passing an orange from chin to chin
- Pushing a peanut with their noses

Try to group families into teams so the families can stay together, but try to keep the teams even. If this is not possible, divide the group into even mixtures of adults and kids.

Other Resources

Music

Music is an important part of the Confident Kids program. Music can provide high-stress families with two needed elements—a fun experience, and reinforcement of God's care and presence.

Music Tape. An audio cassette containing seven short songs written specifically for each Confident Kids curriculum topic is available. Side A of the tape contains music and words; side B is music only. You can order this resource from the Confident Kids office. (See order form on page 391 and 393 for contact information.)

Children's Praise Tapes. Your local Christian bookstore will have many excellent children's music tapes. Look for ones that put the Psalms and other Scriptures to music.

Secular Tapes of Children's Classics. You can include some of the old favorites, such as the Disney music collections or the Wee Sing™ cassette series. Look in the children's sections of any bookstore, toy store, or discount store, such as Wal-Mart, Target, or Costco.

Badge-a-Minit™

Badge-a-Minit manufactures a high-quality badge maker, which will enable you to make your own 2" or 4" pin-back badges. These badges can be used in several ways:

- To make permanent name tags for group participants
- To have kids design their own badges and assemble them immediately
- To make attractive award ribbons for special events

Write or call for a complete catalogue, which lists various sizes of assembly machines, badge parts, and other ideas for using the badges. We recommend the Badge-a-Minit over every other brand of badge maker.

Badge-a-Minit
Box 800
LaSalle, IL 61301
800/223-4103
815/883-9696 (FAX)

"How Do You Feel Today?" Feelings Faces Materials

Use feelings faces posters, mugs, stickers, and buttons to help kids learn to identify and express their feelings. The Confident Kids office offers a variety of these items in several fun formats. Contact the office directly (see page 391 and 393) for more information.

Training Resources

Seminars and Training Tapes. The Confident Kids organization offers a variety of training formats to equip you to administer a successful Confident Kids program and train your program leaders. One-, two-, or three-day training seminars are held throughout the country each year. Audio or video training tapes with six hours of training, a participant's workbook, and additional process activities for use in group settings are also available. Contact the Confident Kids office for more information.

Books. We recommend the following printed resources (listed by topic):

- **Family Systems**
  - —**Bradshaw, John. *Bradshaw On the Family.* Health Communication, Inc., Deerfield Beach, FL, 1988.** This resource reads like a textbook, but has excellent material on how dysfunctional family behavior develops and is passed from generation to generation.
  - —**Satir, Virginia. *The New People Making.* Science and Behavior Books, Inc., Mountain View, CA, 1988 (revised).** Satir was a pioneer in the field of family systems theory and family therapy. Her book is an excellent introduction to the complexities of family relationships, family

communication, and the development of self esteem in the family.

- Legal Issues

  —**Hammar, Klipowicz, and Cobble.** ***Reducing the Risk of Child Sexual Abuse in Your Church.*** **Church Law and Tax Report, 1993. (Order from Christian Ministry Resources, Mathews, NC, 704/841-8066; FAX 704/871-8039)** This is an excellent work that describes how to set policy, screen volunteers, train leaders, and keep appropriate records to reduce both the incidents of and your church or organization's legal liability for sexual abuse. A book, cassette tape, and workbook for church leaders are available.

- Leading Parents Groups

  —**Curran, Dolores.** ***Working With Parents.*** **American Guidance Service, Circle Pines, MN, 1989. (To order, call 800/328-2560.)** This excellent handbook covers topics such as listening to identify parents' needs, conducting groups that empower parents, and dealing with problem parents.

  —**Cynaumon, Dr. Greg.** ***Helping Single Parents With Troubled Kids.*** **David C. Cook Publishers, Colorado Springs, CO, 1992.** This book is an excellent resource for helping parents and kids understand divorce and related issues. I highly recommend this one!

- Resources for Parents

  —**Curran, Dolores.** ***Traits of a Healthy Family.*** **Ballantine Books, New York, 1983.** This text gives an overview of what makes a family healthy, and describes how to begin developing these characteristics in families. (One of the handouts in the Confident Kids unit, *Living in My Family*, is taken from this book.)

  —**Curran, Dolores.** ***Stress and the Healthy Family.*** **Harper Collins, New York, 1989.** This book is a follow-up to her previous work, *Traits of a Healthy Family.*

  —**Faber, Adele and Elaine Mazlish.** ***How to Talk So Kids Will Listen, And Listen So Kids Will Talk.*** **Avon Books, New York, 1980.** This small, practical book was written by two parent group leaders. It addresses common parenting problems and how to deal with them. There are easy-to-understand steps, and interesting cartoons illustrate the authors' points. This book is extremely helpful.

  —**Sanford, Doris and Graci Evans. Heart to Heart Series. Multnomah Press, Portland, OR.** This series of books deals with the difficult issues children face, such as living with an alcoholic parent, sexual abuse, death, divorce, and more. Well written and illustrated, this book will teach adults how to help children deal with these issues. It clearly presents how God's love and presence help us through painful circumstances.

  —**Kondracki, Linda.** ***Going Through Changes Together.*** **Fleming H. Revell (a division of Baker Book House), Grand Rapids, MI, 1996.** I wrote this book to help families grieve losses associated with major life changes. The text coordinates with the Confident Kids unit, *Growing Through Changes*. Each chapter is divided into three sections: Getting Ready (for parents), Read Along (for kids), and Family Activities.

  —**Sanford, Doris.** ***Helping Kids Through Tough Times.*** **Standard Publishing, Cincinnati, OH, 1995.** This text contains reproducible "help" sheets adults can use to guide children through stressful times. Each sheet addresses a tough issue kids face and contains practical help and Scripture support to help kids understand and cope with that issue. Parents groups will find this resource particularly helpful.

  —**Smalley, Gary and John Trent.** *The Blessing.* **Thomas Nelson Publishers, Nashville, TN, 1986.** Smalley and Trent give parents an easy-to-understand, five-part program to help them bond emotionally to their kids. The biblical practice of parents blessing their children provides the foundation for this text.

—**Wright, H. Norman.** ***Helping Your Kids Handle Stress.*** **Here's Life Publishers, San Bernardino, CA, 1989.** Material on causes of stress in children, symptoms of childhood stress, and methods for dealing with specific stressors is included.

- **Secular Life Skills Resources You Should Know About**

All of the following publishers offer free catalogues.

—**American Guidance Service.** This company produces and publishes excellent educational materials in many areas, including self-esteem building, social skills development, chemical dependency prevention, and parenting. Materials are activity centered and include excellent teaching aids such as puppets, activity cards, and discussion starters.

AGS
Publisher's Building
P.O. Box 99
Circle Pines, MN 55014-1796
800/328-2560
800/247-5053 (Minnesota only)

—**Contemporary Health Series. Produced by ETR Associates.** This series of curriculum modules was developed for classroom use. The Into Adolescence series contains a number of modules for grades five through eight on subjects such as: communication, emotions, living in a family, enhancing self-esteem, and more.

Network Publications/ETR Associates
P.O. Box 1830
Santa Cruz, CA 95061-1830
408/438-4080 (order department)

—**STAGES: Education for Children in Transition. Developed by the Irvine, CA school district as a supplementary classroom curriculum for public schools.** STAGES teaches children how to cope with significant change in their lives, particularly divorce. Complete curriculum components for both elementary children and adolescents are included. Also available are student workbooks, a video, and parent materials. One-day training seminars are held in Irvine periodically.

Guidance Projects Office
5050 Barranca Parkway
Irvine, CA 92714
714/552-4882

—**Sunburst Communications.** Sunburst produces videos and filmstrips with accompanying study guides for classroom use on subjects such as self-esteem, skills for living, decision making, drug and sex education, and more. Materials are available for grades five through nine, and high schoolers. They are expensive, but well done.

Sunburst Communications
101 Castleton Street
Pleasantville, NY 10570-3498
800/431-1934

From the Directors of Confident Kids

Who Are We?

Confident Kids is more than the title of this curriculum series. Confident Kids is a national organization that has been promoting Christian support groups for children and families since 1989. From our headquarters on the central coast of California, we equip churches and other Christian organizations to effectively minister to today's hurting kids and struggling parents.

Confident Kids can be of service to you in one or more of the following areas:

- Getting support-group programs up and running in your community
- Providing in-depth training through videotapes and/or live seminars
- Supplying additional resources for ministry to families
- Putting you in touch with other churches or organizations using Confident Kids in your area

We're Here to Help!

Return the Confident Kids Response Form by letter or FAX or contact us by phone or e-mail. We are always happy to hear from you and welcome the chance to answer your questions. Let us be of service to you as you seek to bring God's love, hope, and healing to hurting kids in your church and community!

David L. Sibley
Executive Director
Linda Kondracki Sibley
Resource Development & Training
Confident Kids **Support Groups**
330 Stanton Street
Arroyo Grande, CA 93420
805/473-7945 FAX 805/473-7948
confidentkids@juno.com

Confident Kids

Response Form

I would like help and support with my ministry to hurting kids and their parents.

_____ Place me on your mailing list.

_____ Send me a product list of additional resources.

_____ Send me a schedule of training seminars.

Return form to:
Confident Kids **Support Groups**
330 Stanton Street
Arroyo Grande, CA 93420
805/473-7945; FAX 805/473-7948;
confidentkids@juno.com

Name ____________________

Church or organization ____________________

Address ____________________

City/State/Zip ____________________

Phone ____________________

This is my _____ *home address* _____ *organization address*

Describe your organization if other than a church.

Church or organization ____________________

Denominational affiliation ____________________

Size of church or organization ____________________

How do you plan to use Confident Kids? (for example, as part of a weekly church support-group program)

Confident Kids

Response Form

I would like help and support with my ministry to hurting kids and their parents.

_____ Place me on your mailing list.

_____ Send me a product list of additional resources.

_____ Send me a schedule of training seminars.

Return form to:
Confident Kids **Support Groups**
330 Stanton Street
Arroyo Grande, CA 93420
805/473-7945; FAX 805/473-7948;
confidentkids@juno.com

Name ____________________

Church or organization ____________________

Address ____________________

City/State/Zip ____________________

Phone ____________________

This is my _____ *home address* _____ *organization address*

Describe your organization if other than a church.

Church or organization ____________________

Denominational affiliation ____________________

Size of church or organization ____________________

How do you plan to use Confident Kids? (for example, as part of a weekly church support-group program)